ADDRESSING CULTURAL COMPLEXITIES IN PRACTICE, SECOND EDITION

ADDRESSING CULTURAL COMPLEXITIES IN PRACTICE,

SECOND EDITION
ASSESSMENT, DIAGNOSIS, AND THERAPY

PAMELA A. HAYS, PhD

AMERICAN PSYCHOLOGICAL ASSOCIATION
WASHINGTON, DC

Second Printing, August 2008
Third Printing, June 2009

Published by
American Psychological Association
750 First Street, NE
Washington, DC 20002
www.apa.org

To order
APA Order Department
P.O. Box 92984
Washington, DC 20090-2984
Tel: (800) 374-2721; Direct: (202) 336-5510
Fax: (202) 336-5502; TDD/TTY: (202) 336-6123
Online: www.apa.org/books/
E-mail: order@apa.org

In the U.K., Europe, Africa, and the Middle East, copies may be ordered from
American Psychological Association
3 Henrietta Street
Covent Garden, London
WC2E 8LU England

Typeset in Meridien by Circle Graphics, Inc., Columbia, MD

Printer: Maple-Vail Book Manufacturing, Binghamton, NY
Cover Designer: Naylor Design, Washington, DC
Technical/Production Editor: Tiffany L. Klaff

The opinions and statements published are the responsibility of the authors, and such opinions and statements do not necessarily represent the policies of the American Psychological Association.

Library of Congress Cataloging-in-Publication Data

Hays, Pamela A.
  Addressing cultural complexities in practice : assessment, diagnosis, and therapy / Pamela A. Hays. — 2nd ed.
     p. cm.
  Includes bibliographical references and indexes.
  ISBN-13: 978-1-4338-0219-5
  ISBN-10: 1-4338-0219-8
  1. Cross-cultural counseling. 2. Psychotherapy. I. Title.

  BF636.7.C76H39 2008
  158'.3—dc22

                                                                          2007016025

British Library Cataloguing-in-Publication Data
A CIP record is available from the British Library.

Printed in the United States of America
Second Edition

Contents

V

Acknowledgments

The first person I must thank is Margery Ginsberg, who pulled the word ADDRESSING out of the earlier (and easily forgettable) acronym I had been using. Next, I thank Peg LeVine for her contribution of the capital letter *I* in reference to Indigenous people, which allows for an individual's diversity within this group's identity across nations. I am also grateful for the stimulating discussions Peg and I had early on regarding this new approach to multicultural counseling.

I am equally grateful to the following friends and colleagues for their suggestions and encouragement: Mary Ann Boyle, Richard Dana, Ned Farley, Karen Ferguson, Paul Gatto, Janice Hoshino, Gwen Jones, Tedd Judd, Kamuela Ka'Ahanui, Carolyn Bereznak Kenny, Lina LePage, Anthony J. Marsella, Bob McCard, John Moritsugu, Karen Sanders, Jan Santora, Isadora Arevalo Wong, Lisa Zaidi, and Jawed Zouari. I also thank the staff of the American Psychological Association books department, particularly Susan Reynolds, Genevieve Gill, and Tiffany Klaff, and the outside reviewers.

Finally, none of the case examples in this book is of real people—each is a composite. I deliberately chose to use names rather than initials for these examples, because familiarity with names from diverse cultures is an important part of one's cross-cultural knowledge base.

INTRODUCTION

Seeing the Forest and the Trees
The Complexities of Culture in Practice

1

A t a national psychology conference in 2005, I started a conversation with a young European American psychologist who had recently joined the faculty of a prestigious university. In response to my questions about the diversity of the psychology department, she told me that it consisted of 36 full-time members, one of whom was a person of color. She stressed that they had made significant progress in the hiring of women, but all of the women were White except the one person of color, and none was tenured. I asked her opinion about why this was the case, and she replied, "Well, I think the core faculty put their priority on developing a high-quality research program rather than on hiring for diversity."

This psychologist's statement reflects a commonly held belief that quality and diversity involve competing agendas. However, I argue, as many others have, that the exact opposite is true. A high-quality program by definition includes faculty of diverse perspectives and backgrounds who bring ideas that move a department beyond the mainstream. It consists of diverse teachers and supervisors who serve as role models for a culturally diverse student body and clinical faculty who have firsthand knowledge of the cultures of the clients that their students are seeing. It includes faculty who speak more than one language, read the psychological literature of more than one culture, and are connected to minority groups that they consider and consult in their development of research projects.

Given the relatively culturally encapsulated origins of the field, this is a tall order. However, significant strides have been made. Throughout the fields of psychology, counseling, and mental health, professional organizations have made a clear commitment to increasing the multicultural competence of their members. Specifically, the American Psychological Association (APA; 2000a, 2000b, 2002a, 2002b, 2004), the American Counseling Association (Roysircar, Arredondo, Fuertes, Ponterotto, & Toporek, 2003), and the National Association of Social Workers (2001) have all issued guidelines and taken specific steps to call attention to previously neglected cultural influences and related minority groups. In the United States and Canada, these influences and examples of corresponding minority groups include the following:

- **a**ge and generational influences—children, elders;
- **d**evelopmental disabilities—people with developmental disabilities;
- **d**isabilities acquired later in life—people with disabilities acquired later, for example, from multiple sclerosis or dementia caused by stroke;
- **r**eligion and spiritual orientation—people of Muslim, Jewish, Buddhist, Hindu, and other minority religions and faiths;
- **e**thnic and racial identity—people of Asian, South Asian, Pacific Island, Latino, African, African American, Arab, and Middle Eastern heritage;
- **s**ocioeconomic status—people of lower status because of occupation, education, income, or rural habitat;
- **s**exual orientation—gay, lesbian, and bisexual people;
- **i**ndigenous heritage—American Indians, Alaska Natives, FirstNations, Inuit, Métis, Native Hawaiians;
- **n**ational origin—immigrants, refugees, international students; and
- **g**ender—women, transgender people.

As you can see, the first letters of these influences form the word *ADDRESSING*, which may be used as a reminder of cultural influences that therapists need to be addressing in their work. I use this acronym as a starting point for what I call the ADDRESSING framework, a practitioner-oriented approach that conceptualizes cross-cultural work in two broad categories. The first category of *personal work* involves the therapist's introspection, self-exploration, and an understanding of the influence of culture on one's own belief system and worldview. The second category of *interpersonal work* focuses on the therapist's learning about and from other cultures, which usually involves interpersonal experiences. The importance of both the personal and interpersonal aspects of cross-cultural learning has been emphasized throughout the multi-cultural literature (Arredondo & Pérez, 2006).

This New Edition

Since publication of the 2001 edition of this volume, a number of political events have had implications for the lives of ethnic, immigrant, and other minority group members. These events include the following:

- the attacks on the World Trade Center, the U.S. invasion of Iraq, and international opposition to the war policies of the Bush administration;
- a series of natural disasters including a tidal wave in Indonesia, an earthquake in Pakistan, and the flooding of New Orleans following Hurricane Katrina;
- a growing immigration rights movement in conjunction with the increasing solidarity of the U.S. Latino population, which is now the largest ethnic minority group in the United States; and
- the legalization of same-sex marriage in Canada, South Africa, and the first state in the United States—Massachusetts.

Recognizing these developments, this new edition gives added attention to the impact of the war in Iraq on people of Arab and Muslim heritage and provides information on assessing trauma in people of diverse cultures. A section has been added on multiple relationships and ethical boundaries in relation to minority communities. New information on play therapy includes suggestions for therapists working with children of ethnic minority cultures. And in response to the growing interest in evidence-based practice (APA, Presidential Task Force, 2006), chapter 9 provides guidelines for integrating cultural considerations into the theory and practice of cognitive behavior therapy (CBT). (A recent poll of psychotherapy experts predicted that CBT and multicultural therapy would be the leading theoretical trends in psychotherapy in the coming years; Norcross, Hedges, & Prochaska, 2002.) Although the empirical research base is sparse regarding cross-cultural applications of CBT (as it is with all of the major psychotherapies), chapter 9 of this volume offers suggestions from a growing number of clinically based studies and the few existing empirical studies. All of the diagnostic information has been updated according to the text revision of the fourth edition of the *Diagnostic and Statistical Manual of Mental Disorders* (*DSM–IV–TR*; American Psychiatric Association, 2000).

ADDRESSING Framework Categories

PERSONAL WORK

The ADDRESSING approach begins with an emphasis on understanding the effect of diverse cultural influences on therapists' worldviews. This effect includes therapists' age-related generational experiences, experience or inexperience with disability, religious or spiritual upbringing, ethnic and racial identity, and so on (i.e., the ADDRESSING influences). By recognizing the areas in which they are members of dominant groups, therapists become more aware of the ways in which such identities can limit their knowledge and experience, particularly regarding minority groups of which they are not members.

Therapists are encouraged to pay special attention to the role of privilege in their lives, defined as the advantages one holds as a result of membership in a dominant group (see McIntosh, 1998). This extra attention is important, because privilege tends to limit a person's knowledge of and experience with nonprivileged groups, even when a person belongs to a minority group in one cultural domain and a dominant group in another.

For example, as a result of her membership in a sexual minority group, a middle-class European American lesbian therapist may hold an exceptional awareness of the subtle sexist and heterosexist biases against lesbian, gay, bisexual, and transgender clients. However, she would not automatically have greater awareness of the issues faced by people of color, people who have disabilities, or people of lower socioeconomic status. The privileges she holds in relation to her ethnicity, physical abilities, education, and professional status may work to separate her from people who do not hold such privileges. Furthermore, if her friends and family are relatively homogeneous with regard to ethnicity, social class, and disability, she may need to put extra effort into finding information that challenges her assumptions, biases, and ways of seeing the world.

INTERPERSONAL WORK

Although human beings like to think of themselves as complex, they often regard others as one dimensional, relying on others' most visible characteristics as the explanation for everything they say, believe, and do. The more people recognize the complexity of human experience and identity, the more they will be able to understand those individuals they perceive as different (G. W. Harper, Jernewall, & Zea, 2004; Hinrichsen, 2006; Reid, 2002). By calling attention to these multiple memberships and identities, the ADDRESSING framework helps therapists avoid making inaccurate generalizations on the basis of a client's physical appearance, language abilities, or name.

For example, using the ADDRESSING acronym as a guide, a therapist attempting to understand an older man of East Indian heritage not only would try to obtain a general understanding of the values, beliefs, and behaviors common among East Indian people but also the following specifics:

- What are the **a**ge-related issues and generational influences on this client, particularly given his status as a second-generation immigrant?
- What is this man's experience with **d**evelopmental disabilities or **d**isabilities acquired later in life? That is, might he have a disability that is not immediately apparent, or have experienced the impact of disability as a caregiver for a partner, parent, or child?
- What was his **r**eligious upbringing, and what are his current beliefs and practices? (Reasonable hypotheses would be that he is Hindu or Muslim or Sikh, but none of these can be assumed; see Almeida, 2005.)
- What is the meaning of his **e**thnic or racial identity in an urban area where he is often mistaken by non-Indians to be Pakistani or Arab?
- What is his current **s**ocioeconomic status as defined by his occupation, income, education, marital status, gender, ethnicity, community, and family name, and might this status be different from that of his parents before their immigration?
- What is the client's **s**exual orientation, not assuming heterosexuality simply because he has been married?
- Might **i**ndigenous heritage be part of his ethnic identity?
- What is his **n**ational identity (Indian, that of his country of residence, both, or neither) and primary language (Hindi, English, Bengali, or other language)?
- Finally, what **g**ender-related information (e.g., regarding roles, expectations, and relationships) is significant given the client's cultural heritage and identity as a whole? (See Assanand, Dias, Richardson, Chambers, & Waxler-Morrison, 2005, and Tewari, Inman, & Sanhu, 2003, regarding the diversity of South Asians.)

Around the world, it is now common to find individuals who hold more than one ethnic or racial identity simultaneously. Biracial and multiracial people may identify strongly with the differing minority and majority identities of their parents and grandparents (Root, 1996). People of Indigenous cultures frequently identify with a particular band or community, a larger Indigenous culture, and a national non-Indigenous society simultaneously. For example, in Alaska, a member of the Kenaitze tribe may identify as Alaska Native, Athabascan (one of the Alaska Native groups), Dena'ina (one of the Athabascan cultures), Kenaitze (the Dena'ina people living on the Kenai Peninsula), American, and a member of the global movement of Indigenous peoples simultaneously (Hays, 2006a).

For many people, identity is a complex phenomenon involving a combination of ethnic and nonethnic influences (Reid, 2002; Wang & Sue, 2005). For instance, a gay man of Filipino heritage may identify with a predominantly heterosexual Filipino community and also be involved in a politically active, mostly European American gay community. The salience of these identities can vary depending on the particular environment in which he finds himself over time (C. S. Chan, 1992).

Therapists will not necessarily ask clients all of the questions raised by the ADDRESSING framework, but it can be helpful for therapists to consider the relevance of each influence for every client. Such considerations must move beyond the expectation that therapists will learn about cultures from their clients; expecting clients to educate therapists about their cultures is unfair to clients. Furthermore, a therapist relying on one or two clients to understand a whole culture could result in a very narrow view. It is our responsibility as therapists to be actively committed to the lifelong process of learning about the cultures of our clients outside of the therapy setting.

Fortunately, the multicultural psychology literature has expanded rapidly since the 1970s, including the development of new fields of research regarding specific populations (e.g., disability studies, affirmative therapy with gay and lesbian populations, geropsychology, feminist psychology, and multicultural psychology). Many excellent books have been written on counseling members of specific ethnic and racial minority groups in the United States, including African Americans (Boyd-Franklin, 2003), Asian Americans (Lee, 1997; Uba, 1994), American Indians and Alaska Natives (Droby, 2000; Duran, 2006; Herring, 1999; Swan Reimer, 1999; Swinomish Tribal Community, 1991; Witko, 2006), Latinos and Latinas (Falicov, 1998; Santiago-Rivera, Arredondo, & Gallardo-Cooper, 2002), Arab and Muslim people (Dwairy, 2006), and English-speaking West Indians (Gopaul-McNicol, 1993).

The list of multicultural counseling books that address multiple minority groups within one book is too long to list here. Since 2000 alone, it includes Aponte and Wohl (2000); Fong (2004); F. D. Harper and McFadden (2003); Hoshmand (2006); Ivey, D'Andrea, Ivey, and Simek-Morgan (2001); McGoldrick, Giordano, and Garcia-Preto (2005); Paniagua (2005); Pedersen, Draguns, Lonner, and Trimble (2002); Robinson and Howard-Hamilton (2000); Roysircar, Sandhu, and Bibbins (2003); and D. W. Sue and Sue (2003). In addition, a text by Waxler-Morrison, Anderson, Richardson, and Chambers (2005) focuses on ethnic minority cultures in Canada. This list is far from exhaustive.

Although not quite as abundant, there are also a growing number of counseling and clinical books on specific nonethnic minority populations, including gay, lesbian, and bisexual people (Martell, Safren, & Prince, 2004; Pérez, DeBord, & Bieschke, 2000); people of different religious and spiritual faiths (Cashwell & Young, 2005; Miller, 1999; Richards & Bergin, 2005; Sperry & Shafranske, 2005); elders (Burlingame, 1999;

Duffy, 1999; Knight, 2004; Nordhus, VandenBos, Berg, & Fromholt, 1998); people with disabilities (Maki & Riggar, 1997; Olkin, 1999); people living in rural areas (Stamm, 2003); and people living in poverty (P. Minuchin, Colapinto, & Minuchin, 2007).

So Why This Book?

Given the impressive number of publications on multicultural topics, what more can this book offer? Currently, most of the overview texts on multicultural counseling are organized with each chapter focusing on one minority group at a time. Although this approach works well for some aspects of multicultural education in the United States, it can be cumbersome for therapists who want to learn the specifics of clinical work with people of complex identities in a variety of contexts. In contrast, *Addressing Cultural Complexities in Practice* is organized according to the flow of clinical work, beginning with suggestions for facilitating the personal process of a therapist becoming more culturally aware and knowledgeable, followed by information on establishing a therapeutic relationship, conducting assessments, testing, making diagnoses, and providing psychotherapy (including individual, family, couple, play, and group therapies). I integrate case examples of people who hold complex identities throughout. (For example, the case of an African American client does not focus solely on her ethnic and racial heritage; her disability, gender, experience as an elder, religion, and socioeconomic status are all addressed, too.) I organize practical suggestions and strategies in "Key Ideas" lists at the end of each chapter for both instructors teaching multicultural counseling courses and clinicians to use.

Recognizing the heavy emphasis on U.S. ethnic minorities within the multicultural counseling literature, I include information and case examples of cultures and minority groups not commonly found in U.S. texts (e.g., Indonesian, Tunisian Arab, French Canadian, Haitian, East Indian, Costa Rican, Korean, and Greek cultures, among others). I also address issues related to age (elders and children), sexual orientation, transgender identity, religion, disability, rural environments, and poverty. I set some cases in Canada (setting cases in a variety of countries proved difficult, because what constitutes a minority culture in one country is often a dominant culture in another.)

Organization of This Book

Chapters 2 and 3 describe specific steps and exercises for facilitating your own cultural self-assessment. Chapter 2 focuses on the exploration of personal experiences, values, and biases. I describe strategies for developing compassion and critical thinking skills, and for preventing defensive interactions with clients. Chapter 3 provides an example of the self-assessment process with a particular therapist who discusses the complexity of his identity including generational experiences, ethnicity, sexual orientation, and the other ADDRESSING influences. Chapter 3 also provides exercises to help you understand your own cultural identity and the role of privilege in the context of your work. Under the premise that you are engaged in and committed to the self-assessment process, chapter 4 explains in detail how you can use the ADDRESSING framework to facilitate greater understanding of your clients' identities through the formulation of hypotheses and questions that are closer to clients' experiences.

The remaining chapters discuss the ADDRESSING framework in relation to the specific tasks and processes of assessment, testing, diagnosis, and therapy. Chapter 5 outlines considerations in establishing rapport with a client and demonstrating respect with people of diverse identities. Chapter 6 provides specific suggestions for conducting culturally responsive assessments, including guidelines for working with interpreters. Chapter 7 focuses on standardized testing in mental status, intellectual, neuropsychological, and personality assessments. Chapter 8 addresses cross-cultural issues in the diagnostic process using the *DSM–IV–TR* (American Psychiatric Association, 2000). Chapter 9 provides information about Indigenous and traditional therapies and expressive therapies (e.g., art, music, and play therapies) and suggestions for making family, couple, and group therapies more culturally responsive. In addition, a new section focuses on the integration of cultural considerations into CBT. Chapter 10 illustrates the use of the suggestions in the preceding chapters in the case example of an older African American woman who has a disability and her family, who go to see an African American male psychologist. Chapter 11 discusses future challenges in the education, training, and research of culturally responsive psychologists.

Concepts and Categories in Multicultural Research

People of ethnic minority cultures now make up approximately one third of the U.S. population, and religious minorities include 4 million Jews, 1.5 million Muslims, 1.5 million Buddhists, and 1 million Hindus (American Religious Identity Survey [ARIS], 2001). Interracial couples now constitute 6% of married couples and between 10% and 12% of unmarried (including same-sex) couples in the United States (U.S. Census Bureau, 2000b). The adoption of foreign-born children in the United

States rose from 7,000 in 1990 to 18,000 in the year 2000, and immigration is responsible for 50% of U.S. population growth (U.S. Census Bureau, 2000a, 2000c). Gay men and lesbians are estimated to constitute between 6% and 10% of the U.S. population (Dew, Myers, & Wightman, 2006). Approximately 13% of Americans are 65 years of age or older (Hinrichsen, 2006), and 19% of Americans have disabilities, with American Sign Language being the third most common language after English and Spanish, respectively (Olkin, 1999; Sotnik & Jezewski, 2005).

Every group has its own terms for self-identification. Although this fact may feel overwhelming to nongroup members, learning the terms that people prefer can be helpful to therapists in several ways. Such knowledge increases therapists' awareness regarding these cultural groups and decreases the likelihood of offending someone through one's choice of terms. It can also increase the therapist's credibility, which in turn can help in building the therapeutic relationship. The following sections provide an overview of some of these terms.

RACE

Race is a social construct, not a scientific or biological fact (Sternberg, Grigorenko, & Kidd, 2005). The concept was originally developed by European scientists to classify people on the basis of geography and physical characteristics (e.g., skin color, hair texture, facial features) into groups of genetically related peoples (Spickard, 1992). Over the years, researchers created differing classification schemes that emphasized a wide range of factors including skin tone, tribal affiliations, nationalities, language families, or simply minority status (Thomas & Sillen, 1972). Underlying most of these schemes was the assumption that races were organized hierarchically, with light-skinned Christian Europeans at the top. The politics and beliefs of the time often determined the choice of a scheme, which in turn reinforced racist beliefs and laws. For example, the illegality of interracial marriage in many U.S. states until 1967 reflected the common belief that "White blood" could be tainted by "Black blood." Hence, in nine states at the turn of the century, a child of predominantly European ancestry with even one great-grandparent of African heritage was, for legal purposes, considered a "Negro" (Spickard, 1992).

Researchers in the fields of anthropology and evolutionary biology generally agree that racial distinctions fail on three counts: "They are not genetically discrete, are not reliably measured, and are not scientifically meaningful" (Smedley & Smedley, 2005, p. 16). There are no pure gene pools, as human beings of dominant and minority cultures are genetically quite mixed (Betancourt & López, 1993). Furthermore, racial classifications do not reliably account for the enormous variation in physical characteristics within the so-called racial groups. For example, many people who self-identify as White have skin that is visibly darker than some people who self-identify as Black.

However, many researchers continue to conceptualize race as an independent variable synonymous with culture. *The Bell Curve* (Herrnstein & Murray, 1994) epitomized the problems in using race in this way, using IQ score differences between racial groups to suggest differences in intelligence between races. As Sternberg et al. (2005) noted, because race is a social construct with no scientific definition, and because intelligence has never been linked to a particular gene, attempting to link the category of race to intelligence is erroneous.

At the same time, although race is a socially constructed concept, "the consequences of this construction are real in terms of perceptions of similarity and difference" (Altman, 2007, p. 15). In clinical practice, therapists need to be aware that race has social meanings that are important to many people (as the title of Cornel West's 1993 book states, *Race Matters*). Since the 1960s, when Black pride led to increased interest among many African Americans in family history and cultural heritage (Boyd-Franklin, 2003), some African Americans have used the term *Black* as a positive self-identification. However, during the past 2 decades, the term *African American* has become popular, because it emphasizes a person's ethnic and social heritage rather than physical characteristics (e.g., Moore Hines & Boyd-Franklin, 1996). Because language is continually changing, therapists need to stay flexible and open to clients' preferences. Whether or not a client uses a racial identification, it is helpful for therapists to remember that a racial identity in itself provides little information about an individual (E. E. Jones, 1987). What is most important with regard to racial identity is an understanding of its meaning for the individual, for the dominant and minority cultures, and for the therapist (Wang & Sue, 2005).

ETHNICITY

For the purpose of understanding the beliefs, values, and behaviors of both clients and therapists, the concept of ethnicity often provides more information than that of race. McGoldrick et al. (2005) defined *ethnicity* as the concept of a group's "peoplehood," including the "common ancestry through which individuals have evolved shared values and customs" (p. 2). Although ethnicity is often understood to involve some shared biological heritage, its most important aspects, in terms of individual and group identity, are those that are socially constructed (e.g., beliefs, norms, behaviors, language, and institutions).

But the concept of ethnicity also includes complications. For one, the term holds different meanings in different countries. In the United States, where American Indians joined together early on with African Americans, Asian Americans, and Latino Americans to call for equal rights, the term *ethnic minority* is assumed to include people of Indigenous or Aboriginal heritage. (The terms *Indigenous* and *Aboriginal* are often used interchangeably; Adelson, 2000; Maracle, 1994.) However, in Canada and Australia, where Aboriginal people consider their situations to be different from all subsequent immigrant groups, the term *ethnic minority* is used to describe only cultures with a history of immigration. Because Aboriginal Canadians emphasize their originality in Canadian lands (i.e., they did not immigrate), they do not conceive of themselves as ethnic minority cultures (Elliott & Fleras, 1992). Aboriginal Australians are similar in this regard (see Young, 1995). Some Aboriginal people of Canada self-identify as *First Nations* to distinguish themselves from the *Second Nations* (the French and English people, who came to Canada as colonizers) and the *Third Nations* (all subsequent immigrant groups to Canada; Elliot & Fleras, 1992). However, because the term *First Nations* does not include the Inuit (people of the Canadian arctic) or the Métis (people of mixed Aboriginal and European heritage), the more inclusive term is *Aboriginal* (see http://www.aaanativearts.com/canadian_tribes_AtoZ.htm).

Another problem with the description of people by ethnicity is that ethnic groups are currently labeled very broadly, as in the use of the term *Asian* for people of Japanese, Korean, Chinese, Vietnamese, Lao, Cambodian, Thai, and even East Indian and Pakistani heritage (Uba, 1994). Similarly, the term *Hispanic* combines into one ethnicity the diverse cultures of Central American Indians, South Americans of African and Spanish heritage, Mexican Americans, Cuban Americans, Puerto Ricans, and Dominicans (Novas, 1994). *Native American* includes more than 500 Native cultural entities in the United States (U.S. Department of the Interior, 2002). *Alaska Native* includes 20 Indian and non-Indian language and cultural groups (11 Athabascan language groups plus Aleut, Alutiiq, Yup'ik, Siberian Yup' ik, Inupiaq, Eyak, Tlingit, Tsimshian, and Haida; Rennick, 1996). Although some individuals use the broader terms to identify themselves, many people prefer their more specific identities (e.g., their nation of origin).

Geographic differences may also lead to variations in ethnic self-identification. For example, as Comas-Díaz (2001) noted, the term *Hispanic* (created by the U.S. Bureau of the Census to designate people of Spanish origin) is offensive to some people because it fails to acknowledge Indigenous people and Latin Americans who are not of Spanish origin (e.g., Brazilians whose primary language is Portuguese). Many such people prefer the terms *Latina* (for women) and *Latino* (for men), particularly those from the Pacific Northwest of the United States and California. However, some people (particularly those in California) self-identify as *Chicana* or *Chicano,* whereas many people in Texas use the term *Hispanic* to describe themselves. (As a young man from Texas once explained to me, "Latino makes me sound like I'm a gang member.")

Recognizing the complications of ethnic identification, Phinney (1996) suggested that misunderstandings persist because ethnicity is commonly conceptualized as a discrete categorical variable. For example, one is considered either Latina or not Latina, despite the fact that there are other possibilities. A person may be bicultural, or the salience of their ethnic identity may vary over time, in different situations, or with developmental changes (e.g., a biracial adolescent who begins to identify strongly with only one side of his heritage as he joins an ethnically defined peer group; Kim-Ju & Liem, 2003).

CULTURE

Culture is the most inclusive term and thus the most general. Definitions of culture abound, but today most anthropologists agree that the term *culture* includes traditions of thought and behavior such as language and history that can be socially acquired, shared, and passed on to new generations (Smedley & Smedley, 2005; Triandis, 1996). Although culture is often equated with race and ethnicity, the most commonly accepted definitions of culture say nothing about biological links (which the concept of race implies) and as such are broad enough to include people of nonethnic groups, too (Pope, 1995).

For example, in the United States, Muslim religious communities in many cities include immigrants and nonimmigrants of diverse ethnic groups and nationalities. Nationally, the Muslim immigrant population consists of approximately 26% Arab people, 25% South Asians (e.g., Indians, Pakistanis), 10% non-Arab Middle Easterners (e.g., Iranians), and 6% East Asians; nonimmigrant Muslims include 24% African Americans and 11% European and Native Americans (Ali, Liu, & Humedian, 2004). Across these diverse ethnic groups, a sense of community is reinforced by the shared values of respect, hospitality, caring for one's family, reason, tolerance, and education (Abudabbeh & Hays, 2006; Dwairy, 2006). In addition, the five foundational principles of Islam, known as the *five pillars of Islam*, require that all believers hold a belief in God and Mohammed as his prophet, follow the daily prayer rituals, give alms to the poor, observe the month-long fast of Ramadan, and make the pilgrimage to Mecca if possible (more on this in chap. 9 of this volume). For many Muslims, the mosque functions as a cultural center that brings together people from different countries (immigrants and nonimmigrants), providing social, financial, and spiritual support for its members. Unfortunately, experiences of prejudice and discrimination may also reinforce Muslim people's sense of themselves as separate, misunderstood, and different from the dominant U.S. culture. (Following the attacks on the World Trade Center towers in 2001, hate crimes against Muslims in the United States increased 1600%; Zogby, 2003.)

MINORITY

The term *minority* has traditionally been used in reference to groups whose access to power is limited by the dominant culture (Wang & Sue, 2005).

In this sense of the word, a minority group is not necessarily a numerical minority. For example, Blacks in South Africa during apartheid were a numerical majority but had minority status in relation to the dominant White culture. Similarly, colonization has often involved the dominance of a cultural group that is smaller in number than the cultural group it colonized.

In North America, the term *minority* may apply to ethnic, religious, national, and sexual minorities; elders; people who are poor, less formally educated, or of rural or Indigenous heritage; people who have a disability; and women and children (i.e., those groups highlighted by the ADDRESSING acronym). All of these populations fit the definition of culture as broadly defined, and all have traditionally been excluded, marginalized, or misrepresented by mainstream psychology; in this sense, they may be considered cultural minorities. (European American children and adolescents are somewhat of an exception, in that although they may be considered minorities in relation to the larger society, they have been the focus of much attention in psychology, beginning with Freud's developmental interests; this is not true for children and adolescents of ethnic minority cultures.)

But there is more to being a member of a minority culture than the experience of oppression. Identification with a minority culture or group may also lead to the development of positive traits and qualities that may not develop in people whose lives are buffered by privilege (McIntosh, 1998, p. 101). Minority status may bring with it unique forms of knowledge, awareness, emotional and tangible support, a sense of community, and an opportunity to contribute to others in ways that are deeply meaningful (Newman & Newman, 1999). Therapists need to be aware that describing a group of people as a minority culture is different from referring to a person as a minority. The latter may be perceived as disempowering because it places a label on the individual as well as an entire group.

ADDITIONAL TERMS

The choice of terms is equally important with regard to older people; people who have disabilities; gay, lesbian, bisexual, and transgender people; and women. For example, consider the differences in connotation between the set of descriptors *elderly, old, old man,* and *old maid* and a second set including *elder, older person,* and *senior.* Although the two sets are quite similar, the first may be perceived as patronizing and the second as more respectful.

With regard to sexual orientation, the term *sexual preference* is offensive, because it suggests that one has chosen to be gay or lesbian and thus can "change back." The term *homosexual* may be offensive in some contexts because of its historical equation with sin and sickness. Also off-putting are questions that reflect an assumption that heterosexuality is normal and other orientations are not (e.g., asking a client why he thinks he became gay—therapists generally do not ask heterosexual clients why they became heterosexual; Martin, 1982). More affirmative expressions are *lesbian, gay,* and *bisexual,* often abbreviated as LGB (Dworkin & Gutierrez, 1992). However, these terms are not used by all cultures or individuals. For example, some men in African American and Latino cultures have sex with men but do not identify as gay, and similarly, women in various cultures may be sexually attracted to women but not identify as lesbian (Balsam, Martell, & Safren, 2006). In some Native American cultures, the term *two-spirit* is used in place of LGB or LGBT, which includes transgender individuals (Balsam, Huang, Fieland, Simoni, & Walters, 2004). *Transgender* is an umbrella term for "individuals who do not fit the binary gender categories of male and female" (Maguen, Shipherd, & Harris, 2005, p. 479). The term *transgender* includes people whose gender identity or sense of themselves as male or female differs from that usually associated with their birth sex (APA, 2006).

With regard to people who have disabilities, "people-first" language was adopted in the 1970s to make the point that individuals should be seen as people first. *People with disabilities* replaced *disabled people,* and similar phrasing was used for people with specific disabilities (e.g., *person with schizophrenia* replaced *schizophrenic;* Olkin, 2002). More recently, in Great Britain and the United States, the argument has been made that disability is a social construct and that its use implies oppression rather than defectiveness of the person. One would not say *a person with oppression* but rather *an oppressed person,* so it may be acceptable to say *a disabled person* (Olkin, 2002). As some authors have noted, using exclusively person-first language "ignores the recognition of disability as a cultural identity and the fact that many people are proud to call themselves disabled people" (Mona, Romesser-Scehnet, Cameron, & Cardenas, 2006, p. 200).

Also regarding people with disabilities, emotionally neutral terms are always preferable to those with negative connotations (such as *victim, invalid, afflicted, crippled, suffers from;* Maki & Riggar, 1997b). Saying that someone uses a wheelchair or other assistive device avoids the assumptions embedded in describing the individual as *confined to* or *wheelchair bound,* which focus attention on the person's limitations rather than on the disabling environment. Noting the disabling environment (e.g., *there was no curb cut*) is preferable to describing a person by his or her limitations (e.g., *physically challenged;* Olkin, 1999). People who identify with Deaf culture (the capitalization denotes the cultural category) do not consider themselves to have a disability; rather, it is the hearing world's ignorance of their language that is the problem. At the same time, not all people who are hearing impaired identify with Deaf culture; for most of the people in this latter group, the term *hard of hearing* is more appropriate (Leigh, 2003; Vernon, 2006). And using the terms *blind* and *deaf* as synonyms for ignorance or unawareness is always offensive (e.g., "He was blind to the impact of his behavior," "They robbed him blind," "He turned a deaf ear to her cry").

Caveats and Reassurances

As the preceding discussion indicates, therapists need to be careful not to assume that terms commonly used in their milieu are acceptable to clients, because they may not be. In general, the more specific a term is, the more acceptable it will be, because it shows a greater level of awareness of the uniqueness of groups. However, the most politically aware terminology may still be offensive or confusing to more conservative clients. As a general rule, even when I know a specific term, I wait and listen for how people describe themselves before using a cultural identifier.

At the same time, even when clients use a term to describe themselves, it is not always acceptable for the therapist to use it. Toward the goal of asserting the right to name themselves, some minority groups have reclaimed terms that were once used in a derogatory way by members of the dominant culture (e.g., *queer* for LGBT people, *crip* for people who have disabilities). This decision to take back the dominant culture's labels and define them for oneself is a powerful act (Watt, 1999), as C. B. Williams (1999) explained in relation to her biracial identity:

> The idea that individuals have a right to define their own experience, to create their own personal meanings, to frame their own identity, to claim an "I" that is uniquely their own, shakes up many people's most dearly held beliefs about race. Courage to claim one's own experience despite resistance and judgment from others allows biracial people like me to begin to forge an authentic self. (p. 34)

When used by members of a particular group in reference to themselves, these terms become a form of "in-language." On rare occasions, it may be acceptable for nonmembers to use these terms; however, as a general rule, it is not.

When I do workshops incorporating the preceding information, this is usually the point at which someone in the audience says in a tone of controlled exasperation, "Honestly, Pam, how do you expect us to remember all of this?" My answer is that I don't. Or at least, not right away. What I do hope is that rather than becoming overwhelmed with the memorization of terms and names, therapists will commit to the ongoing process of learning about cultures of which they are not a member.

I emphasize the process aspect of this learning because cultures and languages are changing all the time. Consequently, what one needs to learn is continually changing. With regard to language in particular, it may be helpful to think of this learning process as involving a willingness to (a) seek out information about the broader cultural meanings of terms;

(b) seek out information about the group-specific meanings of terms; (c) listen for the terms each client uses; and (d) when appropriate, ask.

Conclusion

The range of influences and groups I include in this book may seem overwhelming, but I believe that a broader focus is necessary if psychology is to move beyond unidimensional conceptualizations of culture and people. At first, recognizing the complexity of cultural influences is more difficult than either ignoring these influences or simplifying them into a singular dimension. But in the long run, recognizing this complexity can lead therapists to a much deeper understanding of our clients and ourselves. Cultural diversity is less a problem than a challenge that offers the potential for personal growth, creativity, and deeper human connections. The next chapter explores the practical aspects of this challenge in therapists' daily lives and work.

Key Ideas

The ADDRESSING Framework: Summary of Cultural Influences and Related Minority Groups

Cultural Influences	Minority Groups
Age and generational influences	Children, adolescents, elders
Developmental disabilities	People with developmental disabilities
Disabilities acquired later in life	People with disabilities acquired later in life
Religion and spiritual orientation	Religious minority cultures
Ethnic and racial identity	Ethnic and racial minority cultures
Socioeconomic status	People of lower status because of class, education, occupation, income, or rural habitat
Sexual orientation	Gay, lesbian, and bisexual people
Indigenous heritage	Indigenous, Aboriginal, and Native people
National origin	Refugees, immigrants, international students
Gender	Women, transgender people

SELF-ASSESSMENT

Becoming a Culturally Responsive Therapist 2

n looking for wisdom about how life can best be lived, H. Smith (1991) examined the world's major religions: Hinduism, Buddhism, Confucianism, Taoism, Islam, Judaism, Christianity, and Aboriginal Australian spirituality. He concluded that these traditions share an emphasis on three elements, or what he called "virtues": humility, charity, and veracity.

> Humility is not self-abasement. It is the capacity to regard oneself in the company of others as one, but not more than one. Charity shifts that shoe to the other foot; it is to regard one's neighbor as likewise one, as fully one as oneself. As for veracity, it extends beyond the minimum of truth-telling to sublime objectivity, the capacity to see things exactly as they are. (p. 387)

It seems to me that these characteristics are equally important in becoming a culturally responsive therapist. Humility helps me to avoid judging difference as inferior. Charity, or an attitude of compassion toward others, enables me to work with and appreciate people who challenge my beliefs and values. And critical thinking skills, which can guide one toward truths, help me continually question my assumptions and look for explanations that go beyond what appears to be self-evident.

Before one can apply these qualities in therapeutic work, it is important to be familiar with the knowledge base regarding individual and social biases, cultural values, and power structures. An understanding of these concepts is essential in cultivating a humble, compassionate, and critical approach to one's work. Let's begin with the example of Elaine, a European American therapist in her early 30s.

Elaine received a call from a local physician who wished to obtain counseling for his patient, Mrs. Sok, a Cambodian (Khmer) woman in her 50s who had been crying, sleeping poorly, and losing weight since learning 3 weeks earlier that her apartment building was scheduled to be demolished. The physician gave Elaine the name and phone number of Mrs. Sok's interpreter, Han, who would bring Mrs. Sok with her to the mental health center.

Elaine called Han and made arrangements for an initial assessment to be attended by Mrs. Sok, Elaine, and Han. During their meeting, Mrs. Sok spoke in a soft voice and made little eye contact with Elaine. Mrs. Sok could not provide her age, the date, or the name of the building in which they were meeting. Han explained that Mrs. Sok had never learned to read or write in her own language and that she did not keep track of dates by the "Western" calendar. Elaine quickly realized it would be meaningless to ask the other mental status questions she would normally ask in an assessment of this sort (e.g., to spell a word backward, recall three objects, or draw geometric designs). Instead, she chose to focus on obtaining more information about Mrs. Sok's medical and social history.

With Han interpreting her questions, Elaine learned that Mrs. Sok had been widowed when her husband was killed in the war in Cambodia during the late 1970s, and that three of her four children (at the time) also died or were killed. During the years in which she lived in a refugee camp in Thailand, Mrs. Sok had two more children by a man whose whereabouts she no longer knew. In the early 1990s, Mrs. Sok and her two youngest children (now ages 15 and 17) emigrated to the United States, where they had been living in an apartment building next door to two other Cambodian families. The family managed to live on public assistance and the money her 17-year-old son earned from a part-time job in a restaurant.

As Elaine obtained this information, she began to notice that Mrs. Sok's responses in Khmer were much shorter than Han's subsequent interpretations in English. Elaine asked Han if she was adding information, and Han said yes, because she knew Mrs. Sok well and was trying to help by including information that Mrs. Sok was leaving out. When Elaine asked Han in a firm tone to interpret exactly what was said with no additions or deletions and explained that this would allow her to gain a more accurate assessment of Mrs. Sok, Han agreed but appeared uncomfortable.

Although Mrs. Sok showed little emotional response to questions about her history, she became tearful when Elaine asked about the impending loss of her apartment. She said that her friends were there and that she didn't know where else she would go. Elaine made an empathic comment in response but did not ask any additional questions about the housing situation. Instead, she focused on obtaining more information about Mrs. Sok's experiences during the war. As their time was ending, Elaine told Mrs. Sok that she believed she could be of help and wanted Mrs. Sok to return with Han the next week. She added that she would like Mrs. Sok to also see a psychiatrist, who might recommend some medicine to help her sleep. Mrs. Sok nodded her head in agreement. At this point, the session had already taken 2 hours and another client was waiting outside, so Elaine scheduled their second meeting, and they all said good-bye. The next week, Mrs. Sok and Han did not appear for their appointment, and when Elaine telephoned Han to find out why, Han told her that Mrs. Sok did not want to return.

This anecdote describes a situation not at all unusual in mental health practice today. A compassionate and well-meaning therapist tries to understand a new client's needs and explain how the therapist might be of help. At the same time, an individual seeking assistance attempts to assess the trustworthiness and competence of this relative stranger (the therapist) and determine whether the benefits of counseling will outweigh the time, effort, and embarrassment involved. For one or more reasons, the client often decides that therapy will not be helpful and so does not return.

From Mrs. Sok's perspective, Elaine seemed young to be in her position of authority and not especially sensitive to those around her; Elaine's pressing questions about Mrs. Sok's past and Han's apparent discomfort at something Elaine said (the request to interpret verbatim) made Mrs. Sok feel protective of Han and cautious about trusting Elaine. Mrs. Sok had had no prior experience with a counselor or psychotherapist, and when her physician and Han had told her that "counseling can help you," she assumed that such help would address her most pressing problem, namely, the destruction of her home.

Although Elaine was at least minimally aware that Mrs. Sok's and Han's Cambodian heritage influenced how they perceived and presented Mrs. Sok's needs, she did not think carefully about how these influences were relevant to the assessment. Had Elaine systematically considered the role of culture in Mrs. Sok's situation, she might have recognized her own lack of experience and knowledge regarding Cambodian culture, refugees, and older Cambodian women (50 years being "older" among people who survived the war). This realization could have led her to treat Han less as an assistant and more as a peer in the recognition that Han's knowledge of Cambodian people was as extensive as Elaine's knowledge of the mental health field. She might then have seen the need to consult with Han before and after the assessment, an action that would have helped her gain the trust and respect of Han and thus, indirectly, of Mrs. Sok. (See Bradford & Munoz, 1993, regarding the importance of pre- and postassessment meetings with interpreters; Struwe, 1994, regarding clinical interviewing with refugees; and Criddle, 1992, for accounts of Khmer people's resettlement experiences.)

Additionally, Elaine could have facilitated rapport if she had systematically considered the ways in which her own personal and professional experiences might be influencing her conceptualization of Mrs. Sok's situation. For example, Elaine's theoretical orientation, training, and personal beliefs about trauma led her to assume that Mrs. Sok's current symptoms were due to past trauma. As a result, she focused on eliciting information about Mrs. Sok's war-related experiences, despite the fact that both Mrs. Sok and Han were asking for help with something else. If Elaine had recognized the legitimacy of Mrs. Sok's conceptualization, she might then have focused on what Mrs. Sok considered central—that is, the threatened loss of her home—and Mrs. Sok might have felt more understood.

In turn, if Mrs. Sok had felt understood, she would have been more likely to return. With further assessment, it might have become apparent that past trauma was contributing to Mrs. Sok's distress, and in this case Elaine would understandably want to address the subject. However, because Elaine did not establish rapport and trust, and Mrs. Sok did not return, she lost the opportunity for helping the client in this or any other way.

Understanding Bias

One way to think about the mistakes Elaine made is in terms of bias, albeit well-intentioned bias. Although Elaine could have conceptualized Mrs. Sok's case in a variety of ways, her experiences and training biased her toward a particular view that then inclined her to take certain actions and not others. Although Elaine would have been open to considering these biases if someone had pointed them out, she did not see them on her own. Largely because she thought of bias in dichotomous terms (i.e., that one is either biased or not), the possibility that she might be biased did not occur to her.

A more helpful way for one to think about bias is simply as a tendency to think, act, or feel in a particular way. In some cases, these tendencies may guide individuals toward more accurate hypotheses and a quicker understanding of someone. In other situations, they may lead individuals to embarrassingly wrong assumptions, as I experienced in the following situation.

I was visiting a small Unitarian group in a rural area. The circle was talkative and cheery, with the exception of one man. Dressed in a plaid shirt, jeans, and hiking boots, he appeared to be European American and had a long, untrimmed beard. His facial expression was somber, and he didn't say a word, although he seemed to be listening intently. The word *unibomber* popped into my head. During the coffee hour afterward, I avoided eye contact with him when I was speaking.

As I was driving home with a friend, I asked her about this man. She said, "Oh, he's an interesting guy. He works full time as a biologist, and he's a professional musician. He gets up at 4:00 every morning to practice his music before work. He's also a Quaker, so he doesn't say much in the service, but when he does, it's always interesting." Ouch.

It is clear that my biases did not facilitate helpful hypotheses about this man. On the contrary, they sent me in the opposite direction— toward inaccurate assumptions that then led me to behave in a way that reinforced these assumptions. By avoiding eye contact with him, I was denying myself the opportunity to learn anything from him that might have contradicted my misunderstanding.

At the individual level, biases emerge in tandem with two other cognitive processes, those of categorization and generalization. The abilities to categorize information and then generalize this data to new situations help people organize the vast amounts of information they encounter on a daily basis (Hamilton & Trolier, 1986; Stephan, 1989). Usually these cognitive processes facilitate people's learning and social interactions, but they can also contribute to the formation of inaccurate assumptions, as in my previous example. When these assumptions become rigid, people may develop what Holiman and Lauver (1987) called "hardening of the categories" (p. 187), or a tendency toward stereotyping. Whereas *prejudice* refers to "the positive or negative evaluations of social groups and their members," *stereotypes* include "the knowledge, beliefs, and expectations associated with those groups" (p. 1; Sherman, Stroessner, Conrey, & Azam, 2005).

To avoid making inaccurate assumptions about their clients, therapists may decide that the best approach is to assume nothing about a client's culture and allow the client to share whatever she or he believes is important. Although such an approach is well motivated, it contains a problematic assumption, namely, that therapists are able to assume nothing about their clients if they choose. The idea that one can "turn off" preconceptions about groups of people is appealing. However, given the subtle and pervasive nature of our assumptions, such control is extremely difficult, if not impossible. What is more likely to occur when one attempts to ignore the presence of assumptions is decreased awareness that one is making them (Pedersen, 1987).

It may be helpful to think of a lack of experience with a particular group as creating a hole or vacuum inside of yourself (Hays, 2007). As with any vacuum, there is a tendency for all surrounding material to be sucked in. When it comes to minority groups, this material often consists of dominant cultural messages that cause people to assume differences are deficits, sometimes so subtly that individuals do not perceive the process. People then use this information to make generalizations and draw conclusions about individual members of a group, despite a lack of direct experience. It is humbling to recognize that people all carry around their own little vacuum packs of ignorance. Our challenge as therapists and human beings is to recognize these vacuum packs and commit ourselves to opening them up and replacing inaccurate information with real experience and direct learning.

In an initial assessment, if a therapist has already established rapport and trust, clients will often give him or her the benefit of the doubt and overlook or forgive inaccurate assumptions. However, in most assessment situations, therapists do not have the benefit of having established a solid working relationship with the client. Rather, upon meeting an individual or family for the first time, therapists must establish rapport and trust in a relatively short period or risk losing the opportunity to help. Knowledge of a client's culture can facilitate this early work, because it enables the therapist to formulate hypotheses and ask questions that more closely address the client's real experience. The deeper and broader a therapist's knowledge of and experience with a client's culture, the more accurate and relevant these hypotheses and questions will be (S. Sue, 1998). In turn, well-informed hypotheses and questions often increase clients' trust and confidence in the therapist.

Examining Social Bias and Power

The case example of Mrs. Sok illustrates bias at the level of cognitive structures that predispose all human beings to the development of prejudice and stereotypes. However, people cannot fully understand bias at the individual level without knowledge of sociocultural influences (Gaines & Reed, 1995). Perhaps the most central concept to an understanding of the influence of sociocultural biases on individuals is that of power (Kivel, 2002).

Because high-status groups hold more power, they can exert more control over their own situations and the situations of lower status groups (Lott, 2002). One way in which powerful groups exert control is through stereotypes (Fiske, 1993). Stereotypes can be described in terms of two key functions. *Descriptive* stereotypes define how most people in a particular group behave, what they prefer, and where their competence lies. Descriptive stereotypes exert control because they create a starting point for people's expectations. That is, the stereotyped person must choose to either stay within the boundaries of these expectations or go outside of them; in either case, the stereotype places a burden on the person being judged and on his or her interactions with others (Fiske, 1993).

Adding to the effect of descriptive stereotypes, *prescriptive* stereotypes define how certain groups should think, feel, and behave (Fiske, 1993, p. 623). For example, think of the ways in which prescriptive stereotypes shape the dominant culture's expectations regarding people with disabilities. People with disabilities are frequently expected to make daily adjustments to the nondisabled world without complaint and work hard to "overcome" or "transcend" their disability despite inaccessible physical environments and social barriers caused by others' fears and hostilities. Moreover, they are expected to do all of this cheerfully (Olkin, 2002).

Stereotypes, prejudice, and bias, when combined with power, form systems of privilege known as the "isms" (e.g., racism, sexism, classism, heterosexism, ageism, ableism, colonialism; Hays, 1996a). Society socializes unprivileged members of these systems to be acutely aware of the lines separating those who have privilege from those who do not. Unprivileged people need to pay more attention to differences and rules, because the outcomes of their lives are more dependent on those who hold power (Fiske, 1993).

In contrast, society does not socialize powerful groups to perceive the rules and barriers separating the unprivileged because they do not need to; oppressed groups have little impact on their daily lives. For example,

> There are many things that an African American child can do that will get him or her characterized as "acting Black" or "acting White," but there is very little that a European American child can do that will prompt such labeling. . . . Living in a White-dominated society, the average African American child is made aware implicitly and explicitly of these categorizations on a daily basis . . . [whereas] the average European American child rarely is made aware of anything having to do with these categories. (Gaines & Reed, 1995, p. 98)

In the United States, systems of privilege and oppression are intimately tied to capitalism. Sexism and racism support the view of women and people of color as "a surplus labor force" that "can be pushed in and out of employment in keeping with current needs of the economy (depression, expansion, wartime, or a period of union-busting)" (Blood, Tuttle,

& Lakey, 1995, p. 156). Corporate capitalism also pressures men, who, if they are too demanding, can be easily replaced by women or people of color who cost less. Gender and racial stereotypes—often aided by the media, educational institutions, and the legal system—reinforce the belief that this arrangement is fair and natural (Blood et al., 1995).

Members of dominant groups often find it painful to acknowledge the existence of systems of privilege, because the idea goes against fundamental Western beliefs in meritocracy (e.g., "If you work hard enough, you'll succeed") and democracy (e.g., "Majority rule is fair") (Robinson, 1999). It is easier for people to believe that instances of prejudice and discrimination are primarily the fault of individual "bad apples." From his perspective as a European American man, Croteau (1999) explained,

> To me, racist attitudes and behaviors were solely about the moral or psychological failures or shortcomings of individual White people. Although I probably would not have explained it in a way that sounded this judgmental, it really came down to my seeing racism as what "bad" White people do to people of color. I desperately wanted to be a "good" White person. In retrospect, I realize that this exclusively individualistic and highly judgmental perspective on racism left my fragile ego on the line with every interpersonal interaction I had across racial lines. . . . Seeing racism solely through the lens of individualism was an unforgiving perspective that failed to take into account the reality of socially learned racism. (p. 30)

As Croteau (1999) suggested, systems of privilege harm those who hold privilege as well as those who do not (Locke & Kiselica, 1999). Systems of privilege can separate whole domains of information, knowledge, and skills from the members of dominant groups who might also benefit. For instance, traditional healing practices, many of which do not involve the side effects of European American medications and medical practices, were seen as inferior by the dominant medical establishment until 1978, when the World Health Organization and UNICEF officially recognized traditional practitioners (Jilek, 1994). As a result, European American physicians (and the dominant culture) have been slow to accept such practices (e.g., acupuncture), which continue to be less available to patients in U.S. health care settings.

At the level of personal growth and development, privilege can also lead to the internalization of feelings of superiority and elitism, resulting in a restriction of one's capacities for love, trust, empathy, and openness (Hertzberg, 1990, p. 279). Privilege (e.g., in the form of money or powerful social connections) may prevent a person from developing the coping abilities that less privileged individuals develop to survive (McIntosh, 1998). At present, older European American men have the highest suicide rate in the United States (Richmond, 1999); this negative buffer effect of privilege may be one reason why.

Although it may never be possible to completely escape the influence of societal biases, it is possible to gain an awareness and knowledge base that can help individuals recognize the influence of these biases on ourselves and others. Such awareness and knowledge increase the likelihood that individuals' decisions, beliefs, and behaviors will be conscious and well-informed. The key lays in one's commitment to assessing—on an ongoing basis—one's own experiences, beliefs, values, knowledge, and information sources (L. S. Brown, 1994; Lopez et al., 1989; C. B. Williams, 1999). Let's turn now to a consideration of the three elements mentioned earlier—humility, compassion, and critical thinking skills—that provide a foundation for this work.

Staying Humble While Thinking Critically

Over the course of my professional life, I have asked various people what he or she believes is the most important quality or characteristic for someone doing cross-cultural work. The most common response I've received is that the person needs to be humble. The word *humble* comes from humility, which is related to the term *humus,* meaning earth (Merriam-Webster, 1983). Similarly, a humble person is often described as "down to earth." When people are humble, they recognize that other viewpoints, beliefs, behaviors, and traditions may be just as valid as their own. Furthermore, people understand that benefits often come from learning these alternative ways of approaching the world. As Davis (1993) noted, "People with genuine humility are effective helpers, because they are realistic about what they have to offer, aware of their own limitations and accepting of the contribution of others" (p. 55).

It may seem that the idea of critical thinking is opposed to that of humility, because the term *critical* is often equated with negativity or confrontation. However, critical thinking skills are essential to humility, because they involve the abilities to identify and challenge assumptions (one's own as well as those of others), examine contextual influences (on one's own thinking, too), and imagine and explore alternatives (Brookfield, 1987).

For example, I consider myself a feminist, and although I recognize the limitations of this philosophy (particularly its ethnocentric applications), I still subscribe to many of its tenets. Among my values is the belief that women are better off if they can support themselves financially; this has something to do with personal empowerment and a desire for egalitarian relationships.

When I was in my mid-20s, I spent several months interviewing Arab women living in three different environments in North Africa: (a) the cosmopolitan capital city of Tunis, (b) a midsized village that was conservative and traditional in its values and mores, and (c) an impoverished Bedouin community that had gone from a nomadic existence to a settled agricultural life in the previous generation. As part of this research, I wanted to learn how Tunisian women's lives had changed since the country gained independence in 1956 and had enacted laws aimed at improving the status of women. I expected to find some form of economic independence to be associated with greater satisfaction and freedoms, at least for middle-class women. What I found was a bit more complicated (Hays, 1987; Hays & Zouari, 1995).

Nearly all of the middle-class urban women were employed outside the home. They cited mixed reasons for this, namely, that they liked working outside, but that they also needed to bring in extra money because of a higher cost of living in the city. The Bedouin women were poor and had always worked outside the home, in the fields alongside their husbands. This was extremely hard work—bending over for long periods in the hot sun, often with a baby tied to one's back. Not surprisingly, this kind of work did not lead the Bedouin women to feel greater satisfaction with their lives; rather, they expressed the most frustration.

It was the middle-class women in the village who surprised me by their disinterest in outside employment or a personal income. Granted, occupational opportunities were limited, but among those women who did have some personal income, whether by inheritance or sewing, the money was considered theirs. One woman summarized a common attitude: "I already do all the work at home [as one job]. Why would I want two?" She added that she liked having time in the afternoon to do embroidery and visit with her sisters, her mother, and her friends. She was astonished at how hard I chose to work; I think that she even thought I was a little nutty. My learning from her and the other women I spent time with led me to think more critically about my beliefs about women's roles, men's roles, personal empowerment, and relationships. Seeing women who were satisfied with lifestyles that contradicted some of my most firmly held beliefs was humbling, to say the least.

In this way, humility and critical thinking often operate in a reciprocal relationship. Humility opens one to new forms of learning and diverse sources of knowledge, whereas critical thinking about one's knowledge, sources of information, and ways of learning, along with constant testing of alternative hypotheses, can help one to stay open (Lopez et al., 1989).

Sound clinical judgments require the therapist to have both humility and critical thinking. Because a willingness to question oneself is communicated in nonverbal ways, both have the added benefit of facilitating rapport. Consider the example of a European American male therapist working with a single woman of Mexican American heritage and her three children, ages 6, 8, and 12. Following her divorce, the client, who had a 2-year college degree, received no child support and had to move to a lower-income apartment and find a job that would support her family. She came to counseling to obtain help in dealing with her 6-year-old son's bed-wetting. The therapist began working with her to help her son; however, he also had concerns about the 12-year-old daughter, whom he thought of as a "parentified child" (i.e., in the role of the mother's confidante and partner in raising the two younger children).

Because the daughter had no academic or behavioral problems, the therapist decided to consult with a Latina therapist before sharing these concerns with the mother. Through the consultation, he began to realize how his own cultural heritage was influencing his views of what constitutes healthy child rearing. He began to see the possibility that in this family's case, the child's role might not be pathological. Although his concerns did not disappear completely, he did begin to see the family in a more accepting way, an attitude that manifested itself in behaviors that were respectful of the mother and all that she was doing for her children. (See Arroyo, 1997; Falicov, 1998; and Santiago-Riviera, Arredondo, & Gallardo-Cooper, 2002, for more on child rearing in Mexican American and Latina families.)

There are a number of questions that therapists can ask themselves to prevent premature judgments. These include the following:

- How did I come to this understanding?
- How do I know that this is true?
- Are there alternative explanations or opinions that might be equally valid in this situation?
- How might my view of the client's situation be influenced by my age or generational experiences, my ethnic background, and my socioeconomic status (i.e., the ADDRESSING influences)?
- Might there be some information that lends validity to the view with which I disagree?
- Might there be a positive, culturally related purpose for the behavior, belief, or feeling that I perceive as dysfunctional or unhealthy?

These sorts of questions do not prevent therapists from making clinical judgments, but rather slow down the process by encouraging a consideration of the client's context. In addition, they increase the likelihood that the therapist's hypotheses will be closer to the client's real experience.

Returning to my learning from the Tunisian women, although I still hold my feminist beliefs, I now realize that my values are directly related to my identity, my opportunities, and my context. Trying to think critically about my beliefs and why I believe what I believe helps me to be more open to people who hold values that I might see as contrary to mine. The more open I am, the more compassionate and understanding I can be toward others, which in turn helps me to be a better therapist.

Overcoming Obstacles to Compassion

The centrality of compassion in becoming a healthier and happier human being (and thus therapist) was explained by the Dalai Lama, the Buddhist spiritual leader of Tibet:

> If you maintain a feeling of compassion, loving kindness, then something automatically opens your inner door. Through that, you can communicate much more easily with other people. And that feeling of warmth creates a kind of openness. . . . Then there's less need to hide things, and as a result, feelings of fear, self-doubt, and insecurity are automatically dispelled. Also, it creates a feeling of trust from other people.
> . . . Anger, violence, and aggression may certainly rise, but I think it's on a secondary or more superficial level; in a sense, they arise when we're frustrated in our efforts to achieve love and affection. (His Holiness the Dalai Lama & Cutler, 1999, pp. 40, 54–55)

The concept of compassion is not unique to Buddhism, but it is so clearly described that I find it helpful to use Buddhist concepts when thinking about compassion (Chödrön, 2000; His Holiness the Dalai Lama, 2003; Thich Nhat Hanh, 1992). In addition, Patanjali (a 2nd-century BC scholar and author of part of the Yoga Sutras) posited five obstacles to growth that seem equally applicable to compassion. These obstacles include fear, ignorance, aversion (i.e., to pain), desire, and egoism (Frager & Fadiman, 1998, p. 501).

Consider the example of a young European American female therapist who experienced an initial fear of an African American male client despite a lack of experience (positive or negative) with African American men. Because the therapist's fear pulled her away from the client's experience into herself, it impeded her ability to engage with and respond compassionately to the man. Such fear is often related to a lack of experience and knowledge. As the metaphor of the vacuum pack suggests, as long as this hole is unfilled by direct personal experience, it is vulnerable to being filled by dominant cultural assumptions (including fears and negative beliefs) about the particular group.

At present, there is also a great deal of pain surrounding cultural issues, and most people try to avoid pain whenever possible. This aversion may lead a therapist to avoid certain topics, shut down, or emotionally distance her- or himself when the topic arises. For example, a nondisabled European American male therapist was repeatedly hurt by others' assumptions that he was lacking in compassion for people of minority identities. As he attempted to understand the meaning of a particular client's disability from the client's perspective, he found himself to be the target of the client's anger. If he had then focused on his own pain and anger, he would have been more inclined to pull away from the client and to make automatic interpretations (e.g., that the client was overreacting) that would not facilitate a deeper understanding of the client's experience.

On the basis of their work with families of people who have disabilities, Hulnick and Hulnick (1989) suggested the following:

> We have observed many times that there is a sequence that always seems to be present at times of emotional upset. It goes like this. Whenever anger is present and we look beneath the anger, we always find hurt. Anger turns out to largely be a reaction occurring when we feel hurt. And when we look beneath the hurt, we always find caring. We are only hurt when something or someone we care about has been, in some way, desecrated or violated. . . . This sequence gives us the key for effectively handling these types of situations. It is this. Give a client full permission to express his or her deepest pain. In fact, assist clients by actively encouraging them in expressing it. (p. 168)

The fourth and fifth obstacles of desire and egoism can play out in the therapist's attachment to a particular theoretical orientation or outcome. From a Buddhist perspective, attachment to one viewpoint, conceptualization, or idea often leads to unnecessary suffering (Rao, 1988). In the therapeutic setting, allowing one's theoretical orientation to take precedence over a client's concerns may result in an inaccurate assessment or an intervention that is inappropriate or ineffective. For example, in working with a client who has anxiety about an impending move, a present-oriented, cognitive behavior therapist might overlook the importance of the family's multigenerational migration history. Alternatively, in response to a client's depression in dealing with coworkers' racist comments, a psychodynamically oriented therapist might overemphasize the client's early upbringing in his feelings about the situation and fail to address the need for immediate practical changes in the client's environment (e.g., talking to a supervisor, filing a grievance, requesting a transfer).

Fear, ignorance, aversion to pain, and attachment may contribute to the development of defensive interactions. Defensiveness can be thought of as the cognitive and emotional rigidity that occurs when one feels threatened or attacked. As C. B. Williams (1999) noted, it is a frequent reaction among counselors when talking about racial issues across racial groups (and I would add across the other ADDRESSING identities as well).

In the therapeutic setting, feelings of defensiveness may lead therapists to focus on the justification of their own ideas, thus lessening their concern for the client's experience. This shift in one's primary concern is easily perceived by clients, who may then engage in self-protective behaviors such as emotionally distancing themselves from the therapist.

It is probably impossible to eliminate defensive feelings. It may also be undesirable, because emotions often serve as cues that something is amiss. However, it is possible and frequently desirable to refrain from engaging in defensive behaviors, particularly if these behaviors interfere with one's acceptance of and concern for another person.

Preventing Defensive Behaviors

My friend Bob was the principal of a high school in a Siberian Yup'ik village in Alaska. One day a European American male teacher (all of the teachers were European American) came in to see him. The teacher was furious because he said that he had corrected one of his students, and the boy had laughed at him. The teacher considered the boy's behavior to be a sign of disrespect. Bob suggested that he bring the boy in, which the teacher did. As the teacher repeated his complaint in a loud, angry voice, the boy began laughing again. Bob told the teacher to leave. When they were alone, Bob asked the boy what had happened, and the boy dissolved into tears.

The boy hadn't meant to laugh, but like all the students there, he spoke English as a second language and just didn't understand what the teacher had wanted him to do. His laughter was out of embarrassment at the teacher's angry focus on him. Unfortunately, the teacher was too stuck in his own defensiveness to stop the downward spiral of their interactions (i.e., the more the teacher shouted the more the boy laughed). If Bob had accepted the teacher's (dominant cultural) view of the problem, he would have missed the opportunity for seeing what was really happening. But by staying open and looking for alternative explanations, Bob opened the way for a deeper understanding of the boy.

A first step toward sustaining openness is to become more aware of one's experience in the moment, a process known as *mindfulness* in Buddhist psychology. The Vietnamese monk Thich Nhat Hanh (1992) described the importance of mindfulness in resolving defensive feelings:

> The word *samyojana* refers to internal formations, fetters, or knots. When someone says something unkind to us, for example, if we do not understand why he said it and we become irritated, a knot will be tied in us. The lack of understanding is the basis for

every internal knot. If we practice mindfulness, we can learn the skill of recognizing a knot the moment it is tied in us and finding ways to untie it. Internal formations need our full attention as soon as they form, while they are still loosely tied, so that the work of untying them will be easy. If we do not untie our knots when they form, they will grow tighter and stronger. (p. 48)

People may experience these "knots" as physiological sensations that accompany one's feelings of defensiveness, fear, and pain. These sensations can then serve as cues that one is focusing more on oneself than on one's client. If possible, identifying the precipitants of these sensations and feelings may help the therapist predict his or her inclination to behave in a way that will work against his or her real intentions (e.g., to communicate respect, to obtain an accurate assessment).

For instance, in a session with an older client, a young therapist began to experience tension in his forehead and upper back. He used these sensations as cues to recognize that he felt some fear about working with a client who was much older than he was. In recognizing this fear, he was then able to refrain from behaviors that he would normally unconsciously engage in when he felt afraid and inadequate. Rather than the therapist describing his qualifications in such a way that the client perceived him to be bragging (and consequently would feel less connected to him), the therapist openly discussed with the client how his younger age might limit his understanding of the client's situation. Because the latter behavior made the therapist vulnerable and thus communicated his "humanness," it was more likely to facilitate a sense of connection between the two (Kiselica, 1998).

When confronted with feelings of discomfort in an assessment, it may be helpful for therapists to take a deep breath, exhale slowly, and then focus for a few seconds on their breath. This emphasis on breathing as a way of grounding oneself is found in Yogic and Buddhist meditation practice as well as in their behavioral descendent, relaxation training. With this focus, it may then be more possible to ask yourself about the presumed need for two parties to hold the same view. That is, must a client conceptualize a situation in the same way that you do?

It may also be constructive to ask yourself if there are alternative opinions that may be as valid or useful as your own. Might there be some information or experiences that would allow you to appreciate these different perspectives? Finally, how might you go about getting the information or experiences that could lead to a broader vision and understanding of the client and her situation? Note that these questions parallel those offered earlier for thinking critically while staying humble.

To summarize, we can never eliminate defensive feelings. However, we can decrease defensive behaviors by following these steps:

- Be mindful of the physical sensations that accompany feelings of defensiveness, fear, and pain.

- If possible, identify the precipitants of these sensations and feelings to help you predict defensive feelings and behaviors before they occur.
- Use these physical sensations as cues to what you are feeling.
- When you feel defensive sensations and feelings arise, take a deep breath, exhale slowly, and then focus for a few seconds on your breath.
- Refrain from defensive behaviors (e.g., talking too much, emphasizing your own accomplishments, emotional distancing).
- Question the need for clients' views to match your own. Are there equally valid alternative opinions?
- Recognize your need for additional information and experiences.
- If appropriate, discuss the limitations of your knowledge and experience with the client.

Keeping a Sense of Humor

Humor provides an opportunity to step out of one's cognitive set, even if only for a few moments (Mahrer & Gervaise, 1994). This shift can allow one to see a new perspective or appreciate other people even if those people hold beliefs with which one disagrees (Lemma, 2000). I am continually reminded in my day-to-day experiences of the ways in which humor enables people to connect.

A few years ago, I was asked to see Mr. Smith, a married man in his 70s, for questions about depression and cognitive difficulties. As I approached his hospital room, I could hear what sounded like an argument between him and his physician:

PHYSICIAN: Now, George, you're gonna have to start listening to what I'm telling you. If you don't do this, you're going to have bigger problems. Are you listening to me?

MR. SMITH: Oh, why don't you just go find somebody else to pester?

Cringing a little inside, I knocked on the open door, then walked in and introduced myself. Mr. Smith was in a wheelchair and hooked up to an IV. He was hunched over (whether he had osteoporosis or depression or was just angrily facing the floor, I couldn't tell). The physician gave me a warm smile and said, "Well, George, I guess you're the lucky one who gets to stay here and talk with Dr. Hays, so I'll just be heading out." Mr. Smith grumbled something; I couldn't see his face. Just then, the physician turned away to make a quick note in his chart. In that moment, Mr. Smith raised his head, looked right at me, winked, and put his head back down. I immediately relaxed and let go of the negative expectations and defensive feelings I'd been building since approaching the door.

Navigating Ongoing Dilemmas

Therapists who can incorporate these suggestions into their cross-cultural practices will still encounter situations in which finding a good solution remains difficult. One such dilemma is that in which a client says something that would generally be considered racist or similarly offensive. If the comment is the main point and intentionally derogatory, it can often be addressed directly. For example, asking about a male client's homophobic beliefs and feelings would be relevant if he uses a slur to describe his gay employer, whom he believes is treating him unfairly.

However, if a client's comment is incidental to her main point and not intentionally derogatory, then the decision to say something can be more difficult because it involves pulling the client back to the offensive remark and prioritizing the therapist's feelings about it. For example, during the Gulf War, I saw a client who was telling me about her son who was a part of the military action, and as she was talking she made a negative comment about Arab people. Her comment was completely incidental to her main point, and I doubt that she had any idea that what she said was offensive. At the time, I was married to an Arab man, and we were both involved in protesting the war. I had many strong feelings in reaction to her comment, but I chose to say nothing, in part because it seemed to me that saying something would have been calling attention to my issues rather than hers. Also, this conversation took place during an assessment, and I had not yet established a relationship with the woman. At the same time, the value I place on the need to speak out against racist and other oppressive attitudes created pressure inside me to say something.

One guideline for therapist self-disclosure is whether it primarily benefits the therapist or the client (see chap. 5, this volume, on establishing a respectful relationship). Responding to a client's incidental remark seems to lean more toward the therapist. I could have addressed the woman's comment without explicitly stating my personal situation; however, simply calling attention to her comment would have made my political views fairly transparent. But one could argue that it is to the client's advantage to know that she is offending others with her language; also, ultimately, racist attitudes hurt and limit the person who holds them (Hertzberg, 1990). It is important to note that the therapeutic relationship and the therapist's identity are also considerations. For example, if I were Arab and the client made the derogatory comment knowing this, I would want to find out why (e.g., Was she feeling angry toward me, or did she think I might be biased against her? see Chin, 1994; Pérez Foster, 1996).

The complexity of dilemmas like these means that solutions will be highly situation specific. To increase the likelihood that you will make the best decision possible, the first step is to have thought about such issues beforehand as a part of your own ongoing cultural self-assessment (Greene, 1994). (This process and the relationship between therapists' values and their work is explored in chap. 3 of this volume, followed by a more detailed discussion of cross-cultural transference and counter-transference in chap. 4.) When difficult dilemmas occur, using the preceding guidelines regarding defensive behaviors can help you make a decision about how to respond in that particular moment. Afterward, whenever possible, I try to consult with a colleague who belongs to the cultural group being referenced; even if it is too late to do something, at least I can learn from the feedback.

Also, in the moment, when I personally feel offended, it helps me to pay attention to the speaker's intentions. If he or she means well, I try to go with that. In turn, I hope that when I make mistakes, listeners will be generous in their judgments of me. Still, this "coming to critical consciousness" is, as the writer bell hooks (1998) noted,

> a difficult, "trying" process, one that demands that we give up set ways of thinking and being, that we shift our paradigms, that we open ourselves to the unknown, the unfamiliar. Undergoing this process, we learn what it means to struggle and in this effort we experience the dignity and integrity of being that comes with revolutionary change. (p. 584)

Conclusion

Humility, compassion, and critical thinking skills provide a therapist with a foundation for learning more about diverse cultural influences on oneself and one's clients. However, these skills do not ensure culturally responsive practice. There is still the need for therapists to be aware of their own particular knowledge gaps and areas of bias. This topic is explored in the next chapter.

Key Ideas

Becoming a Culturally Responsive Therapist

1. Bias is best thought of as a tendency to think, act, or feel in a particular way, sometimes guiding one toward more accurate hypotheses, but sometimes not.
2. When bias is reinforced by powerful groups and social structures, the results are systems of privilege and oppression (e.g.,

racism, sexism, classism, heterosexism, ableism, ageism, and colonialism).

3. Unprivileged members of these systems are socialized to be acutely aware of the lines separating those who have privilege from those who do not, because the outcomes of their lives are more dependent on those who hold power.

4. Privileged members are socialized to be less aware of the lines and differences related to privilege.

5. Humility, compassion, and critical thinking skills are qualities that facilitate therapists' work across lines of privilege and oppression.

6. The obstacles of fear, ignorance, aversion to pain, and attachment can contribute to defensive interactions.

7. Although defensive feelings can never be eliminated and may even be helpful as cues, defensive behaviors often create emotional distance between the therapist and client.

8. Steps that one can take to minimize defensive behaviors include maintaining mindful awareness of the physiological sensations that accompany one's defensive feelings, focusing on one's breath in the moment, and questioning the need for a client to see things in the same way as the therapist.

9. Cross-cultural work is fraught with challenging dilemmas; the best solution for one situation may not be the best for another.

10. Following a cross-cultural mistake or misunderstanding, it can be helpful to consult with a colleague who belongs to the cultural group being referenced.

Looking Into the Clinician's Mirror
Cultural Self-Assessment

3

One of my friends was in a spiritual growth group whose members became quite close. They provided each other with a warm, supportive environment to share their joy and pain. Everyone except my friend and her husband were European American, but this did not seem to be an issue until one meeting, when my friend shared her pain about what she believed to be a racist comment from someone outside the group. Rather than validate her experience, the group asked her questions about why the person would make such a comment. They seemed to be looking for a way to justify it and, in the process, implied that she was overreacting. As the tension built, one member objected to the time being spent on this issue, saying, "You know, this is a spiritual growth group, not an antiracism group." My friend replied, "But racism *is* a spiritual issue for me." Unfortunately, the group members were unanimous in their inability to see this situation from my friend's perspective; the result was that she and her husband decided to leave the group.

The dictionary defines *privilege* as a right or immunity that gives the individual a distinct advantage or favor; in contrast, the term *oppressed* is described as the state of being burdened spiritually or mentally, suppressed or crushed by an abuse of power (Merriam-Webster, 1983). McIntosh (1998) compared White privilege to an invisible knapsack that White people can count on to make life easier. For example, European Americans can usually choose to be in the company of their own race when they want to be, they are not asked to speak for their race, they rarely have trouble finding housing because of their race, and so on.

However, as discussed in chapter 2, privilege also tends to isolate people, cutting them off from information and experiences related to specific minority groups that could be helpful and enrich their lives. In my friend's case, the privilege experienced by the European Americans in the group led them to believe that racism was not the problem, and because they all agreed with each other, their position of "rightness" was affirmed. The only information they had to contradict their belief was that provided by my friend and her husband, whose views were easily dismissed because they were in the minority.

People all have their own unique identities and experiences, and consequently the areas in which they hold privilege vary. In general, though, these privileged areas are often those in which people hold the least awareness. The challenge then is to recognize one's areas of privilege and commit oneself to the extra work that is required to fill in one's knowledge gaps (Akamatsu, 1998; Roysircar, 2004). Toward this goal, there are a number of practical steps therapists can take to increase their self-awareness and knowledge. These include, but are not limited to, the following:

- investigating our own cultural heritage;
- paying attention to the influence of privilege on our understanding of cultural issues, and hence on our work with clients;
- educating ourselves through diverse sources of information; and
- developing diverse relationships with an understanding of the influence of sociocultural contexts.

Work in each area can be facilitated through the use of the ADDRESS-ING framework.

Investigating Your Own Cultural Heritage

One way to begin thinking about the influence that diverse cultural factors have had on you is by doing the following exercise. First, take a lined piece of paper, and on the left side, write the acronym ADDRESS-ING vertically, leaving space to the right of and below each letter. Next, record a brief description of the influences you consider salient for yourself in each category. If current influences are different from those that influenced you growing up, note the salient influences and identities in relation first to your upbringing, and then to your current contexts.

Also, fill in every category, even those for which you hold a dominant cultural identity, because this too is meaningful information. These categories are not mutually exclusive, so there may be some overlap between them. For example, if you are an American Indian, you may note this under **e**thnicity and/or under **I**ndigenous heritage, depending on how you identify. Similarly, Jewish heritage might be noted under **e**thnicity and/or **r**eligion and spiritual orientation.

Table 3.1 illustrates this process using the therapist, Olivia, as an example. Under **a**ge and generational influences, Olivia wrote, "52 years old; third-generation U.S. American; member of politically active generation of Chicanos and Chicanas in California; first generation affected by post-civil rights academic and employment opportunities in the

TABLE 3.1

The Therapist's Cultural Self-Assessment: Example of Olivia

Cultural influences	Olivia's self-assessment
*Age and generational influences	52 years old; third-generation U.S. American; member of politically active generation of Chicanos and Chicanas in California; first generation affected by post-civil rights academic and employment opportunities in the 1970s.
*Developmental disability	No developmental disability.
Disability acquired later in life	Chronic knee problems since early adulthood, including multiple surgeries; sometimes I use crutches to walk.
*Religion and spiritual orientation	Mother is a practicing Catholic, father nonpracticing Presbyterian; my current beliefs are a mixture of Catholic and secular; I do not attend mass.
Ethnic and racial identity	Mother and father both of mixed Mexican (Spanish and Indian) heritage, both born in the United States; my own identity is Chicana; I speak Spanish, but my primary language is English.
*Socioeconomic status	Parents urban, working, lower-middle-class members of an ethnic minority culture; however, my identity is as a university-educated Chicana; I identify with working-class people, although my occupation and income are middle class.
*Sexual orientation	Heterosexual; I have one friend who is lesbian.
Indigenous heritage	My maternal grandmother was Indian and immigrated to the United States from Mexico with my grandfather when they were young adults; what I know about this part of my heritage came from her, but she died when I was 10 years old.
*National origin	United States, but deep understanding of the immigration experience from my grandparents.
Gender	Woman, Chicana, divorced, mother of two children.

Note. *Connotes dominant cultural identity.

1970s." On the line for disabilities, she wrote, "Chronic knee problems since early adulthood, including multiple surgeries; sometimes I use crutches to walk." She continued through the list, with some overlap between categories, providing a general sketch of both minority and dominant cultural influences and identities salient for her.

The degree to which this exercise is helpful depends on how far one takes the exploration of these influences and identities. For instance, in the first area, **a**ge and generational influences, simply recognizing your age is not particularly informative. However, exploring the generational influences—including historical and sociocultural contexts related to your age and particular developmental phases—offers a rich source of material regarding the meanings of these influences and identities (Rogler, 2002).

The following general questions can help to elicit the meanings of age and generational influences in your self-evaluation:

- When I was born, what were the social expectations for a person of my identity?
- When I was a teenager, what were the norms, values, and gender roles supported within my family, by my peers, in my culture, and in the dominant culture?
- How was my view of the world shaped by the social movements of my teenage years?
- When I was a young adult, what educational and occupational opportunities were available to me? And now?
- What generational roles make up my core identity (e.g., auntie, father, adult child, grandparent)?

The specific details of these questions are shaped by your particular identity, experiences, and contexts. Returning to the example of Olivia, her specific questions were the following:

- When I was born (1955), what were the social expectations for a Chicana growing up in California?
- When I was a teenager (late 1960s–early 1970s), what were the norms, values, and gender roles supported within my family, by my peers, in Chicana culture, and in the dominant culture?
- How was my view of the world shaped by the social movements of my teenage years (e.g., protests by Chicano farm workers, the Civil Rights movement, the Women's Liberation movement, and the Vietnam War)?
- When I was a young adult (1970s), what were the educational and occupational opportunities available to me?
- Currently, how has the growing population and solidarity of Latinos in the United States, plus the anti-immigrant backlash (since 2000), affected my identity and opportunities?

The initial part of this work is individual, but the development of questions aimed at exploring the meaning of diverse influences can be facilitated by participation in a group aimed at increasing self-awareness (see Aponte, 1994, regarding the importance of groups in cross-cultural training). With large groups, I find it most helpful to divide into triads. Individuals in these smaller groups can help you explore the questions, and returning to the large group provides opportunities to share insights and obtain feedback from a broader range of perspectives.

How Privilege and Culture Affect Your Work

In the ongoing process of cultural self-assessment, an understanding of the role of privilege in relation to one's own identity and opportunities is essential. The next exercise can help you recognize the ways in which privilege affects you. The focus is on privilege (rather than oppression) because I have found that therapists' areas of privilege are usually the areas they are less knowledgeable about and less aware of. In contrast, people are usually very aware of the areas in which they feel oppressed, because they have spent more time thinking about their experiences of oppression.

So, for this next step, return to your ADDRESSING outline. Look back over each category and next to the areas in which you hold a dominant cultural identity, put a little star (*). (Look again at Table 3.1 to see the stars next to Olivia's dominant cultural influences.) For example, if you are between 30 and 60 years of age, put a star next to *age and generational influences. If you do not have a disability (i.e., if you are a member of the nondisabled majority), put a star next to *developmental disabilities or *disabilities acquired later in life. If you grew up in a secular or Christian home, put a star next to *religion and spiritual orientation. Continue on down the list, starring *ethnic and racial identity if you are of European American heritage, *socioeconomic status if you were brought up in a middle- or upper-class family or are currently of middle- or upper-class status, *sexual orientation if you are heterosexual, *Indigenous heritage if you have no Indigenous heritage, *national origin if you live in the country in which you were born and grew up, and *gender if you are male.

Now look at your ADDRESSING self-description with attention to the stars. Every individual has a different constellation. However, because a majority of therapists in North America hold membership in dominant ethnic, educational, and socioeconomic groups (e.g., only 8% of mental health providers are of ethnic minority identities; Puryear Keita, 2006), when I do this exercise in the United States, people are often surprised by how many stars—that is, how much privilege—they have. This is true even for therapists who hold a minority identity in one area but are privileged in others (e.g., generational status, educational level, socioeconomic status, sexual orientation, or physical abilities).

As you may notice, this task of recognizing the areas in which we hold privilege is not a simple one. Privilege can change over time—for example, for a person who grew up in poverty but now lives a middle-class lifestyle. Privilege also varies depending on context. For example, a middle-class older Chinese man living in British Columbia may experience little privilege in relation to the dominant Anglo majority. However, within the Chinese Canadian community in Vancouver, the same man's age, gender, and socioeconomic standing may give him significant privilege. In fact, he may be seen as quite powerful in his particular community.

Perceiving one's own privileges can be as difficult as seeing one's own assumptions. As Akamatsu (1998) noted,

> the underlying duality—the coexistence of one's own privileged and targeted positions—is not easy to apprehend emotionally. It requires a more complex view of identity, in which contradictory experiences of advantage and disadvantage form ragged layers. This demands a particular sort of "both–and" holding that relies on the ability to "contain opposites." (p. 138)

Values

As systems of privilege work to maintain the status quo, they also reinforce the values of powerful groups. Because the field of psychology is a privileged profession, its values are often synonymous with those of the dominant culture (Moghaddam, 1990). Many therapists, although recognizing that biases occur in the larger culture, fail to see the biases in their own theoretical orientations and believe that their particular approaches are relatively value-free (Kantrowitz & Ballou, 1992). These therapists are vulnerable to making assumptions without being aware that they are doing so. On the other end of the continuum are therapists who believe that their political and social values are "the healing elements of their therapies"; problems arise when these therapists believe that their views concerning social roles and personal morality are the "therapeutically correct standards for healthy functioning" (Aponte, 1994, p. 170).

Not surprisingly, there is evidence that clinicians' personal beliefs and lifestyles are reflected in their values concerning therapy. In one study (Jensen & Bergin, 1988), religiously oriented therapists rated religious values as more important in mental health than did less religious therapists. Practitioners in their first marriage valued marriage more highly. Psychiatrists and older therapists "valued self-maintenance and physical fitness more than did nonphysicians and younger professionals," and psychodynamically oriented practitioners believed that "self-awareness and growth values were more salient to mental health and psychotherapy than did behavior therapists" (Bergin, Payne, & Richards, 1996, p. 306).

Because the psychotherapy field is so dominated by European American practitioners, European American values are often simply not perceived. Take the example of individualism. A random sample of 229 psychologists (96% were non-Hispanic White) clearly endorsed individualistic values over others (Fowers, Tredinnick, & Applegate, 1997, p. 214). This emphasis contrasts sharply with the greater weight given to interdependence, group cohesion, and harmonic relationships in other cultures (S. C. Kim, 1985; Matheson, 1986).

Furthermore, individualistic values influence the concepts used to measure success in therapy—for example, "*self*-awareness, *self*-fulfillment, and *self*-discovery" (italics added; Pedersen, 1987, p. 18). Although family systems theories offer a potential solution to this individual focus, they, too, suffer from European American biases. For example, the value placed on the individuation of family members may lead a therapist to diagnose an East Indian family as "enmeshed" despite the normality of their behavior within an Indian context (see Rastogi & Wampler, 1998).

Self-disclosure and emotional expressiveness are similarly valued by the field and often seen as central for progress in therapy. However, many clients are cautious about sharing personal information. Among Asian Americans, such reserve may be viewed as a culturally appropriate sign of maturity and self-control rather than as pathological resistance (S. C. Kim, 1985). For Arab and Muslim people, a reluctance to self-disclose may reflect values that emphasize the importance of family over the individual and a desire to protect the family's reputation (Abudabbeh & Hays, 2006; Ali, Liu, & Humedian, 2004). Similarly, among Orthodox Jewish people, avoidance of self-disclosure may represent a culturally appropriate attempt to avoid speaking poorly of one's family (Paradis, Cukor, & Friedman, 2006). And the reluctance of gay and lesbian elders to openly identify as such is often related to social contexts that required (and still require) caution for safety reasons (Barón & Cramer, 2000).

Although behavioral change is often the goal of psychotherapy, clients of minority cultures and religions (and even some clients of dominant groups) may be more interested in obtaining emotional support or developing patience. Helping clients with the process of letting go of the need to control events

> is not a process of passivity, resignation, dependency on authoritarian direction, or obedience to some guru. It is rather a turning loose of the uncontrollable and the unnecessary, a positive spiritual realignment of one's life and a joining of one's

resources with healing and life-enhancing processes of reality.
(E. W. Kelly, 1995, p. 221)

To engage therapists with the exploration of personal values in a
group context, I ask members of the triads to first answer the question,
"What do you value?" Common answers for therapists are hard work,
education, family relationships, community, honesty, and a spiritual
orientation to life. You may share some of these values but also hold
others that are related to your particular cultural identity, family, and
experiences. I remember asking the question of one triad that coinci-
dentally consisted of three women of Scandinavian backgrounds. They
laughingly said that they were all taught, "Work hard, save your money,
and don't enjoy it!" Although humorous, they went on to talk about
how this message affected their lives in the form of a certain seriousness
and stoicism that was helpful to them in some situations but unhelpful
in others.

A second question for consideration is, "How does a particular value
affect your work with clients who may not share this value?" Note the
difference between clinically necessary judgments and judgmentalism;
whereas the former facilitates the therapeutic relationship, the latter
works against it. The challenge in this question is for one to begin to see
value differences less judgmentally and more with an attitude of interest in understanding oneself and others. For instance, the value that
many therapists place on hard work (in school and employment) may
not be rewarded in the culture of a client who comes from an extremely
harsh environment in which there are few jobs, low pay, and no opportunities for advancement (Aponte, 1994; Boyd-Franklin, 1989). The
person who works hard in such a situation may even be seen as identifying with the dominant culture and be punished for trying to separate
him- or herself from the minority group.

Often, what appears to be a value conflict between a therapist and
client is instead related to differences in the degree to which something is
valued. For example, in working with families, therapists may need to
consider the extent to which family cohesion is valued over individual
desires and goals (and vice versa). Both are important in most families;
the differences are primarily in the degree to which one is valued over
the other. Recognizing the shared aspect of these values (i.e., the middle
ground) can help therapists and clients of different belief systems work
together more effectively. In addition, thinking about one's own possible
negative assumptions regarding differences can help.

Returning to the example of the East Indian family, the therapist might
think to herself: "I value independence and egalitarian interactions, but
this family does not. This family is enmeshed, authoritarian, and patriarchal." Such a black-and-white conceptualization focuses on differences as
negative. It also ignores the possibility that the family does value independence and equality but that other values have a higher priority or that

value priorities vary depending on the situation. A more open-minded and accurate reframe would be, "I value independence over interdependence, and I place a higher priority on egalitarian interactions than on respect for authority in most situations. This family places a higher value on respect for the wisdom and decisions of elders. They place a high value on interdependence, family cohesion, and the preservation of cultural and religious traditions." Note the positive connotation of the terms in the latter description. (See Tewari, Inman, & Sandhu, 2003, regarding values in South Asian families.)

The following are a few more examples of judgmental statements with their positive reframes:

Judgmental: I am open. She is closed.
Positive: I am more open regarding feelings and personal information. She is more reserved.

Judgmental: I work hard. He is lazy.
Positive: I place a high priority on my work. He places a high priority on enjoying and appreciating life.

Judgmental: I value free choice. She is resigned to fate.
Positive: I value free choice. She places a higher priority on patience and acceptance.

Judgmental: I value change. He is resistant.
Positive: I place a high priority on behavioral change. He is cautious regarding change and has reasons for preferring patience.

Judgmental: I am honest. She is dishonest.
Positive: I value openness and honesty regarding my feelings and opinions. She considers emotional restraint a sign of self-control and maturity and values harmony between people over open self-disclosure that could offend someone.

The Case of Don

To give you a better idea of how this process of self-exploration and self-questioning can work, consider the responses to the following questions given by one therapist. People would generally see Don as a middle-aged, middle-class White man; however, his identity is much more complex when considered via the ADDRESSING framework. His example is a good one for illustrating the point that cultural influences affect all people in complex ways, regardless of their identities.

Table 3.2 summarizes the ADDRESSING influences in Don's life. The following interview provides the background for understanding the meaning of Don's self-description in Table 3.2.

TABLE 3.2

The Therapist's Cultural Self-Assessment: Example of Don

Cultural influences	Don's self-assessment
*Age and generational influences	Late 1940s, post–World War II baby boomer; I identify with the sense of hopefulness of my generation and a shared history of political and social upheaval in my early adult years (grew up near Berkeley, CA).
*Developmental disabilities *Disabilities acquired later in life	No current disability, but I once had cataracts on both eyes that hindered my work for 1 year; also, I was the primary caregiver for parents both who had a heart attack and/or a stroke in their 50s.
*Religion and spiritual orientation	Grew up in a fairly religious Irish Roman Catholic family; currently a "recovered" Catholic with a strong sense of spirituality as well as a belief in reincarnation, Buddhist philosophy, and earth-based spiritualities.
*Ethnic and racial identity	One-half Irish, one-quarter French Canadian, one-quarter Seneca Indian; adopted at birth and reared in Irish American family; as an adult, reconnected to Native heritage through legal search, academic study, professional work, and social relationships.
*Socioeconomic status	Adopted into a middle-class family that made it into upper middle class; currently upper middle class.
Sexual orientation	Gay, with some bisexual leanings; was married to a woman in my early 20s, had a child with her, then divorced; currently with a male partner and politically active in the gay community.
Indigenous heritage	See ethnic and racial identity.
*National origin	Born and reared in United States; English is first language.
*Gender	Male; roles as son, brother, father, and partner.

Note. *Connotes dominant cultural identity.

Interviewer: How have these cultural influences shaped who you are, how you see yourself, and how clients see you?

Don: Well, clearly they've all influenced me in a great way. I think the most significant factor in my life would probably be having been . . . adopted; I'm hesitating, because the word that comes to mind is *abandoned*, and I do think that's a significant piece, because the abandonment stuff has been pretty big in my life.

I was adopted by my Irish Catholic family at the age of 10 months. My sister was also adopted, but she was 100% Irish. I've known my whole life that I was adopted, but I did not find out more about my background until high school. Then, much later, I did a legal search, not to get in contact with my biological parents, but because I wanted more of a cultural identity, more of a sense of who I was. And that's how I found out about the French Canadian and Seneca piece.

[As for the meaning of this for me,] it's a mixed blessing. Because I found it out as an adult, with a fair amount of education behind me and an interest already in diversity, the first thing that it did was that it slapped me in the face with my own prejudice. What I felt was a lot of pain because I realized how much I had bought into stereotypes growing up. I lived in a family with a father who was pretty bigoted, my mother less so, but still influenced by her culture. I was raised in a pretty privileged, White, upper-middle-class environment on the East Coast, in the Midwest, in the South, and then in California. I went to junior high and high school in Oakland, and that was very diverse; the schools were about 60% students of color. That introduced me to a whole lot more. But I still lived in a White neighborhood.

In finding out more about my ethnic heritage, I had fairly avoidant behaviors, particularly around Native Americans. One, because growing up in the East and Midwest, I didn't see them; even in California, the Native population was not very visible. Seattle is the first city I've lived in where there is a much larger Native population that is urban. I also had a painful awareness of how I had these internalized stereotypes of people who were lazy, who were drunk, who didn't parent very well. And then having to discover that there was a part of me that fit into that group was really hard, and it still is.

I've never felt a part of my family, so to some degree I feel more connected now that I have a sense of my ethnic heritage. But I still feel pretty isolated from a community. Through my adoptive family, I can connect to my Celtic heritage, but there's still this other half of me. I'm trying to find ways to connect with that in more meaningful ways. I battle with feeling like an outsider because, basically, I am. I have been putting out feelers to the Seneca tribe, which is one of the more decimated groups of the Iroquois Nation. They are primarily in upper New York State, Ontario, and Québec. But they've lost their land and don't really have a place.

I've also made some strong connections in the Seattle community. I completed the Native American mental health specialist certification and did a lot of work with the Seattle Indian Health Board, which gave me more of a sense of how to work. I have also spent a lot of time in some rural areas of Mexico, particularly with Zapotec Indians. I did observations with their healers, studying with a translator, as part of my dissertation work.

I had these interests even before I knew the details of my heritage. But it was still pretty painful for me to see that, despite all of that, there was still part of me that avoided Indian people. I don't have this problem when I'm someplace else. But in my own home community, I really have to push myself to change that. It's still a struggle in that I generally want to feel connected, but I also feel like a fraud, because I was not raised with the identity. And clearly the other piece for me is that I look White.

Interviewer: How do these influences affect your comfort level in certain groups and your feelings about particular clients?

Don: There's a double-edged sword. On one hand, they allow me to feel fairly comfortable about being with people I don't know. I resort back to being the quiet observer at the beginning before I move in. The flip side of it is that I can get so introspective and so conscious about how I can best connect that I get in the way of opportunities that are available. It's the fraud thing. I would hate for any person or group of people to think that I'm co-opting them or attempting for all the wrong reasons to be a part of them.

Interviewer: What is the relationship between your visible identity and your self-identification?

Don: Today, they are much more congruent. But I would say historically, I was really good at having a facade of being personable and present, when internally I experienced myself differently. I did a really good job of acting. But I didn't feel as confident inside.

Interviewer: How has your self-identification been influenced by your cultural context?

Don: A lot. I think there's a cultural thing with being an adult adoptee. It comes out in the part of me that realizes the male White privilege I have and how uncomfortable I can feel about that sometimes. Even though I realize it's somewhat uncontrollable. And adding to it is the recognition that I had all of that, and then finding out that I'm not really that at some level, or not all of me. I mean, in the purest sense, I'm not this White middle-class straight male. And that's a whole thing that we haven't even touched on—the gay aspect.

Interviewer: Was there a parallel between the time that you began to recognize that you were gay and the time that you started to learn about your ethnic identity?

Don: The gay part happened much earlier. I mean, I knew, but I didn't have a word for it. But I knew that I was attracted to other boys at about age 6 to 8. Certainly, culturally, it was not just my family, but also the world around me. I didn't really get it—that there were gay people—until I was in college. And that says something about the interaction between the social and family system. I mean, I grew up in the Bay Area, and I had no clue until I moved here. And I spent lots of time in San Francisco, and so, like, where was I? I have no idea. I dated women, and I had these full-blown attractions to men. And I was comfortable about it, but I knew I couldn't talk about it.

I think the hard thing now in my life is that although I feel so much more congruent, I am more aware when I act in opposition to this desire to be authentic. I don't have to or want to hide parts of myself. There are certainly places and situations where I come up against that—hiding myself—where it feels very clear that I should keep my mouth shut, for safety. However, I am no longer willing to consciously lie. Now, I might find creative ways around it that feel safe. Still, being more conscious means being aware of my discomfort.

But that's contemporary, and it's been true for the past 10 to 15 years. Previous to that, it was a real struggle. I mean, my homophobic stuff played itself out in terms of finding ways to avoid having to deal with it. I didn't want to lie, but I didn't want to get in trouble either and I could pass as straight really well. To me, it was particularly evident not so much in my own life and how it had an impact on me, but in the sense that I wouldn't say anything when other people were making jokes or cracks. And now I feel ashamed that I didn't say something—which I'm no longer willing to do, about anybody. And that's true in terms of my ethnic relations stuff, too. If I have anything in my life that haunts me now, that's it—that for a long chunk of time I didn't stand up and say, "This is not OK."

Interviewer: What kind of assumptions are clients likely to make about you based on your visible identity, your socio-cultural context, and what you choose to share about yourself?

Don: I think that my clients are attracted to me because they experience me as being genuine, which includes being willing to talk about my experience openly. And at the same time, I'm willing to say, "I need to learn more about this." So when I'm working with someone who has such a different experience from me, I'm pretty open about the fact that I don't know what those experiences are, and I really want to understand. I think that's why I've had a fair amount of success with diverse clients.

Interviewer: When clients first meet you, and know nothing about you, do you have an awareness of how they perceive you?

Don: I suspect that they perceive me as this middle-aged—oh, I don't like to say that word—this youthful, middle-aged, White guy and assume that I'm straight. I think that once we've chatted for a little while, they have a sense of me that's deeper. And it's not so much about whether my exterior has changed, but their sense of my being that's shifted.

Interviewer: How might your areas of privilege affect your work (e.g., your clinical judgments, theoretical preferences, view of clients, beliefs about health care)?

Don: The biggest piece for me, and I try to keep really conscious of this, is the biases that come out of the givens of my life. It's something that I always have to pay attention to in terms of the expectations I have of people. In other words, when someone is clearly different from me, it's much easier for me to step out of my biases, because I think I'm more conscious of them. I actually struggle more with people who look like me, or are more like me, because then it's easier to make assumptions that I shouldn't make about their experience. On one level, I really do believe that we all have the capacity to do whatever we want to do. And I think that there are tremendous obstacles based on history and all these "isms" we're talking about.

But underneath that, I still really believe the idea that we can all transcend ourselves in some way, even if it's just our attitude. So sometimes I have to be careful that I'm not leaving things out, like the obstacles; that has happened, and I have to catch myself that I don't make these assumptions.

The other thing to pay attention to is values with people of particular backgrounds. The biggest place I get caught is between the value of the group versus the value of the individual, to stay conscious of not placing importance on the individual only. I've also been in situations where there's so much value placed on the group that the individual gets lost. It's not that it's right or wrong; it's just priorities.

Interviewer: How about in terms of your theoretical preferences?

Don: I can't help but assume that because I was raised in this Western culture as a White male, that's influenced me to some degree. I've certainly known that early on, for me, a cognitive–behavioral training program was attractive because it was rational. It was about changing thinking, and that made sense to me. Even though that's not how I operate very well, but I got caught in it, and I was good at it.

I also think that my later attraction to existentialism was influenced by Western culture, which values the individual more than the group. And I think that I was attracted to Zen Buddhism for the same reason. Zen Buddhism is a very rational, individually oriented kind of thing, and I think it's also larger than that. It's about the individual within a group context. When I talk to people who were raised in Buddhist cultures, they have a very different slant on it than I do, yet this doesn't diminish the usefulness of this perspective for me.

I also have a firm belief that both of these theoretical leanings have lots of room to be widened. I think that there are elements of each that address societies and groups and not just the individual. But that has to be conscious, something you do with it, which is most of the work I'm trying to do now. Clearly, I'm still influenced by my experience, which I can't change.

And that's the other big thing I've come to realize: I can't leave behind my context, so how do I adapt it? I think it's a trend now to want to throw it out, because it's "bad," but I can't. We see this now in how many Westerners attempt to co-opt Eastern thought without truly understanding the context. In the process, they have once again done this Western dualistic split— Eastern is good, Western is not.

I can change what I think about things, but I can't change who I am. So I have a hard time with folks out there throwing everything off of their Euro/White, Christian culture and trying to be something they're not. I think we can learn from lots of other things, but we're always going to interpret it in a Western way. We can live in another country for years, and there's still going to be a way in which we perceive things. I think that's one of the reasons why both Zen Buddhism and existentialism offer me so much, because the one thing they do similarly and really well is that they hold the paradox. To me that's so essential. It's not about leaving one behind and moving to another, or either–or. It's about both–and.

It is clear that Don is a person who had thought deeply about cultural influences on himself before the interviewer asked him these questions. But even when one is highly experienced in the area of diversity, there are always areas in which one can learn more. Now that you have read Don's responses, try answering the same questions in relation to yourself. If you can talk about your answers with a friend or a culturally diverse group of people, all the better.

- How have cultural influences shaped who I am, how I see myself, and how clients see me?
- How do these influences affect my comfort level in certain groups and my feelings about particular clients?
- What is the relationship between my visible identity and my self-identification, and how is this influenced by my cultural context?
- What kinds of assumptions are clients likely to make about me based on my visible identity, my sociocultural context, and what I choose to share about myself?
- How might my areas of privilege affect my work (e.g., my clinical judgments, theoretical preferences, view of clients, beliefs about health care)? (The concept of countertransference in relation to particular clients is discussed in chap. 4 of this volume.)

Seeking New and Diverse Sources of Information

Carefully considering the questions and ideas outlined so far, you may come to recognize the key gaps in your experience and knowledge base regarding particular groups. The next step is to begin to search for information that will educate you about the groups with which you have less experience. This search can lead to books, magazines, newspapers, films, theater, workshops, and culture-specific community events. Of course, most people already use these sources of information; what turns them into culture-specific learning opportunities is how one thinks about them and the questions one asks—that is, one's critical thinking.

Critical thinking about one's sources of information involves questions that challenge the information itself and simultaneously expand one's perceptions, beliefs, and attitudes (Brookfield, 1987). For example, when you read newspaper articles about ethnic minority cultures, do you read between the lines for information about the authors' identities and political orientations? Does it occur to you that many articles about minority cultures are written by members of dominant groups, often without comment from members of the group being discussed? If an article was written by a minority group member, do you assume that the person's opinion represents those of the entire group? The following questions may help you think critically about information sources:

- Who are the authors, producers, or editors of this information and what are their identities, political orientations, and alignments?
- Are people of minority identities and views represented?
- Is this information directly from people of minority groups, or only about them?
- Where can I obtain information from more direct or alternative sources?

The views and experiences of people of minority cultures are routinely excluded from the mainstream media. Consider the number of popular films that focus on the love story of a person who has a disability, a hero who is Hindu, or the lives of ethnic minority elders. When minority groups are discussed, it is often from the perspective of members of the dominant culture. For example, despite the plethora of films about the Vietnam War, I have yet to see one written and directed by a Vietnamese person. Similarly, how many U.S. newspaper articles about Iraq are written by an Iraqi?

To counter such imbalances, look for information from publications and other media emanating from minority communities themselves (e.g., *Mouth Magazine* [http://www.mouthmag.com/]; *Able* [http://ablenews.com]; The American Association of Retired Persons [AARP] Magazine; *The Advocate;* National Public Radio/Alaska Public Radio Network program *Native News*). In cities and even in many smaller communities, minority groups often publish their own newsletters and newspapers. Large newsstands and bookstores sell magazines and newspapers from various countries that provide news and perspectives on events often completely ignored by U.S. reporters. Films from Asia, Latin America, and India are available in many video stores. And another enormous resource for psychologists is the large and growing psychological literature on people of diverse minority groups.

However, regarding the multicultural research base, there continues to be gaps; one of the most obvious is the paucity of information regarding social class and people of lower socioeconomic status (SES; Robinson & Howard-Hamilton, 2000; L. Smith, 2005). There are several reasons for this neglect. For one, people of lower SES have historically been labeled as poor candidates for psychotherapy (Jones, 1974). The disinterest in investigating this stereotype and in developing approaches, if indicated, that are more effective may be related to dominant cultural beliefs about the poor. As Lott (2002) noted, poor people tend to be seen as "lesser in values, character, motivation, and potential" (p. 108). Such beliefs justify the exclusion, separation, and devaluation of poor people.

By education, occupation, and income, therapists (of both minority and dominant ethnic identities) are usually middle- or upper-middle class, and hold values consistent with this status (Acosta, Yamamoto, Evans, & Wilcox, 1982; Robinson & Howard-Hamilton, 2000). As Aponte (1994) noted, today's therapeutic models often carry strong social messages and philosophies "that reflect the world of the intellectual and the academic" (p. 246) and contrast sharply with the traditional customs, lifestyles, and religious beliefs that many clients of lower SES hold. These differences can make it difficult for some therapists to understand and effectively help clients of lower SES (Acosta et al., 1982).

Recognizing the need for greater attention to poverty, classism, and the poor population, the American Psychological Association (APA, 2000b) adopted the Resolution on Poverty and Socioeconomic Status. In recent years, a few articles and book chapters have also been published that may be helpful to therapists (for overviews, see C. Campbell, Richie, & Hargrove, 2003; Lott, 2002; P. Minuchin, Colapinto, & Minuchin, 2007; Payne, 2003; L. Smith, 2005). For a wider range of information on this topic, it is useful to look beyond the field of psychology to the areas of political science, history, sociology, anthropology, social work, and some forms of literature: Regarding the latter, novels can provide a rich description of the experiences of people living in poverty (e.g., see Gaines, 1997; Gibbons, 1998; Hogan, 1995; Mistry, 2001).

To learn from—not simply about—people of diverse minority groups, knowledge of culture-specific organizations is also important. Examples of resources therapists should be familiar with include religious institutions (e.g., mosques, synagogues, churches, temples, meeting houses);

support groups; educational institutions; recreational centers for elders and people with disabilities and their families; culture-specific community organizations; language-specific social services; gay, lesbian, bisexual, and transgender counseling services and political action groups; university and community women's centers; and community support groups and activities for parents and children. Some specific organizations include the Association of Multiethnic Americans (http://www.ameasite.org), the Biracial Family Network (http://www.bfnchicago.org), the National Family Caregivers Support Program (http://www.aoa.gov/prof/aoaprog/caregiver/caregiver.asp), the National Gay and Lesbian Taskforce (http://www.thetaskforce.org), Parents and Friends of Lesbians and Gays (http://www.pflag.org), and the American Association of People with Disabilities (http://www.aapd-dc.org).

Relationships and the Influence of Sociocultural Contexts

As a field, psychology is oriented toward individualistic work. However, to increase one's cross-cultural competence, individually oriented work (e.g., introspection, self-questioning, reading, some forms of research) is necessary but not sufficient (Pedersen, Fukuyama, & Heath, 1989). Equally important are therapists' relationships with people of diverse identities and an understanding of how people in their social networks influence their identities and worldviews (Kim-Ju & Liem, 2003). Interpersonal relationships can help to increase self-awareness of one's limitations and biases. However, if the people around therapists hold similar identities and share the same privileges, then they may rarely question the "universal nature" of their beliefs and become what Wrenn (1962) referred to as "culturally encapsulated counselors."

Because the therapist's role in itself confers authority and power (Holiman & Lauver, 1987), therapeutic practice—even with clients of diverse identities—will not necessarily increase one's self-awareness. As therapists, we need to look outside the therapy setting to individuals and groups who differ from us, and who can facilitate our self-assessment process.

Here is another exercise. Take a minute to consider the people with whom you choose to spend most of your time. It can be helpful to make a list of these individuals (e.g., your partner, spouse, friends, coworkers, fellow students, and particular family members). Now look back at

TABLE 3.3

Recognizing the Influence of Sociocultural Contexts

	Confidantes' names				
Cultural influences: Are my confidantes different from me in	Jan	Habib	Max	José	Nadya
Age and generational influences?					
Developmental disabilities?					
Disabilities acquired later in life?					
Religion and spiritual orientation?					
Ethnic and racial identity?					
Sexual orientation?					
Socioeconomic status?					
Indigenous heritage?					
National origin?					
Gender?					

the ADDRESSING outline and the cultural influences you starred as areas of privilege. Think about the individuals in your intimate circle and ask yourself, "How many in my circle differ from me in these areas of privilege?" (See Table 3.3 as a guide). If you are in your 30s, do you have any close friends who are in their 60s? If you do not have a disability, do you have any close relationships with people who do? If you grew up in a Christian or agnostic home, do you have any intimates who are Muslim, Buddhist, or Jewish? If you are heterosexual, is anyone in your closest circle gay, lesbian, bisexual, or transgender? If you are of European American heritage, do you have any confidantes of ethnic minority cultures?

Of course, everyone's situation is different, but for many people, this exercise highlights the homogeneity of their social circles. This homogeneity is particularly common when one belongs to a majority group. Research suggests that people tend to be attracted to those they perceive as similar to themselves, particularly with regard to mates (see Kail & Cavanaugh, 2000). (Although interracial partnerships are increasing in the United States, they still constitute only 6% of marriages and 10%–12% of gay and lesbian partnerships; U.S. Census Bureau, 2000b.)

There is some evidence that people of ethnic minority identities marry outside their groups more often than do European Americans. For example, by the 1990s, between 54% and 80% of Asian American women married non-Asians (Kitano, Fujino, & Takahashi, cited in Hall, 2003). Perhaps because they are fewer in number, minority members often have no choice but to develop relationships with people who are different from themselves. In contrast, people of majority groups can more easily find friends and partners of their own cultures because there are more of them (McIntosh, 1998).

Direct personal experience with people who differ culturally from oneself is an important element in gaining cross-cultural sensitivity and understanding (Mio, 1989). But it is not enough to simply be around people of diverse backgrounds. Traveling to different countries, eating in ethnic restaurants, and attending cultural events can set the stage for interaction, but deeper learning comes from relationships between people that are sustained over time.

In addition, it is important to remember that power differentials can affect what and how much is shared in a relationship. Relationships with people who are in a less powerful position than oneself (e.g., clients, students, support staff) may involve learning, but power differences generally mean that one person is in a more vulnerable position and thus less able to speak freely. One can better learn from peer-level, intimate relationships in which both parties hold enough power to honestly and safely share their feelings and thoughts.

The development of such relationships is a natural outgrowth of the personal work I have described so far. However, if members of dominant cultural identities are not engaged in this personal work, their attempts to develop relationships with people of minority identities may backfire. Choosing to develop a friendship because the person holds a particular identity may be offensive, because it suggests a greater interest in obtaining cultural information than in knowing the individual.

Conclusion

Culturally responsive practice begins with the therapist's commitment to a lifelong process of learning about diverse people across cultures and life spans. A first step in this process is to explore the influence of one's own cultural heritage on one's beliefs, views, and values. Related to this work is the therapist's need to recognize the ways in which privilege can limit one's experiences and knowledge base. Equally important is the therapist's willingness to seek out new sources of information that enable him or her to learn from and with (not simply about) people of diverse cultures. Forming intimate relationships with people of diverse identities is an important part of this learning. The reward for these efforts is a deeper understanding of one's clients, an appreciation of the richness of diverse people's experiences, and an ability to provide more effective and culturally responsive mental health services.

Key Ideas

Engaging in One's Own Cultural Self-Assessment

1. Recognizing the ADDRESSING influences on one's own life is a first step in the exploration of one's cultural heritage.
2. Recognizing the areas in which one holds privilege is key to understanding the impact of these influences on one's work.
3. Privilege is contextual: A privileged identity in one cultural context may not be privileged in another.
4. Because privilege tends to cut people off from information and experiences related to specific minority groups, the areas in which people hold privilege are usually those in which people hold the least awareness.
5. Psychology is a privileged profession that reinforces many dominant cultural values.
6. Therapists' personal beliefs and lifesyles are often reflected in their values concerning therapy.
7. Individually oriented work (e.g., introspection, self-questioning, reading, some forms of research) is necessary but not sufficient for increasing cross-cultural competence.
8. What turns mainstream sources of information into culture-specific learning opportunities is how one thinks about them and the questions one asks—that is, critical thinking.
9. Peer-level intimate relationships with people of diverse identities are a rich source of cross-cultural learning.
10. Humor is a valuable tool in reducing the conflict that often comes with cross-cultural relationships and interactions.

CONNECTING WITH YOUR CLIENT | III

Entering Another's World
Understanding Clients' Identities and Contexts

4

L aura is a 45-year-old woman of bicultural heritage whose European American father met her Japanese mother in Japan just after the end of World War II. The couple decided to settle in Hawaii, where mixed marriages were more accepted. Laura and her younger sister attended public schools, and the family lived in a neighborhood where bicultural children were so common as to be the norm. Looking back on her childhood, Laura remembered being referred to as *hapa*, the Hawaiian word for *part*, meaning part Japanese. However, as she reached her teenage years, she was more inclined to see herself simply as "local," meaning born and reared in Hawaii. This identity gave her a feeling of comfort with friends of mixed ethnicities.

After high school, Laura left Hawaii to attend a university on the mainland. Her school was located in a rural area with few people of color. She was frequently asked where she was from and was not sure if the person meant "what state" or "what country." Although she perceived herself to be visibly bicultural, everyone seemed to assume that she was Asian. She began to think of herself more as Japanese American and became interested in connecting with the few Japanese American and Asian American students on campus.

After college, Laura moved to San Francisco, where she worked for a large bank. When she turned 30, she married a

Chinese American man named Dan. Her daily interactions with Dan's large family contrasted with her predominantly Anglo work environment, and heightened Laura's sense of herself as an Asian American woman, although among her in-laws, she was also strongly aware of her Japanese roots.

In her late 30s, during the birth of her second child, Laura had a stroke caused by a brain aneurysm. Because of moderate cognitive and physical impairments and the paralysis of her right arm and leg, she had to go on leave from her work. Her mother came to stay with her and care for the children. Members of Dan's family came daily to bring meals and offer support.

Laura regained her cognitive abilities within a month. However, the right-sided paralysis persisted, and during this time Laura became depressed and anxious. She worried about whether she would ever regain the mobility she had had before. She worried about her ability to take care of her children over the long haul. And she worried about their finances, because although she was receiving disability insurance income, it did not match her previous salary. Her husband was clearly stressed from coping with the ordeal while maintaining his usual 55-hour-per-week job. It seemed that the disability dominated her entire existence, and only in negative ways.

Laura received both group and individual counseling through a rehabilitation program that lasted 6 months. During this time, she gained the use of her right arm, but her right leg remained weak. After 3 months in the program, her depression began to lift—not solely because her previous abilities were returning, but also because she began to see new ways of looking at her life. Through counseling, she realized that a big missing piece for her was a spiritual practice. She had been brought up in a Protestant church and, during college, was very interested in "the deeper questions," but she had let go of this part of herself when she entered the workforce. She could see now how she had been "caught up in the busy-ness" of working, rearing children, and maintaining a marriage and family relations and had had little time to think about the meaning of these activities for her.

After 1 year, Laura continued to use a cane to walk. She returned to work part time, and she and her husband and children moved into a smaller house to decrease their expenses. Laura became actively involved in a culturally diverse church that one of Dan's siblings attended. The new relationships she made with church members provided an additional sense of purpose and meaning in her life. Despite the family's lowered income and her difficulty walking, Laura described herself as happy with her life.

With regard to her identity, Laura continued to experience shifts in her sense of self, depending on her situation. At her core, she still felt "local" (i.e., born and reared in Hawaii). With Dan's family, she experienced her Japanese ethnicity as most salient because it contrasted with their Chinese culture. With friends who had disabilities (most of them European American), she was more aware of herself as an Asian American woman, but in her culturally diverse church group, she thought of herself more as a person with a disability. Permeating all of these identities was a strong sense of herself as a spiritual person.

The Complexities of Identity

During the past 20 years, psychologists have given a great deal of attention to describing the development of identity. Although this work initially focused on racially based identities of "Blacks" and "Whites" in the United States (W. E. Cross, 1991; Helms, 1995), attention soon shifted to include the development of identities related to ethnicity (D. W. Sue & Sue, 2003), gender (Downing & Roush, 1985; Kimmel & Messner, 1992; Wade, 1998), sexual orientation (Cass, 1979; McCarn & Fassinger, 1996; Troiden, 1979), disability (Olkin, 1999), and minority status in general (Atkinson, Morten, & Sue, 1993).

These new fields of study heightened awareness of individuals and groups that had been marginalized from and by mainstream psychology. However, they also assumed a cultural homogeneity within the specific groups that did not exist (e.g., gay and lesbian studies focused on people who were European American, disability studies focused on European Americans with disabilities, and multicultural counseling focused on ethnic minorities who were heterosexual and did not have disabilities). This unidimensional conceptualization of identity no doubt reflected dominant cultural assumptions that a person is either a minority or not. Only in the past few years have researchers begun to address the complexities of identity for most people.

With regard to people who hold more than one racial identity, Root (1996) described a framework for understanding self-identification. Drawing from Anzaldua's (1987) ideas regarding "racial borders," she noted that biracial people may identify in one of the following four ways:

> (1) An individual may solidly identify with both groups, simultaneously holding and merging multiple perspectives;
> (2) The individual may experience a shift in one identity, from foreground to background, depending on the sociocultural context. That is, in one setting, one identity may be experienced as primary, whereas in another setting, the other identity may be;
> (3) The individual may identify primarily as a biracial or multiracial person, thus using the "border between races" as a central reference point; or

(4) The person may identify primarily with one group but, over an extended period of time, move in and out of identification with a number of other groups. (pp. xxi–xxii)

Early studies (pre-1980s) of biracial and multiracial people (hereafter referred to as "multiracial") looked for and found negative effects of a multiracial heritage. However, more recent research indicates that multiracial people's self-esteem is positive or similar to that of monoracial individuals and that multiracial people are increasingly likely to identify themselves as biracial or multiracial (Hall, 2003). These shifts probably reflect changes in the numbers, power, and status of multiracial people. As interracial relationships have increased, the number of multiracial children has grown. Multiracial people have formed numerous support and social action groups, and they were successful in lobbying the U.S. government to allow individuals to choose more than one racial category on the 2000 U.S. Census form (Hall, 2003).

As Laura's example illustrates, ethnic and racial identities can interact in complex ways with other self-identifications, too. Early on, Laura identified as biracial largely because of her social environment (i.e., Hawaii), where multiracial identities are common. In contrast, the predominantly rural European American college environment pushed her to think of herself in more dichotomous terms (Asian American vs. European American). In marrying a man of Chinese heritage, she became increasingly aware of the differences between her Japanese heritage and that of her in-laws. The stroke and disability brought another layer of complexity, including identification with people with disabilities and a religious community. In sum, the salience of each identity varied with her social situation and her personal and generational experiences.

The Significance of Identity in Assessment

Why is it important to be aware of the varied identities clients experience? Perhaps the most obvious reason is that knowledge of clients' salient identities gives the therapist clues about how clients see the world, what they value, how they may behave in certain situations, and how others treat them. The more a therapist knows about a particular client's cultures and the variations within, the closer her or his inferences and hypotheses will be to the client's reality (Lopez et al., 1989). And the closer the therapist's hypotheses and questions are to a client's true situation, the greater his or her credibility, efficiency, and accuracy.

Consider another example. An African American therapist was seeing a married, male client in his 30s who had recently immigrated to the United States with his family from Kenya. The assessment and two therapy sessions had gone well, and the therapist experienced a sense of mutual respect between them; because of their common African heritage, she also assumed that she held a deep understanding of his experiences in the United States. However, the therapist found herself becoming increasingly annoyed that the client called her a couple of times between each session to confirm some agreement or arrangement that the therapist had considered firm from their in-session discussion. These behaviors were not representative of any obsessive tendencies in the client; to the therapist, it felt as though the client did not consider her reliable and so was checking up on her.

During the third session, the therapist tactfully asked the client about his need to call. The client explained that in his country, he often had to remind people to do things they said they would do, especially people working in government or institutional settings. He added that things worked slowly and if you wanted something, you had to keep checking on it. The therapist, who had never been outside the United States, recognized the assumptions she held based on her own experiences with institutions and agencies in the United States: People in such settings usually do what they're supposed to do, even if it's slowly, and if they don't, there are usually alternatives. Her annoyance subsided as she and the client had a straightforward discussion of their different expectations.

In an initial assessment, the simplest way to learn about a client's self-identification is often to ask. However, at times, asking about a client's identity can be difficult. It is still considered impolite and even risky in many North American settings to discuss race, social class, sexual orientation, age, or certain disabilities. In an initial session, clients may assume that a therapist holds the dominant culture's biases. Hinrichsen (2006) described a poignant example of this expectation when, as a young psychologist born in rural Illinois and raised Catholic, he was gently asked by an older Jewish woman, "Have you heard of the Holocaust?"

In addition, the way in which the therapist asks an identity-related question can subtly determine the client's response. Depending on the context, the question, "What is your ethnicity?" may be perceived as ridiculous or odd, because the client believes the answer to be obvious. Or, when the client's ethnic identity is not self-evident, such a question may be offensive, because in the dominant culture, questions about identity have historically been used to decide how people will be treated (Root, 1996). People of minority and mixed identities may be especially sensitive to such questions from a therapist who appears to belong to a dominant cultural group.

A less direct form of this question, such as, "Would you tell me about your cultural heritage or background?" is more likely to elicit helpful information without giving offense. Similarly, asking clients to describe their "religious upbringing" and then inquiring about their practice today allows for a richer response than simply asking, "What is your religion?" This suggested phrasing implies that heritage is not a uni-dimensional, static phenomenon, and that one may have been brought up in a particular culture or group but may currently identify with another. In addition, unlike more specific questions (e.g., "How is it for you as an African American in your school?"), such phrasing does not assume an identity for the client that the client does not hold for him- or herself.

In working with people who have disabilities, Olkin (1999) recommended avoiding questions such as, "What's wrong with you?" or "What happened?" The first question assumes that only people without disabilities are normal, and the second suggests a search for something or someone to blame. Similarly offensive is the question, "How might you have been different without your disability?" which is like asking someone who they would be if they weren't a man, African American, Jewish, and so forth. More appropriate inquiries are, "What is the nature of your disability?" and, if the client has not brought up the subject of disability following a discussion of the presenting problem and current situation, "Are there ways in which your disability is part of this [presenting problem]?" (Olkin, 1999, p. 167).

With heterosexual and lesbian, gay, bisexual, and transgender (LGBT) clients, therapists generally want to know each individual's sexual orientation and relationship history. However, the degree to which a therapist can ask directly about these topics varies depending on the setting and client population. For example, in rural community mental health settings, a therapist directly asking a person's sexual orientation may be perceived as embarrassing, offensive, or intrusive. Homophobic heterosexual men may take the question as implying that the therapist thinks they might be gay, resulting in defensiveness; older clients may be put off by direct questions about their sexuality; and LGBT individuals may feel threatened about disclosing such information. In such settings, it can be helpful to obtain this information indirectly—for example, through questions about the client's relationship history. Through this process, it is always important to avoid assuming heterosexuality in one's questions (e.g., by using the term *partner* rather than *husband* or *wife* and avoiding such questions as "Are you married?").

With clients who openly identify as lesbian, gay, bisexual, or transgender, the therapist may be able to ask direct questions regarding the individual's attractions; how and when the person disclosed to others and important events in this process; how "out" the client is; how accepted the client feels in his or her social environment and about the individual's experiences of discrimination, harassment, or victimization (Balsam, Martell, & Safren, 2006). A key aspect of these questions involves the therapist making an assessment of the degree to which sexual orientation plays a role in the client's presenting problem; in some cases, it may be the focus, whereas in others, it may have little to do with the problem (Balsam et al., 2006).

Therapists also need to be aware of the influence of European American cultural assumptions on the psychological literature regarding sexual orientation and gender identity among LGBT people. For example, some of the work regarding the coming-out process for lesbian, gay, and bisexual people assumes (a) that it occurs in a linear progression of specific stages, (b) that it occurs only once in a person's lifetime (i.e., a person is either "out" or "still in the closet"), and (c) that the end result is usually positive (i.e., that there is an increased self-acceptance and integration of one's sense of self; A. Smith, 1997). However, the coming-out process may be a very different experience for a person of color. More specifically, disclosure of one's sexual orientation may involve the contradiction of cultural norms regarding personal and family privacy and the potential loss of support from one's cultural group. It may also add another form of oppression that, for an individual already affected by racism and possibly sexism, represents an unbearable burden (Greene, 1994). In such a context, a person's reluctance to disclose may be an adaptive, self-protective response (A. Smith, 1997). (See American Psychological Association, 2000a, for "Guidelines for Psychotherapy With Lesbian, Gay, and Bisexual Clients," and American Psychological Association, 2006, for information regarding transgender individuals.)

Straightforward questions about a client's identity may also be inappropriate when clients perceive the concept of identity to be an abstraction unrelated to their presenting concerns. In fact, identity is an abstraction—one that may be useful to therapists but not necessarily of interest to clients. Recall the case of Mrs. Sok (the Khmer woman in chap. 2 of this volume), who would no doubt have found a discussion of her identity to be even less relevant to her presenting complaint than the questions she was asked.

In general, when a client does not wish to explore the relationship of personal and cultural identities to his or her current situation, it is wise to respect this wish, especially before a trusting relationship has been built. However, this initial avoidance of the subject does not mean that the therapist should not consider identity issues and discuss these issues later in therapy once a respectful relationship has been established. Assessment and therapy will invariably be facilitated by an understanding of clients' identities (Comas-Díaz & Greene, 1994a) and by a consideration of the interaction between the therapist's own identity and that of the client (Pérez Foster, 1996). Exhibit 4.1 lists questions

---

EXHIBIT 4.1

Understanding Clients' Identities: Questions for Clients

1. How would you describe yourself?
2. Would you tell me about your cultural heritage or background? (Follow up with questions about ethnicity, racial identification, national origin, Indigenous heritage, and primary language, as relevant.)
3. What was your religious upbringing? Do you have a religious or spiritual practice now?
4. What was your family's economic situation growing up?
5. Do you have experience with disability, or have you been a caregiver for someone who does?
6. Are there ways in which your disability is part of [the presenting problem]? (Olkin, 1999)
7. What did it mean to grow up as a [girl or boy] in your culture and family? (L. S. Brown, 1990)
8. Do you currently have a partner? Could you tell me about the significant intimate relationships you have had?

---

therapists can use to inquire about cultural influences with clients, and Exhibit 4.2 offers questions therapists may consider even if they cannot ask them directly.

Turning Assumptions Into Hypotheses and Questions

At the beginning of any assessment, information about a client's identity and situation is usually provided by the referral source (e.g., "Mrs. Cheng is a 55-year-old, widowed, Asian American woman who presents with . . ."). Using this introductory information, the therapist then engages in "a con-

---

EXHIBIT 4.2

Understanding Clients' Identities: Questions for Therapists

1. What are the ADDRESSING influences on this client (i.e., age and generational influences, developmental disabilities, disabilities acquired later in life, etc.)?
2. What are this client's salient identities related to each influence? What are the possible meanings of these identities in the dominant culture, in the client's minority culture(s), and from the personal perspective of the client?
3. How are my salient identities interacting with those of the client?
   a. How am I being perceived by this client, on the basis of my visible identity?
   b. Am I knowledgeable about those groups with which the client identifies?
   c. How might my identity and related experiences, values, and beliefs limit my understanding of this client?

---

tinuous cycle of hypothesis formulation and hypothesis testing about the particular individual. Each item of information . . . suggests a hypothesis about the person, which will be either confirmed or refuted as other facts are gathered" (Anastasi, 1992, p. 611).

For example, a therapist who has experience with Asian American people would immediately recognize that Mrs. Cheng's surname is Chinese. This realization would then allow him to begin to form hypotheses about the client's cultural context that are more likely to be useful (i.e., hypotheses that are relevant to a widowed Chinese American woman living in the area). At the same time, the therapist's experiences would keep him aware of the diversity of possible influences in this client's life, including, for example, the possibility that despite her name, the client is not Chinese American.

Of course, once the therapist and client meet, a great deal more information is usually available about a client's identity. The client's language fluency, national or regional accent, physical appearance, body posture, preferred physical distance during social interactions, mannerisms, clothes, grooming, and apparent age all serve as cues for the therapist's hypotheses about the client's possible identities. Here again, the usefulness of such information depends on the knowledge base and experience of the therapist.

To illustrate this point, consider a less knowledgeable therapist's inferences regarding Mrs. Cheng's report that she was born in Vietnam and came to the United States with her husband and children at the age of 30. From the perspective of the second therapist, this piece of information would raise questions about the client's experiences of immigration and the Vietnam War and adjustment to life in a new country, and these would be reasonable areas of inquiry. However, because the therapist is unfamiliar with Asian names and people, her observation that Mrs. Cheng appears to be of Asian heritage, combined with Mrs. Cheng's statement that she was born in Vietnam, might lead the therapist to assume that the client is ethnically Vietnamese, when in fact she is not. In this situation, the therapist's lack of knowledge of the existence of a Chinese minority culture within Vietnam (as well as any information about this culture) could lead to questions, hypotheses, or interventions that are irrelevant or inappropriate (e.g., consultation with a Vietnamese individual who holds negative attitudes toward people of Chinese heritage). (See Rumbaut, 1985, for information on Chinese Vietnamese refugees.)

There is no substitute for culture-specific knowledge and experience in providing culturally responsive services. Moreover, what one needs to learn is therapist specific and dependent on the therapist's own cultural identifications, experiences, and contexts. For example, to work effectively with a gay African American client, a therapist who is gay and European American would need to expand his knowledge and experience in ways that are different from the ways in which a heterosexual African American therapist would need to expand hers.

HOW THE ADDRESSING FRAMEWORK CAN HELP

For therapists engaged in the cross-cultural learning process, the most basic level of attention in an initial assessment involves considering what identities may be relevant for a given client. The ADDRESSING framework can be helpful with this process, because it provides an easy-to-remember list of minority and majority identities that correspond to each of the ADDRESSING influences. The following example describes the systematic consideration of the ADDRESSING influences and related identities with one client.

Jean (pronounced *Zhahn*), a 35-year-old Haitian man, immigrated to Québec at the age of 13 with his uncle and the uncle's wife, who had no children of their own. Jean completed university in Montréal but had difficulty finding employment with his degree in political science. After many months, he "settled" on a position as assistant manager of a large, nationally franchised hotel. He subsequently married a French Canadian woman who also worked in the hotel. They had a son, but after 2 years they divorced because, as Jean put it, "she looked down on my family."

Jean was referred to a counselor by his physician, who could find no medical reason for Jean's recurring migraines. Six months before the referral, Jean had taken a new position as manager of a midsized hotel, a significant move up. The position was so demanding that he had not had a weekend free in 3 months, and many times he stayed overnight at the hotel. His former wife was pressing to change their joint custody arrangement, because she knew that Jean was frequently leaving their 8-year-old son with his aunt and uncle. Jean described his headaches as extremely painful and said that he had missed several days of work and was feeling anxiety and even some panic that he might lose the job.

In the initial assessment, the therapist, Marie, a 40-year-old French Canadian woman, spent the first few minutes talking socially with Jean. She told him that she had visited one of the French-speaking islands (St. Martin), which prompted Jean to talk about the similarities and differences between it and Haiti. Marie was aware of the prejudice toward Haitians in Québec (see Menos, 2005) and the need for her, as a Québecoise, to demonstrate her respect for Jean fairly quickly. Because she knew he had a university degree, she asked him what he had studied, thus acknowledging his educational status. His response allowed her to draw a connection between their experiences, as her partner also had a degree in political science with a focus on immigration issues. In sharing this information, she communicated her view of Jean as a peer.

Once a beginning rapport had been established, Marie explained the purpose of the assessment and asked Jean if he agreed to proceed. He did, so she went on to ask if he would describe himself to her, including "any information that you think I might need to know in order to understand you and your situation better." He replied,

> My father is a successful businessman in Port au Prince, and my mother was a teacher before she retired. I have one sister, who is also a teacher, and two brothers, who work with my father in his business. My brothers also attended university in Montréal, but they returned to live near our family. We have a large family, and I have many aunts, uncles, and cousins, and my grandparents are still living, too. I stayed here because my son is here.

Reviewing the ADDRESSING influences in her head, Marie noted those areas in which Jean provided information regarding his identity. The most consistent aspect of his summary was his emphasis on family. In addition, he provided information about his generational and socioeconomic status through the details about his parents' occupations, his sister being a teacher, and his brothers' university educations. From this brief description, as well as other observed cues (e.g., his physical appearance, dress, language abilities, and social skills), the therapist hypothesized that Jean's identity was closely tied to his family relationships, that he considered himself middle class, and that his national origin was a central part of his identity. These hypotheses were accurate primarily because they reflected the information Jean provided (see Table 4.1).

TABLE 4.1

ADDRESSING Clients' Cultural Influences and Identities: The Case of Jean

Cultural influences	Jean's influences, as noted by Marie
Age and generational influences	35 years old; born in 1972 and grew up under the oppressive Duvalier government (1957–1986).
Developmental disability	None reported or apparent
Disability acquired later in life	None reported or apparent
Religion and spiritual orientation	Self-identifies as Catholic; I did not ask about, and he did not mention, any voodoo beliefs or practices.
Ethnic and racial identity	Haitian; reports he "does not feel Canadian," although he has landed immigrant status (i.e., permanent residency).
Socioeconomic status	Middle-class parents, has a university education, underemployed probably as a result of discrimination; speaks French fluently (a class-related ability).
Sexual orientation	Probably heterosexual
Indigenous heritage	None
National origin	Haitian; speaks Haitian Creole and French fluently; immigrated to Québec, Montreal, Canada in 1985.
Gender	Male, single (divorced), father of one son; also a brother and uncle.

Marie also noticed that Jean did not mention a religious or spiritual identity, his sexual orientation, his gender, or the presence of any disability. She hypothesized that he had not mentioned gender, sexual orientation, or disability because he assumed that these were obvious. She also recognized that he might not conceptualize sexual orientation in the same way as the dominant culture (i.e., research suggests that for Haitians, sexual behavior between people of the same gender "is often not correlated with a self-definition as gay or bisexual"; Bibb & Casimir, 1996, p. 103). She asked if he had had a "partner" since his divorce, and he said that he had gone out with a few women but that he had not developed a serious relationship with anyone. Marie refrained from further questions in this initial assessment but still considered the possibility that Jean could be gay or bisexual. Later, as she learned more about his life and relationships, she ruled out this hypothesis.

Marie still needed to find out about religious influences in Jean's life, because this could be a source of support and positive coping behaviors. She asked, "What was your religious upbringing?" Jean said that he was Catholic but attended mass only when he was home (in Haiti), although he prayed "during hard times, like now." Marie was aware that many Haitians integrate voodoo rituals into Christianity and that such rituals might be helpful to him, providing some relief from the burden he was feeling. However, she also knew that some people associate voodoo with lower social class, and Jean might interpret such questions as stereotyping or as an indirect way of checking his class status (Bibb & Casimir, 1996). So instead, she asked what he thought was contributing to his migraines and what he had tried in order to change these contributing factors or to decrease the pain. He did not mention any voodoo beliefs or practices, so she refrained from asking specifics about this. (See Nicolas, DeSilva, Grey, & Gonzales-Eastep, 2006, regarding explanations of illness and symptom presentations among Haitian people.)

UNDERSTANDING THE MEANINGS OF IDENTITIES

Even when a therapist has a clear description of a client's self-identification, this information will not necessarily lead to a deeper understanding of the client. What is important is knowledge of the meaning of these identities (L. S. Brown, 1990). Depending on one's reference point, there may be more than one meaning for the same identity. That is, a particular identity may have one meaning in the dominant culture, another in a minority culture, and still another person-specific meaning for the individual.

Information about the person-specific meanings of identity usually comes from the client, either indirectly (through descriptive information and views shared by the client) or in response to direct questions (e.g., regarding Jean, "What does your identity as a Haitian man mean to you, in your present situation?"). However, to understand these person-specific meanings, it is important that therapists also understand their culture-specific meanings.

To understand the meaning of Jean's identity as a Haitian man living in Canada, it is necessary to have at least a general knowledge of Haitian culture and history. Haiti became the world's first independent Black republic when slaves overthrew French colonizers in 1804. From 1915 to 1934, Haiti was occupied by the United States, and the first group of Haitians immigrated to the United States. Many of them settled in Harlem and integrated into the African American community (Menos, 2005). From 1957 to 1986, Haitians endured the oppressive regimes of Papa Doc Duvalier and his son Baby Doc. The Tonton Macoutes, a secret military police, routinely tortured and persecuted dissenting professionals, politicians, and students. The second wave of immigration to the United States began during this period and consisted primarily of the well-educated upper and upper-middle classes, resulting in the loss of many professionals from Haiti. Later groups, from the mid-1960s to 1971 and during the 1980s, consisted mainly of middle-class and poorer people. In the early 1990s, another 65,000 risked their lives to escape political persecution and economic devastation but were intercepted according to a U.S. policy that ordered the Coast Guard to turn away all Haitian boats without screening passengers (i.e., for refugee status; Menos, 2005). Between 1980 and 2001, thousands of Haitians immigrated to Canada. As of 2001, approximately 82,000 Canadians identified as Haitian, the vast majority residing in Montréal, Toronto, and Vancouver (International Policy Coordination, Citizenship and Immigration, 2004).

More recently, Haiti has continued to experience armed uprisings (e.g., the ousting of the democratically elected Jean-Bertrand Aristide in 2004), foreign intervention (e.g., a U.S.-backed government until 2006), natural disasters (e.g., Hurricane George in 1998 killed 140 people and displaced 160,000; in 2004 flooding killed 1,000 people, with another 2,400 missing or dead); and disease (approximately 4% of the population has AIDS; World Almanac Education Group, 2007). Today, Haiti remains the poorest nation in the Western Hemisphere. Class divisions among Haitians both inside and outside the country are strong. Fluency in French and lighter skin color (related to family histories of intermarriage with the French and thus alignment with French colonial values) are associated with higher social status. In Québec, Haitians who are fluent in French have the advantage of language (i.e., in contrast to Haitians in Vancouver, Toronto, or the United States, who must learn English). However, they are not accepted in the same way as French speakers of European origin; color-based job discrimination is not uncommon (Bibb & Casimir, 1996; Glasgow & Adaskin, 1990).

Jean was a lighter-skinned Haitian man who was fluent in French, held a university degree, and came from a middle-class family. In his culture of origin, he held privilege and status. In contrast, in a Canadian context, the same cultural identities held a different meaning. Being Haitian (or, from the dominant cultural perspective, Black) meant that he was seen primarily as an immigrant and a foreigner. The most salient aspects of his identity in Haiti—gender and social class—were eclipsed by his ethnic identity, which visibly set him apart from the majority of Canadians.

Although it might at some point be appropriate for the therapist to ask Jean about his personal experience as a Haitian man living in Québec, it would not be appropriate for the therapist to expect Jean to educate her about the general cultural meanings of his identity (i.e., the information provided in the preceding paragraphs). Nor would it be wise, because information about a whole culture from the client's sole perspective is often quite limited. Obtaining this kind of information is part of a therapist's own personal learning, most of which should occur outside the therapy setting.

As an analogy, consider a therapist who has no direct experience with people who have dissociative disorder; she would not expect the first client she sees with this disorder to educate her about its common characteristics. Rather, she would obtain this information herself outside the therapeutic relationship and then use the assessment time to explore the client's personal experience of the disorder.

If, with regard to Jean, the therapist is unfamiliar with the general history and culture of Haiti, the impact of political events on Jean's generation, and the position of French-speaking "visible minority cultures" in Canada, she would be more likely to maintain her credibility by admitting these gaps, at the least to herself, and, depending on the circumstances, possibly to Jean as well. She could then commit herself to expanding her knowledge for the benefit of her client. This commitment would lead her to seek information and experiences outside the therapy setting and to educate herself about these general meanings. As her knowledge and experience increase, her understanding of Jean's identity would still be framed as hypotheses, but these hypotheses and the questions that emanate from them would be much closer to the realities of his life.

Client–Therapist Interactions: Beyond Traditional Transference

Early psychoanalytic approaches emphasized the therapist's role as a blank slate or mirror onto which the client's feelings about parental figures could be projected. The client's emotional reactions to the therapist, known as *transference,* were seen as "projections by a client of expectations and distortions based on past experience" (Chin, 1994, p. 207). However, when one introduces the concept of culture into an analysis of therapist–client interactions, it is clear that the emotional reactions of clients to therapists, and vice versa, often reflect differences and power imbalances in the real world.

As Pérez Foster (1996) noted, "the fact is that analysts are neither neutral screens nor simple clay for transferential transformation. They are, in fact, formidable characters who often have robust prejudices" (p. 15). A client's reaction to a therapist of another cultural identity may be less related to the client's feelings about her parents than to the client's daily experiences with people of the therapist's culture. Recognizing this reality, psychodynamic theorists have broadened definitions of transference and countertransference in ways that open up a consideration of cultural influences (Chin, 1994; Muran, 2007). For example, from the perspective of self psychology, Hertzberg (1990) noted that the internal representations people of minority identities hold include "both the experience of self within a particular subculture, as well as the experience of the self as an outsider of a larger, dominant culture" (p. 276).

Consider the situation of a 60-year-old married woman of Guatemalan heritage who is referred to a much younger, European American female therapist. Because the client's most intimate and long-lasting relationships have been with her husband and children, and because she is older than the therapist, she may be more likely to see the therapist as a daughter than as a parental figure. Similarly, the therapist's experience of the client may involve feelings associated with her own mother or grandmother. (See Newton & Jacobowitz, 1999, for more on transferential and countertransferential processes with older clients.) But the reactions of this client and therapist to one another may be more complex than those related solely to age. For example, what if the therapist is from a well-educated, upper-middle-class family and the client is from a poor, rural, Mayan (Indigenous) background? In this case, the client may remind the therapist more of the maid that she has hired to help with household responsibilities and child care, and the therapist may remind the client of the powerful Spanish-speaking landlords in Guatemala or of a demanding employer in her new country. Conceptualizing the client's distrust as solely a projection of her feelings overlooks the client's history and day-to-day experiences of oppression by members of the therapist's culture (see Gleave, Chambers, & Manes, 2005, regarding the sociopolitical history of and U.S. role in suppressing democracy in Guatemala).

Despite the negative emotions often associated with the topic, it is important that therapists be comfortable bringing up the topic of culture (including race and other differences) if it appears to be relevant to the therapeutic relationship. For example, a European American therapist's straightforward question to a Black family (e.g., "How do you feel about working with a White therapist?") makes available for discussion what is probably already on everyone's mind (Boyd-Franklin, 1989). Of course, if the therapist does raise the topic, it is essential that she has "seriously thought through its relevance" (p. 25); otherwise, the question may be perceived as patronizing (Greene, 1994). In addition,

> White therapists need to be prepared for the possibility that this question may elicit feelings of anger, and some family members may even verbalize their reluctance to work with a White therapist. The more able a therapist is to remain nondefensive and nonapologetic while discussing this issue with the family, the greater the likelihood of a therapeutic connection. (Boyd-Franklin, 1989, p. 102)

Before raising these questions with clients, consultation and supervision with people of diverse identities can be helpful. As C. B. Williams (1999) noted with regard to race,

> the task in training White counselors is to desensitize them to talking about their feelings about race. For counselors and trainees of color, on the other hand, this usually is not the problem. Much of their experience . . . has been marked by frequent, lively discussions about racial issues with other people of color. However, White people have typically been missing from these discussions. The counselor education classroom or professional workshop, thus, becomes a forum for an unfamiliar enterprise that is rich with opportunity for growth for everyone: discussing race across racial groups. (pp. 34–35)

At the same time, with some clients, it may not be appropriate to bring up the topic before a feeling of trust has been established. Many older people, of both dominant and minority cultures, grew up in a time when one was expected to hide or minimize differences related to race, social class, sexual orientation, and disabilities (Sang, 1992). In addition, many individuals are uncomfortable with direct discussion about another person's abilities or limitations, fearing that such discussion might suggest that the therapist is not competent. Finally, as mentioned earlier in the case of Mrs. Sok, some clients simply do not see the relevance of the therapist's identity or their own, and making it an issue before a relationship is established may feel forced.

Just as clients' feelings about therapists may originate in their experiences with members of the therapist's culture, so too are therapists influenced by their experiences with clients' cultures. Chin (1994) discussed common manifestations of countertransference in therapists of minority and dominant ethnic identities. When the therapist is a person of color, countertransference may involve overidentifying with clients' experiences and thus underdiagnosing or minimizing psychopathology when it is present. A similar phenomenon can occur for any therapist who shares a minority identity with her client (e.g., a lesbian therapist may assume similarities between herself and her lesbian client that are unwarranted; Morrow, 2000). Chin advised therapists of color to beware of "interventions that promote an agenda for personal change regarding cultural and gender roles that is not the client's" (p. 212). However, the strong identification of therapists of color with their clients frequently facilitates the therapeutic relationship.

In contrast, countertransference in European American therapists often involves issues related to power and difference (Chin, 1994). Out of a desire to form an alliance with clients of color, European American therapists may minimize cultural differences (Quiñones, 2007). And out of a lack of knowledge, they may assume similarities that do not exist. As a result, clients may feel misunderstood or alienated. However, countertransference may facilitate the therapeutic relationship if the therapist acknowledges the differences and her lack of knowledge regarding the client's culture but also holds a strong willingness to be helpful and to learn (Chin, 1994, pp. 212–213).

Returning to the case of Jean, the therapist's assessment could be facilitated by an understanding of the interaction between her own identity and that of Jean. She could first use the ADDRESSING acronym to identify those aspects of her identity that are different from Jean's and thus most salient in this particular setting; these would include religion, ethnicity, national origin, and gender. Recognizing her own identity as a Canadian-born feminist Québecoise, this therapist would want to think critically about how her inexperience with Haitian people increases her susceptibility to dominant cultural assumptions about Haitian men. She would want to consider the possibility that her own European American feminist philosophy, which she considers relatively unbiased, might contribute to any prejudice she holds (see Exhibit 4.2).

Although the therapist might identify with Jean's experience as a member of a minority group because she holds minority status as a woman and as a French Canadian, she would want to be cautious about assuming similarities in this regard. When considered from a national perspective, her French Canadian ethnicity certainly constitutes a minority status. French Canadians make up approximately 23% of the total Canadian population of 33 million, and as a group they have traditionally been in a subordinate position relative to the Anglophone majority (World Almanac Education Group, 2007). However, within Québec, French is the official language, and French Canadians constitute a powerful majority. Thus, relative to Jean, and in the context of Québec, the therapist is a member of the dominant culture.

Since the revision of discriminatory immigration laws in 1962, the proportion of European immigrants to Canada has decreased (Elliott &

Fleras, 1992). Between 1991 and 2001, 3% of Canadian immigrants came from the United States, 58% from Asia and the Middle East, 20% from central and eastern Europe, 11% from Latin America and the Caribbean, and 8% from Africa (International Policy Coordination, Citizenship and Immigration, 2004). Members of the non-U.S. and non-European groups, referred to as "visible minorities" in Canada, commonly experience problems related to language, employment, finances, and the bureaucracies of the social services, health care, and immigration systems (Waxler-Morrison & Anderson, 2005). Although U.S. and European immigrants experience these problems, too, the barriers are often less formidable for their children, who physically resemble Anglo and French Canadians.

Along with this background information, Marie's awareness of her perceived visible identity would help her understand Jean's behavior in the therapeutic setting. If Jean initially appears defensive, Marie could consider the possibility that his self-protective behaviors may be in reaction to her visible identity as a Québecoise. Given the prejudice and discrimination he has experienced from members of her culture, it would not be surprising that he feels defensive with her. However, Jean's reaction may have more to do with the therapist's identity as a woman. What appears to be defensiveness may be discomfort about sharing his particular problems with a woman or with a woman who belongs to the dominant culture. Whatever the case, the more knowledgeable the therapist is regarding her own and Jean's identities, the more able she will be to understand his reactions and then behave in ways that facilitate their interactions. Facilitative behaviors are discussed in more detail in chapter 5.

Conclusion

Identity is a complex phenomenon that includes both group-specific and person-specific meanings. Although the concept of identity is not always of interest to clients, it can be helpful to therapists who want a deeper understanding of their clients. Knowledge of a client's identity allows the therapist to more accurately infer what cultural influences have been important in that person's life. In turn, such information helps the therapist to form hypotheses and ask questions that are closer to the client's reality.

Although information about a client's personal experience of culture usually comes from the client, it is generally not fair to expect clients to educate the therapist about the broader cultural meanings of their identity. Obtaining the latter information is primarily the therapist's responsibility and often involves work outside the therapeutic setting.

The more committed therapists are to this outside work, the more able they will be to use this background information to understand the client's personal experience and respond in ways that facilitate assessment and the therapeutic process.

Key Ideas

Understanding Clients' Identities and Contexts

1. Identity is a multidimensional phenomenon that varies across cultures, contexts, and time.
2. Knowledge of clients' salient identities gives the therapist clues about how clients see the world, what they value, how they may behave in certain situations, and how others treat them.
3. In an initial assessment, the ADDRESSING framework can be helpful because it provides an easy-to-remember list of minority and majority identities that may be salient in a client's life.
4. Even if a client does not wish to explore the relationship of personal and cultural identities to his or her current situation, it is important that the therapist considers identity issues, including the interaction between the therapist's own identities and those of the client.
5. A particular identity may have one meaning in the dominant culture, another in a minority culture, and still another person-specific meaning for the individual.
6. Information about the person-specific meanings of identity usually come from the client; however, obtaining knowledge of culture-specific meanings of identity is a part of the therapist's own personal learning and ought to occur primarily outside the therapeutic relationship.
7. The reactions of clients and therapists to one another (transference and countertransference) often reflect cross-cultural relationships, conflicts, and power imbalances in the real world.
8. Awareness regarding one's own cultural identity is essential for understanding cross-cultural transference and countertransference in therapy.
9. The therapeutic relationship may be facilitated by an honest discussion of cultural differences between the therapist and client, if the client is open to such a discussion.
10. Consultation, supervision, and ongoing self-assessment are important steps in building one's confidence and experience in addressing cross-cultural differences with clients.

Making Meaningful
Connections
Establishing Respect and Rapport

5

M r. Ortega, age 32 and of Costa Rican heritage, arrived for an appointment with the physician in his company's outpatient clinic. In fluent English with a Costa Rican accent, he explained that during the past 5 months he had had pains in his stomach, had not eaten well, and had lost about 20 pounds. The physician, a European American man in his 60s, did a thorough medical examination and then asked Mr. Ortega if he was experiencing some stress in his life. Mr. Ortega said yes, that he and his wife had not been getting along, that she had gone back to Costa Rica with their daughter to visit her family, and that he was afraid she might not come back. The physician responded that this sounded like a very stressful situation. He went on to explain that Mr. Ortega's problem appeared to be heartburn, which can be aggravated by stress. While writing a prescription for a medication, the physician asked Mr. Ortega if he would be willing to see the "nurse practitioner therapist" for a few minutes "to talk about stress and diet in relation to your stomach problems and get some suggestions regarding your health and what you can do to feel better." Mr. Ortega agreed, so the physician found the nurse practitioner, Sharon, introduced her to Mr. Ortega, and left the two to talk.

Sharon, age 38 and of Italian American heritage, greeted Mr. Ortega with a firm handshake and some informal conversation about how difficult traffic had become in the two areas of town in which they each lived. Sharon's friendly manner and mention of traffic on the way to her children's day care led Mr. Ortega to talk about his own 2-year-old daughter. During the course of this conversation, he told Sharon that his first name was Manuel. Sharon observed to herself that Manuel was casually but neatly dressed and wearing dark-rimmed glasses. He showed a full range of affect and was friendly, although his facial expression and posture suggested anxiety.

Following this casual conversation, Sharon began the formal part of the assessment by describing her training as a nurse practitioner and psychotherapist who works with people who have stress-related problems. As she explained her particular, eclectic approach to therapy and gave a few examples of how she had helped people in the past, Manuel's facial expression became increasingly tense. He told Sharon that he had thought that this meeting "was just to talk to the nurse to get more information about my stomach problems; the doctor was the main one helping me." Sharon could see that he was feeling embarrassed about the suggestion that he might need counseling. She recognized her own feelings of embarrassment and irritation—embarrassment that he obviously didn't see how she could be of help, which felt like a jab at her competence, and irritation emanating from her belief—an assumption—that he wouldn't be reacting this way if she were a man.

Taking a deep breath to slow her own reactions, Sharon apologized for the misunderstanding about the meeting's purpose. She then validated Manuel's feelings by saying that she could see how he would be confused by the situation and that she and the physician had not been as clear as they could have been. This seemed to ease the tension slightly, so Sharon went on to explain that in their clinic, she and the physicians worked closely together, because so many health problems involve both the body and the mind. She talked about how "physical" problems like headaches, stomachaches, and body pains are often related to stress—for example, losing one's job, making a major move, or being in the middle of a family conflict. She also gave examples of problem solving that clients had done in counseling that helped them feel less worried, which in turn decreased their physical symptoms. Manuel still appeared tense, but he was listening. Realizing the need to establish her own credibility, Sharon said she would like to ask the physician to join them for a few minutes.

Sharon went down the hall and returned with the physician, who also apologized to Manuel for the misunderstanding. The physician went on to repeat in his own words the clinic's intention to help people solve whatever problems might be affecting their health. He said that he and Sharon consulted regularly with each other to provide the best possible care for their patients and that if Manuel were willing to talk further with Sharon, he was sure she could give him some useful ideas on controlling his stomach pain and even eliminating the heartburn. Much of the tension subsided with this, and the physician left. Manuel indicated his willingness to stay for another half hour to "consider" some of Sharon's suggestions. They talked informally again for a few minutes and then resumed the assessment.

As this case illustrates, the establishment of some form of meaningful connection is an essential first step in the assessment process. With it, the therapist can proceed to gather information, but without it even the most basic questions may lead to the downward spiral of defensive behaviors. From the beginning, Sharon laid the foundation for a working relationship when she engaged in social conversation with Manuel. This initial accommodation to Manuel's culturally related expectation of *personalismo* (a friendly, personal approach; more on this concept later in this chapter) and *respeto* (respect) increased the likelihood that he would stay engaged even if a conflict arose (Organista, 2007). When a conflict did occur, the therapist was able to set aside her own inclination to respond defensively, which allowed her to think about what the client might need to feel more at ease. She hypothesized that Manuel might have more respect for the older male physician, so she chose to involve the latter despite the feelings that this brought up for her. (See Hernandez, 2005, for more on working with Costa Rican clients.)

Building the Therapeutic Relationship

A great deal of research attention has been given to elucidating behaviors aimed at building the therapeutic relationship. Early on, this work focused on the development of specific helping skills including verbal skills (e.g., paraphrasing, open questions, reflection of feelings) and nonverbal skills (e.g., eye contact, body posture). Much of this work originated from a Eurocentric frame of reference (Ivey, Ivey, & Simek-Morgan, 1993). For example, the skills taught to demonstrate attending and listening were those commonly valued by European American culture (e.g., direct and steady eye contact, forward-leaning posture to indicate interest, and a neutral tone of voice even when a client shares disturbing information). In addition, dominant cultural norms permeated beliefs regarding appropriate touch, therapist self-disclosure, the use of titles of address, expectations regarding time constraints, and therapist availability between sessions (L. S. Brown, 1994).

In recent years, research on helping skills training has declined significantly (Hill & Lent, 2006). This change may be due, in part, to the increasing recognition of cross-cultural variations in helping behaviors and to the complexities involved in teaching these behaviors. The following information focuses on verbal and nonverbal relationship-building skills that multicultural researchers have described as important, particularly in minority cultures. Because behavior can vary as much within a culture as between cultures, many of these approaches will be relevant to members of the dominant culture, too. It is helpful to remember that information about specific cultures does not explain the behavior of all members of that culture; however, it opens up new hypotheses that the therapist might otherwise have ignored.

The Importance of Respect

European American culture places great emphasis on egalitarianism in relationships. In individual interactions, differences in power related to social class, ethnicity, disability, and so on are supposedly ignored. Peer-oriented exchanges are preferred and "talking down to" or interacting with someone in a patronizing way is considered just as undesirable as being patronized. It may be for this reason that (predominantly European American) psychotherapy researchers have focused primarily on behaviors that build rapport rather than respect.

However, the concept of respect is just as important, if not more so, than that of rapport in many cultures, including Latino, African American, Asian, Arab, and many Indigenous cultures (Abudabbeh, 2005; Iwamasa, Hsia, & Hinton, 2006; S. Kelly, 2006; Organista, 2007; Swinomish Tribal Community, 1991). This assertion does not mean that respect is unimportant to European Americans or that the concept of rapport is irrelevant in these cultures. But it does mean that what is considered a core element in a relationship may vary across cultures as well as across individuals and families.

It can be helpful to think of respect in two ways: (a) as an internal orientation to the world (i.e., a set of attitudes or a worldview) and (b) as a set of overt behaviors. One of the best definitions I've found for the attitudinal form of respect is that of Matheson (1986). From an American Indian perspective, she described the internal orientation of respect as

> a quality which one carries with him/her, as constantly as his/her heart or spine . . . not a reactive phenomenon, only stimulated in response to specifically measured behaviors or status . . . but a conscious and active awareness . . . between an individual and his/her universe. (p. 116)

What I like about this description is that the person starts by respecting others rather than waiting for people to earn it.

Sometimes the value placed on respect reflects traditional beliefs about the importance of honoring those in authority (Iwamasa et al., 2006). For example, within Arab cultures, respect is determined by a number of interactive factors, including age, type of work, family name and reputation, and socioeconomic status. Specifically, greater status and respect are accorded to older people, those with higher levels of education, and those seen as having personal integrity (e.g., families that have lived in the area for many generations, families with a good reputation because of their benevolent works or religious practice; Abudabbeh & Hays, 2006; Barakat, 1993).

In Mexican families, *respeto* is a central value in parent–child relationships and often connotes "more emotional dependence and dutifulness" (p. 235) than does the English *respect* (Falicov, 2005). Respeto may also be used to reinforce the authority of men over women and children, although increasingly, immigration and social changes have resulted in a wider variation of structures and processes in Latino marriages and family life (Bernal & Shapiro, 1996; Falicov, 1996; Martínez, 1999).

Assuming that one holds the attitudinal orientation of respect, how does one demonstrate it behaviorally? One of the most basic behaviors in the demonstration of respect is the form of address used in an initial encounter. However, what constitutes a respectful address varies as much within as across cultural groups. Members of the dominant culture often assume a first-name basis in an attempt to decrease the social distance between people (Pauwels, 1995). But many people of ethnic minority and European American heritage, particularly elders, consider such informality to be offensive (Morales, 1999). For instance, African American adults may interpret the use of first names without permission as disrespectful, because such behavior is seen as related to the demeaning attitudes during and since slavery of European Americans "who refused to use their names, renamed them, and referred to them with terms intended to convey low status (e.g., boy)" (Moore Hines & Boyd-Franklin, 1996, p. 79). Because of the wide variation in customs regarding titles even within cultures, the general rules I go by are as follows: (a) initially use a formal title with elders of all cultures; (b) generally follow the norms of the client's culture, if you know them; and (c) when in doubt, ask clients at the initial meeting how they prefer to be addressed.

In his work with parents of children with chronic illnesses or disabilities, Davis (1993) demonstrated respect by making parents the complete focus of attention during their time together, "allowing them to speak freely, listening to what they have to say and valuing it" (p. 54), even if he and the parents disagreed. Davis noted that such respectful behaviors involve using all of a therapist's knowledge and skills to help, but not "taking over for [clients] or denying their role in the process of change" (p. 54).

Inaccurate assumptions on the part of the therapist are a potential source of problems, because clients may interpret them as disrespectful. For example, an African American woman may judge a therapist to be disrespectful if she suspects that the therapist assumes she understands the woman's family solely on the basis of a general knowledge of African

American culture (Boyd-Franklin, 1989). The therapist's assumption that she understands without really knowing the client or her family suggests that the therapist is failing to recognize the enormous variations within African American culture—in other words, that she is stereotyping. In this situation, the therapist needs to distinguish between her general knowledge of African American culture and the person-specific and family-specific experiences of the client. Although she would not expect the client to educate her about the general cultural meanings of the client's identity, she would recognize the need to learn about the client's personal and familial experiences from the client.

Therapist–Client Ethnic Match

In their attempts to understand why ethnic minority populations underuse mental health services, researchers have investigated the question of whether clients prefer and do better with ethnically similar counselors (Kearney, Draper, & Barón, 2005). Early studies that used a simple choice method (e.g., "Do you prefer an ethnically similar counselor to an ethnically dissimilar counselor?") found that people often chose the former. However, when more specific choices were posed (e.g., "Which is more important to you—ethnic similarity, similar attitudes and values, a more educated counselor, an older counselor, a similar personality, socioeconomic status, or gender?"), people ranked ethnic similarity as less important than one or more of these factors (Atkinson, Wampold, Lowe, Matthews, & Ahn, 1998, p. 103).

In a recent overview of the literature on ethnic matching, the researcher concluded that of the studies available, "most suggest that ethnic matching does not affect the outcome of therapy" (Karlsson, 2005, p. 124). Rather, what appears more important is cultural match—that is, similarities in values, attitudes, beliefs, and worldview (Kim, Ng, & Anh, 2005; Maramba & Nagayama Hall, 2002). Therapists of diverse ethnicities may be able to provide culturally competent services to diverse clients (Maramba & Nagayama Hall; 2002), provided that the therapists understand, respect, and accept clients' different perspectives.

Some clients may specifically prefer a therapist who is dissimilar from themselves on particular dimensions. Among clients of minority identities, the preference for a therapist of the dominant culture may reflect negative transference toward a therapist (and internalized racism)—for example, believing that the therapist will be preoccupied with race or less competent because he or she is a woman or person of color (Chin, 1994; Comas-Díaz, 2007). In other situations, clients may prefer a therapist of any cultural group other than their own because their ethnic community is small and they do not fully understand or trust the therapist's commitment to maintaining confidentiality (Tseng, 1999).

Diverse Communication Styles

Common to many cultural and other minority groups is the expectation that informal social interaction will precede a formal procedure such as an assessment. This more casual type of interaction is known as *personalismo* in Latino cultures (recall the positive interaction between Sharon and Manuel; Organista, 2007). It has also been described as the establishment of a sense of *mutuality* among older women (Greenberg & Motenko, 1994), a *person-to-person connection* among African Americans (Boyd-Franklin, 1989), and *respect and reciprocity* among American Indians (Matheson, 1986). Often, this expectation takes the form of what I call *who-you-know* exchanges. This form of interaction involves asking the other person if they know so-and-so, with the goals being to find common connections and gain a sense of the person's context. It is distinguished from the European American practice of "name dropping" in that it is generally not intended to impress or reinforce power.

I remember one such interaction between my friend and colleague Gwen, an African American woman, and a Native American man, who were meeting for the first time. Both had lived in Seattle for many years and knew many Native people in the mental health field. The conversation went something like this:

> "So, you're at Antioch. Do you know S?"
> "No, but did he use to work at ——?"
> "Yes."
> "Oh. I had a friend who worked there for a couple years. Do you know her?"
> "No, but I know her husband. He's at ——."

The exchange ended when they had found several people that they both knew; we then went on with the business parts of the meeting.

Hornby (cited in Allen, 1998) described this type of initial interaction among Lakota people as *common basing*, which occurs with the shared understanding that "people and relationships are not viewed in isolation but instead as parts of an interconnected community" (p. 34). Upon meeting, people engage in casual conversation that may touch on social events, activities, or people that the speakers have in common (Allen, 1998). Among people of Indigenous heritage, connections are often similarly made on the basis of one's familial heritage and geographic origin. This form of connecting is also common among immigrants and among people in rural areas.

With clients, however, who-you-know connections are tricky, because acknowledgment of the connection may imply that the therapist and the third party have a therapeutic relationship. In very small communities, this may be less of a problem, because everyone knows everyone anyway, and a therapeutic relationship is not necessarily assumed. In other settings, when clients want to make such connections, it may be helpful to focus the discussion on events and places that one has in common, rather than on people, and then if necessary to explain the limits of confidentiality as matter-of-factly as possible to avoid embarrassing the client. In any case, I mention such interactions because they are a very important form of communication for many people, and therapists should be aware of and prepared for this possibility.

Directness is another communication style valued by the dominant culture. Research comparing more individualistic cultures with more collectivist cultures suggest that the latter more often use indirect forms of speech, particularly when conflict is possible, to avoid embarrassing others (see P. B. Smith & Bond, 1999, for a review). Reframing "indirectness" as "politeness" is more accurate and can help therapists to avoid judgmental assumptions about clients' responses.

The use of psychological jargon is a potential barrier that therapists should minimize, especially with clients who speak English as a second language (Holiman & Lauver, 1987). For instance, consider the use of the term *dysfunctional* to describe a particular pattern of family interactions. Although assumptions are often made about the meaning of this term, cultural norms that define functionality are rarely taken into account. But beliefs defined as functional in the family-systems literature are not necessarily functional in the contexts of many low-income African American and European American families. For example, in one study, the dominant cultural definition of functional communication as open and direct was challenged by these families' equally valid belief that "communication involves a time to speak and a time to be silent" (Westbrooks, 1995, p. 141).

To understand the meaning behind a client's use of language, it may be necessary to ask the client to define a term (e.g., "Tell me what you mean by a 'functional' family or a 'dysfunctional' one"). This sort of inquiry is equally important for therapists to ask themselves. Therapists' use of theoretically based terms or concepts (e.g., "providing a container," "outlining contingencies," or "cognitive distortions") may be familiar and comfortable for therapists but alienating to clients. Equally obscure from many clients' perspectives are phrases such as "getting in touch with your feelings," "sharing personal issues," and "learning to accept all parts of yourself."

Whether the use of theoretically based language and idioms originates with the therapist or the client, it is important to consider the assumptions underlying such phrases (e.g., "What does 'being in touch with one's feelings' mean, and how do I know if I am or am not?"; Holiman & Lauver,

1987). It can be helpful for therapists to ask the questions, "What does that mean?" and "How do I know?"

For instance, once when I used the term *manipulative* to describe a client, my supervisor questioned what I meant by the word. I said something to the effect of "trying to get one's needs met and not caring if you take something away from someone else in the process." However, my supervisor pointed out that we all have needs that we're trying to fulfill but some people have less education, less effective social skills, a brain impairment, or live in a particular environment that decreases their ability to meet their needs in ways that do not infringe on other people. It is clear that the judgmental tone of this word did not facilitate my understanding of, or compassion for, the client.

Therapist Self-Disclosure

Part of what distinguishes a more personalized approach from an engaging professional demeanor is the therapist's willingness to self-disclose. However, therapist self-disclosure has traditionally been viewed suspiciously, primarily related to early psychoanalytic assumptions about the processes of transference and countertransference. As Pérez Foster (1996) noted, "the trend in most analytic work has been to avoid exploration and weighted consideration of a patient's views of the therapist, outside of their transferential context" (p. 15).

I recall being chastised by a psychoanalytic supervisor once when I chatted about the weather with a very nervous 85-year-old female client on our way from the lobby to my office. He told me that everything I said was material for therapy, so I should have waited until we were in the office to say anything to her. I understood his point from a psychoanalytic perspective; however, my client did not hold this worldview and seemed to need the reassurance of a more personal connection.

In an initial assessment, the client is also assessing the therapist (e.g., Mrs. Sok, who decided that the therapist would not be able to help her). In figuring out what and how much to self-disclose, a useful question for therapists to ask themselves is, "How do I share personal information in a way that respects and empowers my clients?" In the earlier example, Sharon's comment about traffic on the way to her children's day care casually communicated the information that she had children—something she had in common with Manuel. Of course, she might not share such information with everyone, but Manuel was a regular patient of the clinic and a longtime employee of the referring company, and Sharon felt safe in sharing this piece of information with him. In sum, her willingness to share something about herself led to a more personalized interaction (Organista, 2007).

Opportunities for self-disclosure may also arise during the course of therapy. A common situation is one in which a client who is worried about the normality of certain behaviors or feelings asks the therapist, "Have you ever experienced this?" Often, such a question is simply an attempt by the client to normalize his or her behaviors in relation to a respected "standard" (i.e., the therapist). Flipping the question back to the client (e.g., "Let's talk about why it is important to you to know this") may be perceived as insulting or patronizing, or as making a mountain out of a molehill.

At times, however, it may be therapeutic for the client to explore the meaning of the question he or she asks, if the client can tolerate it. Lovinger (1996) advised taking this approach in work with religious clients, particularly Christian clients who ask, "Are you saved?" However, if the client is unable to explore the significance of the question, he advised not avoiding the question and answering it directly.

What therapists choose to share about themselves is highly person specific and situation specific. For example, although feminist therapy comes from a consumer orientation in which therapists are expected to share personal information that may inform their professional work, the extent of this sharing varies depending on how the therapist defines her boundaries regarding privacy. Thus,

> One feminist therapist will be quite comfortable letting clients know that her capacity to work with incest survivors derives in some part from the fact that she is herself a survivor of incest; another will experience this level of sharing as a disrespect of self and will prefer to refer to other sources of knowledge. (L. S. Brown, 1994, p. 214)

Although sharing a personal experience that parallels the client's may be intended to communicate empathy, it may be seen by some as undercutting the uniqueness of, or pulling away from, the client's experience. Some clients prefer a more formal approach, and the therapist's self-disclosure may be perceived as "intrusive" (Ivey et al., 1993, p. 58). There are also clients with whom therapists choose to share little or nothing personal about themselves out of self-protection (e.g., clients who are potentially dangerous or who have difficulty with personal boundaries).

Multiple Relationships and Ethical Boundaries

The preceding points about self-disclosure assume that therapists can choose to disclose personal information, but for therapists working in small communities, this is not always an option. For example, in the small Alaskan town where I live, it is not uncommon for me to meet my clients at the bank, grocery store, post office, or in restaurants and other social gatherings. My parents have lived in this area for over 30 years, so many of my clients know them, and sometimes a person comes to see me because they know of me through a family member or friend.

Many therapists (myself included) began their training with the belief that one should avoid such contact so as to avoid any possibility of multiple relationships. However, in recent years, therapists working in diverse settings (many of them members of the minority group that they are serving) have acknowledged that in some cases, multiple relationships are unavoidable (Lazarus & Zur, 2002; Younggren & Gottlieb, 2004). Furthermore, active involvement in one's community, which increases the likelihood of multiple relationships, may even increase a therapist's effectiveness. Particularly in rural areas, a therapist's trustworthiness and competence may be judged by his or her involvement in and contributions to the community (Schank & Skovholt, 2006). Therapists working in and as members of lesbian, gay, bisexual, and transgender (LGBT); Deaf; ethnic minority; and other communities may encounter similar situations (Guthman & Sandberg, 2002; Kertesz, 2002; Kessler & Waehler, 2005).

The "Ethical Principles of Psychologists and Code of Conduct" (American Psychological Association [APA], 2002a; see also http://www.apa. org/ethics/code2002.html; hereinafter referred to as the Ethics Code) clearly states that sexual relations and exploitative relationships between clients and therapists are unethical. However, the Ethics Code is less clear regarding nonsexual multiple relationships. A multiple relationship is defined as existing when a therapist holds a professional role and a secondary role with a client, is in a relationship with someone closely associated with the client, or plans to begin a secondary relationship with the client or someone closely associated with the client. Ethics Code 3.05 states that "Multiple relationships that would not reasonably be expected to cause impairment or risk exploitation or harm are not unethical" (APA, 2002a, p. 1065).

In deciding whether a multiple relationship is ethical or not, Kessler and Waehler (2005) offered the following suggestions with regard to LGBT clients, and that are relevant to other small communities:

1. If the potential for a multiple relationship exists, openly discuss with the client the possibility of this occurring, the pros and cons of such a situation, the potential impact on therapy, and the topics of privacy and boundaries.

2. Develop a clear rationale for your behaviors. For example, although I have found that group-oriented social relationships with clients and friends of clients are impossible to avoid in a small town, I have a clear boundary that I will not develop an individual friendship with a client or a former client. This rule allows for the possibility that clients may return 2 or 3 years after therapy has

terminated, a not-uncommon occurrence in the 7 years I've been back in this area.

3. Be familiar with and specifically adapt an ethical decision-making model from the literature (e.g., Ridley, Liddle, Hill, & Li, 2001). Such models involve consideration of the type, duration, and clarity of termination of the therapeutic relationship and the type and severity of the client's presenting problems (Schank & Skovholt, 2006).

4. Consult with therapists in similar communities regarding their suggestions, and be open to feedback from community members regarding typical ways that they address problems.

Schank and Skovholt (2006) provided additional advice regarding rural and other small communities:

5. Engage in scrupulous documentation that clearly demonstrates careful consideration of the ethical issues involved in any decision to enter into a multiple relationship with a client. As with any ethical issue, the client's needs should always come first.

6. Know yourself, including your own weaknesses and vulnerabilities. Ask yourself whose needs are being met by a secondary relationship—the client's or your own. Watch for cues that your boundaries are slipping—for example, a lack of sleep, illness, increased self-disclosure, or overidentification with clients (p. 187).

Nonverbal Communication

It is important to remember that therapists' self-disclosure may occur in nonverbal as well as verbal forms (Pauwels, 1995). The greater therapists' knowledge of and comfort level with different cultures, the more aware they will be of the nonverbal ways in which they are communicating and of the subtle types of information that people of different cultures look for.

An initial handshake can communicate a wealth of information. For example, in European American culture, a firm handshake is meant to convey a sense of self-assurance, sincere happiness at seeing someone again, or (if very firm) an air of dominance. In contrast, among many American Indians and Alaska Native people, a handshake involves a more gentle touch, with the point being to receive information about the other person (Hays, 2006a; Swinomish Tribal Community, 1991). Not realizing this, non-Indians may interpret an Indian handshake as weak or unfriendly, whereas the Indian person may interpret the non-Indian handshake as aggressive or disrespectful. Furthermore, an Indian client may assess a therapist's knowledge of and experience with Indian clients by his or her handshake. That is, "when a non-Indian shakes hands in the usual non-Indian manner with an Indian, the Indian person knows that this non-Indian is probably not very familiar with Indian culture" (Swinomish Tribal Community, 1991, p. 190).

Nonverbal communication may also take the form of bodily movements, preferences for physical space, and facial expressions (Berry, Poortinga, Segall, & Dasen, 1992). Physical gestures show considerable variability across ethnic cultures (P. B. Smith & Bond, 1999). In addition, people who have disabilities often use facial expressions and bodily movements to augment spoken or sign language (e.g.,the term *guilt* is changed to *paranoia* in sign language by adding eye movements back and forth; Olkin, 1999, p. 194).

In European American culture, direct eye contact is commonly considered a measure of one's self-confidence or mental health. In therapeutic settings, indirect eye contact is often interpreted negatively as shyness, a lack of assertiveness, deception, or depression (D. W. Sue & Sue, 1999). However, in many cultures, indirect eye contact not only is normal but also considered the appropriate and even respectful behavior toward people in positions of authority (e.g., among Navajo students speaking to professors; Griffin-Pierce, 1997).

With regard to physical space, early research suggested that Arab, Latin American, and southern European cultures (i.e., those with Mediterranean roots) preferred less physical distance in personal interactions (Hall, 1966). However, subsequent research found significant intracultural differences on the basis of social class and situational determinants. For example, in one study, Japanese students sat farther apart when speaking in Japanese than did Venezuelans speaking Spanish. But when both spoke English, they sat at distances similar to those of students in the United States (Berry et al., 1992; Sussman & Rosenfeld, 1982).

With people who have disabilities, it is important to note the inappropriateness of touching someone's assistive device (e.g., walker, wheelchair, or prosthetic) without permission. An assistive device functions as an extension of a person's body. As Olkin (1999) noted, "Wheelchairs are like one's legs, and I can only presume you don't rub a client's legs" (p. 194) so don't touch a person's wheelchair without being asked.

Adding to the cultural variations in preferences for physical space, individual and family differences make generalizations even more difficult. If therapists do not have experience with a client's particular cultural group, it is important to stay aware that there are differences so that automatic misinterpretations are less likely to occur. It can be helpful for therapists to consider the arrangement of their office furniture, such as how close seats are placed and who sits where (D. W. Sue & Sue, 1999, p. 78), and to have chairs that are easily movable to allow for client- and family-specific adaptations.

Nonverbal communication may also occur in the form of silence. In European American culture, silence is often taken to be a sign of anger or an indication that the speaker is finished and the next person may speak. In contrast, in Chinese, Japanese, Alaska Native, and American Indian cultures, silence is often used to communicate respect for what has just been said or for the speaker (e.g., for elders); it may also be a signal that one is forming thoughts or waiting for a sign to speak (Allen, 1998; C. T. Sutton & Broken Nose, 1996). To avoid misinterpreting a client's silence, it may at times be helpful to ask the client about its meaning.

Related to silence is the phenomenon of turn-taking in conversation: "Knowing when to talk and when to remain silent or pause, how long to talk for and how to indicate that one wants to talk" (Pauwels, 1995, p. 20). Overlapping speech, in which the second person begins speaking before the first finishes, is common in many families and cultures. However, it is offensive to many people, who consider it "interrupting" (Pauwels, 1995). To avoid offending in this way, it may be helpful to allow the client to set the pace of the conversation (D. Brown, 1997; Trimble & Fleming, 1989).

Two other nonverbal behaviors are important to mention. One is note-taking by therapists in sessions. With American Indian and Alaska Native clients, taking notes may be perceived as disrespectful, because clients may assume that the therapist is not listening carefully (Herring, 1999, p. 37). Although it is often necessary to take notes during assessments, particularly in mental health centers, I try to keep my focus on the client as much as possible, even suspending the paperwork when clients are sharing particularly emotional information. The other nonverbal behavior is that of giving gifts. In many cultures, giving gifts is an expression of appreciation. Turning down a small gift from a client may unnecessarily offend the client and is not recommended (Abudabbeh & Hays, 2006; Morales, 1999).

Environmental Cues

Environmental cues are another form of nonverbal communication. For example, information about a therapist's cultural connections and relationship to the community may be communicated by the location and accessibility of his or her office. For example, when a therapist's office is accessible only by climbing a flight of stairs, clearly, the therapist cannot see clients with certain types of disabilities there.

Within the therapist's office, the magazines in the waiting room, a calendar in a particular language, desktop photographs, wall hangings, and the books on the shelves all say something about the therapist's interests and concerns. When thinking about the range of clients who may be looking for the therapist's sensitivity to their own cultural contexts, it can be helpful to ask oneself, "How do aspects of my office communicate my awareness of and interest in people of different ages; people who have disabilities; religious or spiritually oriented people; people of various ethnicities; gay, lesbian, bisexual, or transgender people; and so on, using the ADDRESSING acronym?"

Time

One of the most common generalizations regarding time is that people of Indigenous, Latino, and Arab cultures are more past or present oriented, whereas European Americans are more future oriented. The future orientation of the United States and European Americans was provided some support by the early work of Kluckhohn and Strodtbeck (1961), which compared value orientations in five cultures. However, subsequent research suggested a more complex situation. For example, the idea that European Americans are future oriented is contradicted by "the massive violation of natural resources" to the neglect of future generations (Robinson & Howard-Hamilton, 2000, p. 30).

Within a particular culture, individuals of different ages may experience time differently. For example, how long a week feels to a young child, a middle-aged adult, and an older person may be quite different (Dator, 1979). People's experience of and the meanings they attach to time may also vary depending on the presence of a disability; the person's socioeconomic status, occupation, or religious culture; or what one is doing in the moment (Dator, 1979; Gonzales & Zimbardo, 1985).

The profession of psychotherapy holds relatively rigid ideas about time, which is grounded in dominant cultural conceptions. Clients and therapists are expected to be on time for appointments and meet during a set number of minutes (Holiman & Lauver, 1987). When clients do not follow the time rules for therapy, therapists may assume that they are not committed to change; clients, however, may feel that the therapist is disrespectfully rushing them (D. W. Sue & Sue, 1999).

There are many reasons why a client is not on time or fails to appear for an appointment. Low-income clients who do not have a car may use public transportation, which is not always on time; they may not have day care for children or older parents or easy access to a telephone to cancel; and health and family crises understandably take priority over a 1-hour appointment with the therapist (Acosta, Yamamoto, Evans, & Wilcox, 1982; Aponte, 1994). Clients who have disabilities must also contend with the extra time it takes to do everything. Having a disability also creates tasks that require more time (e.g., ordering and buying a wheelchair or scooter, maintaining it, finding accessible services and entrances; Olkin, 1999).

Given the variability of attitudes toward time, it is difficult to make accurate generalizations about how a client will perceive the time constraints embedded in psychotherapy. But keeping in mind the possibility of differences and clearly explaining to clients how flexible you can or cannot be will help to minimize misunderstandings.

Conclusion

With clients of diverse identities, making meaningful connections is complex, requiring familiarity with a wide range of relationship-building behaviors and attitudes. Of particular importance are the abilities of a therapists to be respectful of and responsive to diverse communication styles, language preferences, and value systems. When clients feel respected and appreciated, they are more likely to share pertinent and accurate information and be open to the possibility of therapeutic intervention. Although a meaningful connection does not guarantee the accuracy of an assessment or the effectiveness of therapy, it is certainly a key element.

Key Ideas

Guidelines for Establishing Respect and Rapport

1. In working with clients, keep in mind the centrality of respect in many cultures.
2. Do not assume a title of address; ask the client what they prefer (e.g., Mr., Mrs., Ms., Dr., family or given name).
3. Even if you are knowledgeable about the client's culture, do not assume that you are therefore knowledgeable about the client's personal experience of culture and identity. Use the ADDRESSING acronym to remind yourself of within-group variations.
4. Regarding the ethics of multiple relationships, adapt an ethical decision-making model from the literature, develop a clear rationale for your behaviors, consult, scrupulously document your decision-making process, and know your own weaknesses and vulnerabilities.
5. Stay aware of the different meanings of physical gestures, eye contact, silence, and other forms of nonverbal communication.

6. Be aware of differences in preferences for physical space, including your own, and if possible, use easily movable furniture to allow for different preferences.
7. Do not touch the assistive device (e.g., walker, wheelchair, prosthetic) of a person who has a disability without asking.
8. Consider what your office location, accessibility, and furnishings communicate about your awareness of people of different ages, people who have disabilities, religious or spiritually oriented people, people of various ethnicities, people who are part of the LGBT community, and so on, using the ADDRESSING acronym.
9. Avoid psychological jargon, and if clients use it, ask about its meaning.
10. Continually use critical thinking skills to evaluate your own assumptions in relation to clients' communication styles, including verbal and nonverbal communication.

CULTURALLY RESPONSIVE ASSESSMENT AND DIAGNOSIS

IV

Sorting Things Out
Culturally Responsive Assessment

6

During the 1980s and 1990s, Kim worked as a fourth-grade teacher on the Texas side of the Rio Grande River in an area known as "the Valley" (the region that Anzaldua, 1987, wrote about in *Borderlands/La Frontera*). The Valley is a politically conservative area with widespread poverty. Most of the children in Kim's classes spoke English as a second language. Some were the children of migrant workers who, during harvest season, moved north with their families to states like Washington and Oregon to harvest farm crops. This work involves hard labor under the hot sun, low pay, poor living conditions (often without running water), daily exposure to pesticides, no paid sick leave, no health or disability insurance, and limited if any access to medical care. Moreover, because the majority of people doing this work (53%) are not authorized to work in the United States, they are easily exploited and have little power to protest poor working and living conditions (Mapes, 1998; U.S. Department of Labor, Employment and Training Administration, 2002).

During the 12 years that Kim was in the Valley, drugs and gangs moved in. The Valley became an even rougher place to grow up, especially for the "migrant kids," who were often assumed to be poorer students because they moved a lot. But Kim said that the exact opposite was true: The children of migrant families were the hardest workers and the most motivated. Their families instilled in them a strong work ethic, respect for education, and, most importantly, a sense of hope. They usually spoke English more fluently than other students because they had spent time in northern schools. Some went on to college and returned to the area, where they now contribute to their communities as bilingual teachers who understand firsthand the challenges their students face.

Because the dominant culture so often assumes the worst about people of minority identities, it is important that therapists actively look for the strengths in their clients. The significance of this focus in clinical assessment is emphasized in the new area of positive psychology (Lopez & Snyder, 2003) and serves at least three purposes. First, a strengths-oriented approach adds to the therapist's understanding of the client by providing a fuller picture of the individual in his or her familial and cultural context. Second, in contrast to the dominant cultural conceptualization of differences as bad, it recognizes the positive aspects of diversity. Third, culture is often a resource for healing and self-help (T. L. Cross, 2003). Therapists may use culturally related strengths and supports as interventions that build on those aspects of the client's life that are already working—a fundamental principle of solution-focused and cognitive behavior therapies.

In the preceding chapters, I consider several steps and processes that lay a foundation for culturally responsive assessment, including the following:

- ongoing involvement in one's own cultural self-assessment and learning about other cultures,
- recognition of the possible significance of diverse cultural identities and influences in a client's life,
- consideration of the interaction between the therapist's and the client's identities, and
- establishment of meaningful connections with clients.

When these initial conditions are met, therapists can turn their attention toward specific actions to increase their effectiveness and accuracy during the assessment process. This chapter describes these actions, with attention to clients who speak English as a first language and those who do not. The chapter focuses on a strengths-oriented approach in which therapists actively look for culturally related strengths within the individual and supports outside the individual.

Obtaining the Client's History

The first main task of any assessment involves gathering information—a fairly straightforward process if the client responds according to dominant cultural expectations (i.e., by providing quick, brief, clearly articulated answers that directly respond to each question in sequential order). However, not all clients respond in this way; those who do not may include elders, people who speak English as a second language, individuals who have disabilities that slow or impair their speaking, people who are less verbally oriented, and people who are very verbal and provide a great deal of detail.

For example, some Alaska Native elders have a narrative way of speaking and thus may perceive intake questions to be offensive (D. Dillard, personal communication, September 15, 2003, cited in Hays, 2006a). In such situations, one way for the therapist to obtain information without offending the elder is to allow the elder to provide the information that he or she deems important. The obvious risk with this approach is that not all of the standardized questions will be answered; however, if the client feels bombarded by questions, he or she will probably not return, and the opportunity to help will be lost. When allowing a client to direct the flow of information, the therapist can still obtain a great deal of information through observation and careful listening. Once rapport has been established, the therapist may then be able to ask questions to fill in the gaps or obtain releases of information so that significant others can provide additional information.

Another challenge is the reluctance of some clients to answer certain types of questions for cultural reasons. Paradis, Cukor, and Friedman (2006) described the case of a depressed young Orthodox Jewish man who did not want to answer questions about his father's mental health out of fear that speaking of his father's depression would dishonor his father. The therapist recognized and respected the cultural norm against speaking badly about a parent and did not press the issue. Later, when trust had been established, and the client understood that the information about his father would be helpful in understanding family dynamics that contribute to his own depression, he was more willing to talk about it.

Questions about spirituality and religion may also be perceived as intrusive to some clients. For example, among American Indians, the degree of openness about spiritual knowledge and practices varies widely. Information may be considered public or highly personal depending on the particular individual, group, or type of information (Swinomish Tribal Community, 1991). The need for spiritual privacy can have a strong cultural basis related to the desire to

(a) preserve one's special relationship to a spiritual being;
(b) avoid loss of spiritual power;
(c) avoid potential misuse of spiritual knowledge;
(d) avoid ridicule or persecution from non-Indians; and
(e) demonstrate respect. (Swinomish Tribal Community, 1991, p. 131)

The use of spiritual rituals, concepts, or symbols by non-Indians (and even by some Indian people) may be considered sacrilegious. Therapists are advised to be cautious as they are learning about Indian people's spirituality. The best approach is a "quiet and non-intrusive interest" with few questions, allowing the individual to share when and what he or she chooses (Swinomish Tribal Community, 1991, p. 132).

A SYSTEMS PERSPECTIVE

Reliance on a client's report as the sole source of information is risky, especially if the client is distressed and thus thinking narrowly about his or her situation. For this and other reasons, a culturally responsive assessment is facilitated by an active approach toward learning about the multiple, overlapping systems relevant to a client's life. These systems include extended family and nonkin relationships, cultural and political contexts, and physical and natural environments.

Clinicians working with children and elders are especially attuned to the need for multiple perspectives in assessment. With children, a comprehensive assessment requires information from the "school, the parents, significant family members, and the child" in addition to culturally related information (Johnson-Powell, 1997, p. 350). Similarly, the assessment of older adults is commonly expected to include information from multiple sources (e.g., the older adult, family members, and other concerned individuals) that is obtained in multiple ways (e.g., clinical interviews, standardized testing, behavioral observation, and team meetings of health care providers) and with regard to multiple areas of the elder's functioning (e.g., activities of daily living, social skills, physical and mental health, spirituality, financial status, and environmental stressors and supports; American Psychological Association, 2004). Such an approach can enhance one's work with diverse clients of other age groups, too.

In many cases, clients come to the initial assessment with family members. Children, for example, are often brought by parents, and older adults are often accompanied by partners or adult children. Obtaining information from others requires special attention to respecting the person being identified as the client, especially when family members have complaints about that person. For example, an older man who is having memory lapses may feel defensive about his wife's concerns (Hays, 1996c). When more than one person comes to an initial assessment, I often meet with the family initially, and then, depending on the makeup of the family and the type of problem, I may meet separately with each individual, followed by a brief summary meeting with everyone at the end.

The choice of whom to meet with (or speak to) first is an important one and should be determined through the therapist's consideration of the cultural identities and ages of those involved (e.g., see Rastogi & Wampler, 1998). S. C. Kim (1985) advised therapists' to follow the family's current hierarchical arrangements, an idea I usually use initially as a demonstration of respect. With clients of ethnic minority cultures, this strategy usually involves speaking to and meeting with the elder first or, in the case of a parent with a young child, addressing the parent first. If I will be working primarily with one individual and family members are present only for the initial assessment, I also clarify the issue of confidentiality and obtain releases of information when needed.

With some clients, including family members in therapy is inappropriate. For example, I would not ask a woman whose husband is abusing her to bring him in, particularly when her goal in therapy is to build her self-esteem and strength so that she can leave the marriage. (But even this is a complicated issue with women of cultural minority groups; more on this issue in chap. 9 of this volume.) There may also be culturally related reasons why particular family members should be seen separately. For example, many people of Asian heritage would consider it inappropriate for parents to discuss their concerns with one another in front of their children (Hong, 1988).

Although it may not be possible or appropriate to obtain information from multiple sources for every client, setting this practice as a standard reinforces the view of clients' problems as multidimensional and complex. More "up front" work is involved (e.g., obtaining releases of information, making telephone calls), but in the long run the advantages usually outweigh the extra time. For one, the reliability of an assessment is increased when more than one source is consulted. Second, rapport with the client may be facilitated when the therapist is willing to connect with significant individuals in the client's environment. And third, because the involvement of others can be used to reinforce therapeutic interventions, the likelihood of success in therapy is often increased.

PERSONAL HISTORIES IN A HISTORICAL CULTURAL CONTEXT

The following was written by an older woman using the pseudonym Schoonmaker (1993):

> I became 18 years old at the close of World War II. It was a time when men came back from the war to reclaim their "rightful" place in society, i.e., one of dominance. A new wave of homophobia swept the nation as men sought the jobs held by women during the war, expecting the women to return to their previous subservient roles. College deans expelled students for lesbian attachments; my college was no exception. . . . I isolated myself from fellow students and was terrified that discovery of my sexual orientation would end my hopes for a medical career. If even the word *homosexual* was used in my presence my mouth got dry and my heart pounded. I carefully wiped out any traces of a personal life in my conversations with co-workers, and refused all social invitations. I continued to be alone with my shame. (Schoonmaker, 1993, p. 27)

In mental health assessments, a client's personal history is commonly organized into a developmental and social history that includes information regarding the individual's education, family upbringing, significant relationships, work experience, medical and psychiatric history including substance use, and psychiatric or psychological treatment. Questions aimed at eliciting information in these categories typically assume a passive stance toward clients' cultural histories. But as Schoonmaker's (1993) experience illustrates, understanding the cultural events during the historical periods of a client's life adds to the therapist's understanding of a person (Rogler, 2002). It can be helpful to think of the historical cultural context as a sort of template into which the individual's personal history fits—a template that deepens one's understanding of the individual.

Consider another case of a college-educated, married 72-year-old Japanese American man during an assessment conducted in 2007. Calculating the client's date of birth immediately leads to questions about the client's personal history in relation to historical events. A general knowledge of the dominant cultural attitudes toward Japanese Americans during World War II, the probable internment of the client's family, and the socioeconomic losses of Japanese Americans after the war would lead the therapist to make hypotheses about the impact of the war on the client that are different from those the therapist might make about an older European American man.

Furthermore, the greater a therapist's knowledge of historical events that are significant in the client's culture, the more relevant his or her questions will be. For example, this Japanese American client turned 18 years old a few months before the Korean War armistice was signed. Did he serve in the military, and if so, what was his experience as a visibly Asian American man? How did the assimilationist attitudes of the late 1940s and 1950s affect him? He was a young adult when the Civil Rights Act became law in 1964; did this event have an impact on his employment opportunities? As an Asian American, what was his experience of the Vietnam War? Recognizing the illegality of interracial marriage in many states until 1967 (Root, 1996), did he marry a Japanese American woman or not? What did the women's movement in the dominant culture mean for his marriage? These questions are similar to those suggested for therapists in their own cultural self-assessments. Although it may not be appropriate to ask the client all of these questions, the therapist's consideration of them can open up a wider range of hypotheses about the client.

The answers to such questions depend to a great extent on the client's immigration history, including where he, his parents, and his grandparents were born and grew up. This particular client's history raises the following questions: Does he identify as *issei* (the first generation of Japanese American immigrants) or *nisei* (the second generation, and the first born in the United States)? Or might he identify as *kibei*, a subset of the *nisei* who were born in the United States, were sent back to Japan for their education, and then returned to the United States (Matsui, 1996; Takaki, 1993)? If he grew up in Hawaii, did his parents work in the sugar cane fields, as did many Japanese people living in Hawaii in the 1930s? Or were they immigrants to the mainland United States during a time when anti-Japanese sentiment was building in the form of the San Francisco School Board Segregation Order of 1906, the California Alien Land Law prohibiting Japanese immigrants from buying land, and the Immigration Act of 1924, which essentially halted Japanese immigration to the United States (Matsui, 1996)? Finally, the therapist should think about and possibly ask the client how it was for him to move into the identity of an older man within his own family, keeping in mind the variety of attitudes toward aging in Japanese, Japanese American, and European American cultures.

Although the therapist might not know about all the specific events mentioned in the preceding paragraph, all it takes is a few minutes after an assessment to look up a particular era in a history book to get a feeling for cultural events of the times. Takaki's (1993) and Zinn's (2005) books on the history of ethnic minority groups in the United States are excellent resources. For Canadians, I recommend *Unequal Relations: An Introduction to Race and Ethnic Dynamics in Canada* by Elliott and Fleras (1992). With regard to people who grew up in other countries, the annually updated *World Almanac* (World Almanac Education Group, 2007) is a convenient resource with information on the languages, religions, economic conditions, ethnic identifications, and political events of every country in the world. A good resource for practical descriptions of different religions is *The World's Religions* by H. Smith (1991).

One way to call attention to the historical influences on a client's life is to construct a timeline that notes sociocultural events in addition to personal events. Figure 6.1 provides an example. As with any timeline, intersecting marks on a horizontal line denote significant dates.

FIGURE 6.1

Example of Timeline for Older Japanese American Man

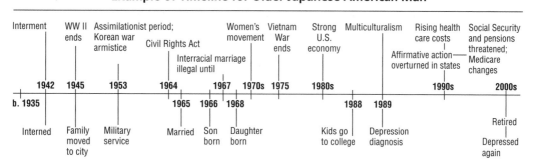

However, with this timeline, personal events are written beneath the line and historical cultural events above the line. Some clients may like drawing the timeline with the therapist, and longer legal-size paper or flip charts are convenient for this work. It is important to note that most of the questions concerning the client's cultural history (i.e., the top side of the timeline) should not be asked directly; it is the therapist's responsibility to learn such information outside assessment sessions.

MEDICAL AND OTHER HEALTH CARE INFORMATION

Equally important sources of information are other health care providers (e.g., physician, nurse, physical therapist, occupational therapist, audiologist, speech therapist) and, in some cases, individuals in the client's community (e.g., religious leader, traditional healer, or teacher; Weissman et al., 2005). With older clients, consultation with medical providers is especially important, because it communicates respect for the client's physical complaints and provides the therapist with an opportunity to learn more about the person's specific needs (Sanders, Brockway, Ellis, Cotton, & Bredin, 1999). Because older adults are more likely to have physical problems and take medication, a thorough medical examination is important to rule out or clarify the effects of physical illness, disability, and medication on the client's mental health and cognitive functioning (see Gatz, 1994). For these reasons, I usually recommend a medical evaluation for clients of all ages.

When gathering information about a client's medical, psychiatric, and psychological history, it is important to remember the historical changes in conceptualizations of illness, health, and disability (Westermeyer & Janca, 1997). Within the dominant culture, certain behaviors that were viewed as normal or treated with a bemused tolerance in earlier decades (e.g., alcohol abuse and intoxication) are now seen as indicative of a serious problem. In contrast, some behaviors considered pathological in past years (e.g., sexual behavior between people of the same gender) are now viewed as normal.

In addition to historical changes, therapists should also be aware of cultural differences in the conceptualization of health, illness, and disability. Understanding these conceptualizations (or what Kleinman, 1980, called *explanatory models*) is important, because what a therapist sees as problematic may not be so from the client's perspective. Clients may engage in certain health care practices that to therapists appear useless or even dangerous; however, it is important that therapists recognize the possible function of these practices so as to avoid overpathologizing.

For example, Muecke (1983b) described dermabrasive procedures commonly used by Khmer and Vietnamese people for a wide range of problems including headache, muscle pain, nausea, and cough. Sub-cutaneous hematomas (i.e., bruises) are made

> by firmly pinching the epidermis and the dermis between two fingers while pulling on the skin, by rubbing an oiled skin with the edge of a coin, spoon or piece of bamboo, or by placing a cup from which the oxygen has been burnt out over the affected area for 15 to 30 minutes. As the air in the cup cools, it contracts and draws the skin and "air" up and out, leaving an ecchymotic area on the skin. (p. 838)

Such practices reflect Asian theories about health as a state of balance and the role of hot and cold in maintaining this balance. Whether or not the therapist believes they work, such self-care practices may help the person to feel nurtured and more in control (i.e., able to do something about the illness). And none of these practices do any permanent damage (Muecke, 1983a). Moreover, one needs to allow for the possibility that such practices work, even if Western medicine does not understand how.

Even within European American culture, the meaning of health and disability can vary. As a person with a disability, Weeber (1999) talked about the different meanings of health and disability for her, her family, and the larger culture in relation to her use of a scooter:

> We are taught that to walk, no matter how distorted or exhausting, is far more virtuous than using a chair—because it is closer to "normal." Never mind that my galumphing polio-gait twists my muscle into iron-like sinew that only the hardiest of masseuses can "unknot." Never mind that my shoulders and hands, never meant for walking, have their future usefulness limited by 40 years of misuse on crutches.
> . . . My using a scooter is an act that scares my family. They are afraid that somehow giving up walking will make me give up—period! It makes them think that I am losing ground, becoming dependent on the scooter, when they and society need me to act as if I am strong and virile.
> . . . I have begun to use a scooter for mobility. What an act of liberation—and resistance—this has been! I felt like a bird let out of a cage, the first time I used one! I could go and go and not be exhausted! I was able to fully participate in the conference I was attending, rather than just be dully present. (p. 22)

Even when therapists and clients agree on how they see a situation or problem, their solution preferences may vary depending on what they consider the origin of the problem. For example, in a situation in which anxiety is clearly the problem, the therapist and client may see its cause to be any of the following: (a) sinful thoughts or actions; (b) external stressors such as poverty, loss of a job, or an oppressive work environment; (c) bad spirits or supernatural forces; (d) a deficit in the client's personality or character; (e) working too hard; (f) poor coping skills; (g) a lack of social support; (h) a difficult upbringing; (i) a need for more physical activity and exercise; or (j) side effects of medication. Obviously, whichever cause is perceived to be primary will strongly influence the course of action taken. To increase the likelihood that the therapist and client are working together toward common goals, it is important that therapists ask about clients' understandings and about their health care practices. This is not to say that therapists and clients must always agree on the cause; however, if they don't, it's better to know this from the beginning to avoid misunderstandings later.

THE ASSESSMENT OF TRAUMA

Early research and clinical work on trauma focused primarily on male war veterans using the definition of a traumatic experience as that which is outside the range of usual human experience. Feminist therapists challenged this definition by pointing to the commonality of physical and sexual abuse, domestic violence, and sexual assault in the lives of women (L. S. Brown, 2004). Largely in response to these critiques, the definition of trauma has been expanded, and increasing attention is being given to the concept of complex posttraumatic stress disorder (complex PTSD; Herman, 1992).

Complex PTSD can be defined as "a type of trauma that occurs repeatedly and cumulatively usually over a period of time and within specific relationships and contexts" (Courtois, 2004, p. 412). Child abuse and other forms of domestic violence fit this definition, as may traumatic experiences related to armed conflict, experience as a prisoner of war, natural disasters, displacement through forced migration and genocide, human trafficking, prostitution, torture, diagnosis of a severe illness such as AIDS, and the witnessing of violence and life-threatening events.

Despite this broader definition and the recognition that PTSD appears to be a cross-cultural response to trauma, most of the research still focuses on people of Western industrialized nations (Foa, Keane, & Friedman, 2000). The research that does exist is limited by the English-language focus of instruments, traditional diagnostic categories that overlook syndromes that do not fit these categories, small sample sizes, and problems in lumping together smaller ethnic cultures into larger ethnic groups (e.g., combining Vietnamese refugees with third- and fourth-generation Asian Americans; Norris & Alegría, 2006, p. 322).

Fortunately, most people who experience a traumatic event do not develop PTSD. However, given the large number of people who have experienced trauma related to armed conflict, war, or natural disasters, combined with those who have been traumatized by childhood physical and sexual abuse, therapists should be prepared for the possibility of PTSD in relation to their clients.

Within the United States, there is evidence that in response to the same traumatic events, members of ethnic minority groups often suffer more than members of the dominant culture. This difference should not be surprising, given the lesser access to resources and political power that go along with minority status. For minority groups, trauma-related losses may also be spiritual and cultural in nature. For example, Alaska Native people were found to have higher rates than non-Natives of depression, generalized anxiety, and PTSD following the Exxon Valdez oil spill (Palinkas, Downs, Petterson, & Russell, cited in Norris & Alegría, 2006, p. 323). The most likely explanation for this difference relates to the interruption of Native people's subsistence activities, which exacerbated fears of losing cultural traditions that defined their identities and communities.

In an attempt to understand the experience of trauma for many minority group members, Root (1992) called attention to the concept of *insidious trauma,* a form of trauma associated with characteristics of a person's identity that are devalued by the dominant culture (e.g., race, gender, sexual orientation, disability). Insidious trauma often begins early in life at a time when one does not have the psychological capacities to understand its sociocultural context (e.g., a child is excluded from play because he is not the right color or social class or because she has a physical disability). Daily exposure over a person's lifetime to such subthreshold traumatic stressors then leads to the development of particular vulnerabilities (although one may also develop unique coping strategies and resilience, too; L. S. Brown, 2004).

The effects of insidious trauma are cumulative, and as a result, events that are not life threatening (e.g., sexual harassment or racial discrimination) may trigger a chain of insidiously accumulated trauma that the client experiences as life threatening. Insidious trauma may also involve the intergenerational transmission of "unresolved trauma and attendant defensive behaviors and/or helplessness" as the result of an ancestor's traumatic experiences (Root, 1992, p. 241). Examples include trauma passed down to the descendents of those who survived the Holocaust, the forced labor under the Pol Pot regime in Cambodia, the loss of whole families and large segments of communities because of AIDS in some African countries, and the disease epidemics and loss of sacred lands and traditions among Native people.

The following suggestions may be helpful when assessing the possibility of trauma, particularly with people who hold a minority status:

1. Be cautious about making judgments as to what constitutes a traumatic experience until you fully understand the individual's family and cultural histories. Recognize that an event that is not life threatening may appear so to a client who has a life history of insidious trauma.
2. Keep in mind that clients' perspectives regarding traumatic events, particularly those related to armed conflict, may differ from those of the dominant culture. For example, following the attack on the

World Trade Center of September 11, 2001, one study found that people of color were more likely than White people to attribute the cause of the attack to acts of omission (e.g., U.S. failure to protect its citizens through poor immigration laws, a false sense of security or arrogance such as the belief that "it could not happen here"; K. L. Walker & Chesnut, 2003).

3. When asking about trauma during the psychosocial assessment, do not assume that the client will disclose. Many individuals are reluctant to share such information until they firmly trust the therapist.

4. If the client is willing to answer such questions but begins to decompensate as the questions proceed, stop or titrate the questions to avoid overwhelming the client (Courtois, 2004). This action also serves to communicate caring.

5. Deliberately look for the client's internal and external strengths and resources. This strategy can help to empower the client, and for therapists, it facilitates a fuller and more realistic understanding of the person. A group-based treatment program for Liberian and Sierra Leonean torture survivors used this idea in helping participants work through the trauma of their loved ones' deaths, many of them involving torture (Stepakoff et al., 2006). Group participants were encouraged to remember as much as possible about their loved ones' lives toward the goal of cultivating a positive, life-affirming image of their loved ones, which acted as a counterbalance to the horrifying images of their loved ones' deaths. (Ways to look for culturally related strengths are described later in this chapter.)

6. Recognize the normality of emotional distress in response to trauma, and avoid pathologizing the individual. Instead, reinforce the client's capacities for healing and growth.

7. With children who lack the psychological and verbal abilities to conceptualize and express their experiences, be aware that they may reexperience the trauma through repetitive play that reenacts the traumatic experience (e.g., sexual abuse or violence they have witnessed; American Psychiatric Association, 2000).

8. Do not limit your assessment of trauma to the individual. Also consider trauma related to the client's culture and community. Examples include trauma caused by civil wars that tear apart families of mixed religions and ethnicities, natural disasters that destroy communities, extreme poverty that forces the men in a community to leave in search of economic opportunities elsewhere, or the loss of cultural traditions and connections in Native communities living in areas where dams have been built resulting in the loss of ancestral lands.

As I noted earlier in this chapter, such information can serve as a template into which individual- and family-specific information can be (cognitively) placed. To facilitate the gathering of such contextual information, it may be helpful to develop a historical trauma timeline with the client. Such a timeline can help some clients visualize how trauma is passed down across generations. Balsam, Huang, Fieland, Simoni, and Walters (2004) used the historical trauma timeline in their work with two-spirit people who had experienced individual and intergenerational trauma. (*Two-spirit* is a term signifying the embodiment of both female and masculine spirits within one person, used by American Indian, Aboriginal Canadian, and Alaska Native people of diverse gender and sexual orientations.) I have found drawing a genogram to be similarly helpful (see McGoldrick & Gerson, 1985, for a discussion of genograms, and see chap. 10, Exhibit 10.1, this volume, for an example).

Working With Interpreters

For a while, I had a tutor for Spanish. She was an Argentinean woman who was fluent in English but wanted help with some of the pickier points of English, so we exchanged services. During one of our lessons, she was quite distressed about a series of events that had occurred. As she was describing her day (in English), she said something about feeling like she was just "going forth and back." I interrupted to tell her that in English, the phrase is "going back and forth." She was annoyed by this and said, "Well, in Spanish, it's *para adelante y para atras,* meaning 'going forward and then back,' because you cannot go back until you've gone forth!" I could see her point; the English was confusing. Furthermore, the illogic of it only added to her annoyance and distress.

When clients are using their second language in the therapeutic setting, emotional distress may affect their ability to describe a stressful or traumatic situation accurately (Bradford & Munoz, 1993; Westermeyer & Janca, 1997), thus increasing the potential for miscommunication and misunderstanding (Westermeyer, 1987). Among bilingual individuals, there is evidence that certain memories may not be retrievable in a second language, not because they are repressed but because they were encoded in the first language and thus are accessible only through use of the first language (Santiago-Rivera & Altarriba, 2002). A greater reliance on pencil-and-paper tests in English generally does not solve the language problem either. Although clients can take their time reading, their results will still reflect language abilities confounded with whatever construct is being measured (Geisinger, 1992; Kaufert & Shapiro, 1996; Wilgosh & Gibson, 1994).

When a therapist does not speak the client's primary language, the ideal solution is usually referral to a therapist who does. However, when such a person is unavailable, the therapist and client may need to work with a qualified interpreter. Clients on public assistance may have case managers who act as their interpreters. (Note that *interpretation* refers to spoken language and *translation* to the written form.)

In the United States, Title VI of the Civil Rights Act of 1964 states that all individuals and organizations receiving federal funds (including Medicaid and Medicare payments) must provide meaningful access to individuals who have limited English proficiency (Snowden, Masland, & Guerrero, 2007). Meaningful access includes the provision of competent interpretation services and translation of documents. Few states have adopted standards for assessing the competence of health care related spoken language interpreters, but the National Council on Interpreting in Health Care (NCIHC) has developed national standards (see http://www.ncihc.org). There are university- and hospital-based programs that train interpreters—for example, the National Center for Interpretation at the University of Arizona (see http://nci.arizona.edu)—and the Cross Cultural Health Care Program offers a training program called Bridging the Gap (see http://www.xculture.org). Information about interpreters for the Deaf can be obtained through the national Registry of Interpreters for the Deaf, which also provides certification of qualified interpreters (see http://www.rid.org).

There are two main forms of spoken interpretation: (a) *simultaneous,* in which the interpreter speaks simultaneously with the client, interpreting the client's words as the client speaks and (b) *consecutive,* in which the interpreter waits for the client or therapist to stop speaking before interpreting his or her words. (Sign interpretation involves different terminology, as sign interpreters do not use consecutive interpreting.) For spoken language, simultaneous interpretation is the favored method in the United Nations, and it has been shown to be effective in therapeutic practice (Bradford & Munoz, 1993). However, in the mental health world of limited resources, individuals with this high level of skill plus mental health expertise are not in great supply. In my experience, though, consecutive spoken interpretation does have one advantage: It gives the therapist extra time to think and observe the client while the interpreter is interpreting what he or she just said.

A number of suggestions may be helpful in working with an interpreter. The first concerns the task of choosing an individual. To avoid problems with confidentiality, it is important that the interpreter not have a close social relationship with the client. The use of family members as interpreters is never appropriate, because such an arrangement places an unfair load on the person acting as interpreter (M. K. Ho, 1987). It also risks offending older family members, who are placed in a lower position when children or grandchildren interpret for them (Itai

& McRae, 1994). And family interpretation may even be dangerous—for example, in cases of domestic violence in which the abuser assumes the role of interpreter for the victimized partner, child, or elder.

The second suggestion is for the therapist to schedule a preassessment meeting with the interpreter to establish rapport and discuss expectations and goals (Bradford & Munoz, 1993). Ideally, this meeting will be face-to-face and held a day or two before the session with the client. Scheduling this initial meeting with the interpreter at a separate time eliminates the need for the therapist and interpreter to meet at the beginning of the assessment session, which could require clients to wait and lead them to feel as though they are being colluded against. Ideally, interpreters will have training in mental health or medical issues; however, if they do not, this meeting allows for the opportunity to review concepts or vocabulary that may be unfamiliar to the interpreter and any forms that will need to be completed.

During the preassessment meeting, it is helpful to learn about the interpreter's background. If raised with polite interest, questions about the interpreter can help to increase rapport and demonstrate respect for the interpreter's expertise. At the same time, such information increases the therapist's understanding of any cultural, social class, or political differences that could inhibit the interpreter's work with a particular client (Sundberg & Sue, 1989). This is where the therapist's personal learning and information-seeking outside the therapeutic setting are important. For example, when I consulted with the leaders of a particular Vietnamese community in which I was going to work, I was advised that there were two main political groups and that if I hired an interpreter who was even loosely connected to one, I should also hire another who was not, because people aligned with one group would not work with an interpreter who was aligned with the other.

Frequently, the gender of the interpreter is also important. With some groups, the choice of a male interpreter may add authority to the therapeutic endeavor, particularly if the therapist is a woman. However, as a general rule, do not expect a woman client to share intimate relationship or physical health details with the therapist or interpreter if either one is male. (See Waxler-Morrison, Anderson, Richardson, & Chambers, 2005, regarding gender preferences for health care providers in Cambodian, Lao, Vietnamese, Iranian, Central American, and other cultures.)

The preassessment meeting is also a good time for the therapist to make sure that the interpreter understands the commitment to confidentiality (Bradford & Munoz, 1993). Any information the interpreter can provide concerning the client's cultural context will be helpful, too.

During the initial assessment with the client present, allowing extra time is important because of the extra speaking time involved (Paniagua, 1998). This extra time may include a get-acquainted conversation between the interpreter and client, which can help to decrease the client's anxiety.

The physical positioning of chairs is important in an interpreted assessment. With spoken languages, the therapist usually sits directly in front of the client, with the interpreter visible but positioned to one side so as to facilitate direct interaction between the client and therapist. It is important that the therapist avoid discussions with the interpreter when the client is present. If the interpreter needs to explain a concept or idea that the therapist has not understood, the therapist should let the client know what is being discussed; otherwise, the client may wonder why the therapist is talking so much about the client's reply to a particular question. In general, it is preferable to hold a debriefing session with the interpreter afterwards to discuss any possible misunderstandings or conceptual inequivalencies.

When the formal assessment session begins, it is helpful to restate in front of the client the commitment to and limits of confidentiality for both the therapist and interpreter. Depending on the interpreter's skill level, it may be helpful to use short sentences and avoid complex language and terms (Paniagua, 1998; Struwe, 1994). Simple one-part questions are easier to interpret and answer than are two-part questions (Pauwels, 1995). For example, "How often have you experienced this dizziness, and when did it start?" may be easier to understand as two separate questions. With consecutive interpretation, it is important to pause after expressing each main idea to allow the interpreter time to interpret.

In addition, the interpreter should use the same pronoun as the speaker. For example, if the therapist says, "I recommend this," the interpreter should say, "I recommend this" (not "She recommends this"). To avoid confusion, skilled interpreters refer to themselves in the third person. For example, if the therapist says, "I recommend that the interpreter set up a medication evaluation for you," the interpreter should interpret this verbatim as "I recommend that the interpreter set up a medication evaluation for you." This example also illustrates that the therapist should speak directly to the client (i.e., rather than saying to the interpreter, "Tell him to get a medication evaluation").

Although it may be well intentioned, therapists are advised not to attempt to work in the client's language without an interpreter unless they have near-native fluency (Westermeyer, 1987). The poor use of a client's language puts the client in an awkward position. Clients may be afraid of insulting the therapist by suggesting the need for an interpreter.

The complexity involved in speaking a second language fluently was underscored by Pollard (1996) with regard to American Sign Language (ASL). Noting that ASL is a conceptually based language (i.e., not English or aurally based) with its own vocabulary, grammar, and patterns of discourse, Pollard observed the following:

> Like German, ASL verbs are often at the end of statements. Like
> Spanish, ASL adjectives follow the nouns they modify. Like

Hebrew, ASL does not employ certain forms of the verb "to be." Like Japanese, feedback signals from the listener are expected in ASL. Like French, there is reflection in ASL sentences and discourse.

. . . Too many individuals (and program administrators) wrongly assume that a few courses in "sign" enable one to converse with, or worse, interpret for, a primary user of ASL. (p. 391)

As a former student of mine noted on the basis of her experience as a Japanese–English interpreter, interpretation is a demanding job (P. Nagasaka, personal communication, January 1999). It is thus unfair to expect bilingual individuals who are not paid for their interpreting services to do interpretation on an as-needed basis for agencies and hospitals. In this case, an informal approach to interpretation is another way in which people of minority cultures are expected to do extra work while the dominant culture fails to educate itself (see Exhibit 6.1).

EXHIBIT 6.1

Guidelines for Working With Interpreters

1. Schedule extra time for the assessment.
2. If the interpreter is not the client's case manager (i.e., they do not have a prior professional relationship),
   (a) be sure that the interpreter speaks the client's dialect (i.e., not just his or her language);
   (b) be sure that the interpreter is certified or similarly qualified; and
   (c) allow the interpreter and client time to talk together before the assessment begins to increase the client's trust and decrease his or her anxiety.
3. Do not use family members or social acquaintances as interpreters.
4. Arrange a preassessment meeting with the interpreter to
   (a) discuss expectations and confidentiality;
   (b) ask the interpreter to interpret verbatim (as much as is possible) and tell you when you may be misunderstanding the client because of conceptual or language difficulties; and
   (c) obtain information (with a release of information when applicable) about the client's particular context if the interpreter knows the client.
5. For spoken language, position chairs so that the therapist and client directly face one another, with the interpreter to the side, to facilitate direct interaction between the therapist and client.
6. Reassure the client about confidentiality and its limits when both you and the interpreter are present.
7. Avoid discussions between you and the interpreter during the session. If such a discussion is necessary, let the client know that you are discussing a conceptual or linguistic difference.
8. Avoid using complex phrases (e.g., two-part questions) and language that is more difficult to interpret.
9. With consecutive interpretation, pause after each main idea to give the interpreter time to interpret.
10. Be aware of cultural, class, and political differences between the interpreter and client that might affect the interpreter's work.

Looking for Strengths and Supports

I ask clients about their strengths and supports toward the end of the assessment, because if they are unable to state any, by the end of our time together I have usually learned enough about them to be able to name something that I have observed or heard. Asking this question also forces me to actively look for a client's strengths. People of Asian, American Indian, and Alaska Native cultures may be reluctant to state personal strengths because of a cultural value of being humble, and if this is the case, I may name something positive that I have observed or heard from the person and watch for a sign of agreement. An additional approach includes asking the individual, "What would your mother [or son or best friend or partner] say they like about you?"

Although most therapists are aware of the usefulness of recognizing the positives in clients' lives, if a therapist differs culturally from the client, it may be difficult for the therapist to perceive or even think of culturally related strengths and supports. It may be helpful to conceptualize culturally related strengths and supports in terms of three categories (Table 6.1). The first category, personal strengths, includes characteristics, beliefs, and abilities that reside within the individual—for example, pride in one's culture; a sense of humor; and artistic, musical, and language abilities. Personal strengths may also include coping abilities related directly to a person's minority status. As McIntosh (1998) noted,

> Those who do not depend on conferred dominance have traits and qualities that may never develop in those who do. . . . In some groups, those dominated have actually become strong through not having all of these unearned advantages, and this gives them a great deal to teach the others. (p. 101)

When looking for personal strengths, I always ask clients if they have a religious affiliation or spiritual beliefs (including any strong connection to nature) that are a source of strength for them. Spiritual beliefs and support from a religious community can be a powerful help, providing clients with meaning, purpose, and a sense of connection to something bigger and greater than themselves (Royce-Davis, 2000).

The second category consists of interpersonal supports. Included in this category are family, friends, group-specific networks, and activities that involve one's cultural group (e.g., traditional celebrations, political or social action groups, recreational activities). A child who is excelling in school may be a special source of pride for a family. And family may include kinship networks that are broader than traditional definitions of family traced by bloodlines (Moore Hines & Boyd-Franklin, 1996). Because low satisfaction with social support has been found to be a sig-

TABLE 6.1

Culturally Related Strengths and Supports

Type of strength	Example
Personal strengths	Pride in one's culture
	Religious faith or spirituality
	Artistic and musical abilities
	Bilingual and multilingual skills
	Group-specific social skills
	Sense of humor
	Culturally related knowledge and practical skills (e.g., fishing, hunting, farming, using medicinal plants)
	Culture-specific beliefs that help one cope (e.g., with racism, prejudice, discrimination)
	Respectful attitude toward the natural environment
	Commitment to helping one's own group (i.e., through social action)
	Wisdom from experience
Interpersonal supports	Extended families, including non-blood-related kin
	Cultural- or group-specific networks
	Religious communities
	Traditional celebrations and rituals
	Recreational, playful activities
	Storytelling activities that make meaning and pass on the history of the group
	Involvement in a political or social action group
	A child who excels in school
Environmental conditions	An altar in one's home or room to honor deceased family members and ancestors
	A space for prayer and meditation
	Culture-specific art and music
	Foods related to cultural preferences for cooking and eating
	Caring for animals
	A gardening area
	Access to outdoors for subsistence or recreational fishing, hunting, or farming or for observing stars and constellations in the night sky
	Communities that facilitate social interaction by location or design

nificant predictor of depression and general psychopathology (Fiore, Coppel, Becker, & Cox, 1986), knowledge of clients' social support is essential to an understanding of their mental health. At the same time, therapists must be careful not to assume that people of color or of other minority identities have good support networks. The stressors that go along with minority status may also work against the formation of close and stable relationships. In one study, McAdoo (1978) found that

African Americans of lower socioeconomic status had less activity within kin networks than did African Americans of higher socioeconomic status.

The third category includes sources of support and strength in the client's physical and natural environments. Some of these sources can be created—for example, an altar in one's home to honor ancestors, a space for prayer and meditation, music, art, or a garden where foods and medicinal plants are grown. In addition to meeting cultural and taste preferences, culture-specific foods may also act as a protective factor in one's health (Marsella, Kaplan, & Suárez, 2002).

Other sources of support may be anchored in the client's sense of place in the natural world (e.g., see Cruikshank, 1990, and McClanahan, 1986, for richly described first-person accounts of the importance of place among Alaska Native elders). Clients of rural origin or Indigenous heritage may find involvement with or nearness to animals, plants, mountains, and bodies of water to be important sources of spiritual strength (C. T. Sutton & Broken Nose, 1996).

Griffin-Pierce (1997) emphasized the importance of place to Navajo people in her description of the emotional trauma many Navajo individuals experience upon leaving their homeland for college or medical care. She noted that such trauma "goes beyond mere homesickness because it is based on an often unconscious sense of having violated the moral code of the universe" by leaving the land, which is considered "a vital source of spiritual strength" (p. 1). The importance of understanding health and illness in relation to losses because of dislocation from the land has also been noted with regard to Aboriginal Australians (Acklin et al., 1999, p. 9).

The importance of outdoor activities, including traditional (e.g., hunting, berry picking) and nontraditional (e.g., snow machining) activities among some Alaska Natives, was documented by Minton and Soule (1990), who found these activities to be the most common response to the question, "What makes you happy?" When such activities are not available because of environmental changes (e.g., pollution, industrialization, a person's institutionalization), therapists and clients may need to think creatively about alternative ways to get these needs met (e.g., visiting a park, setting up a bird feeder, finding a new place to go fishing or watch the stars at night).

As solution-focused therapists like to point out, even if solutions do not appear to be directly related to the problem, simply increasing the strengths and supports in clients' lives often has a positive effect on their view of the problem, which in turn helps them to feel better (deShazer, 1985). Moreover, recent research in the area of positive psychology suggested that a sense of meaning, control, and optimism can be protective of one's physical as well as mental health (Taylor, Kemeny, Reed, Bower, & Gruenewald, 2000).

Assessing Unusual Perceptions and Experiences

One of the most difficult tasks in a cross-cultural evaluation involves the assessment of beliefs and behaviors that are unusual in the dominant (and sometimes minority) culture but that are seen as positive and healthy in certain contexts (e.g., belief in the supernatural, communication with spirits, trance experiences). Westermeyer (1987) offered several criteria for distinguishing pathological from nonpathological behaviors and beliefs, noting that nonpathological behaviors and beliefs are usually characterized by the following:

(a) community and family support;
(b) time limitations from a few hours to a few days;
(c) socially appropriate, productive, and coping behavior before and after the experience;
(d) a resultant gain in self-esteem and social prestige;
(e) the absence of psychopathological signs and symptoms; and
(f) culturally congruent visions or auditory experiences. (p. 473)

Psychopathological conditions are distinguished by the opposite of these criteria.

Although clients' presentations do not always fit this list (in part because some of the criteria apply to beliefs, some to behaviors, and others to experiences), the criteria can be useful as a general guide. Take the example of a Christian client who told his therapist that God spoke to him on a daily basis. This man was a member of a fundamentalist church that conceptualized the Bible as the literal word of God. His experience of direct communication with God was supported by his family and church community and was "contained"—that is, the communication was of an expected duration and did not interfere with other activities. In addition, the content of the communication was constructive and perceived as helpful. Although the client was experiencing anxiety and depression, his spiritual experiences seemed to be a source of support and strength, not a maladaptive response. Attention to the cultural aspects of this client's presentation prevented the therapist from misinterpreting the client's experience as pathological.

In contrast, just as therapists risk pathologizing and overdiagnosing clients whose cultures are unfamiliar, therapists may also overlook pathology and underdiagnose because they frame a belief, behavior, or experience as cultural and thus automatically accept it (Paniagua, 1998). This mistake almost occurred on a geropsychiatry hospital unit when an older Filipina woman was admitted for treatment of "probable depression." Although the woman was noted to be "talking to the spirits of dead people," the intake nurse decided that these were not pathological hallucinations because she knew that "in some Asian cultures, people talk to their deceased relatives."

In this case, however, the nurse's limited knowledge was misleading. A closer look at the accompanying behaviors and experiences of the client revealed that she was distressed by these "conversations," that she was coping poorly both before and after them, and that the voices inhibited her ability to care for herself and engage with her family and caregivers. In addition, the voices were telling her to do destructive things that were not congruent with her culture and Catholic faith.

A more thorough evaluation found the client to have moderate dementia and hearing impairment that were contributing to her auditory hallucinations and depressed mood. Antidepressant medication subsequently lifted her mood and antipsychotic medication eliminated the voices. The client refused to wear a hearing aid, but her impairments resulted in her admission to a nursing home, where she had more auditory stimulation (i.e., more people around her who would speak loudly).

Kemp and Mallinckrodt (1996) discussed similar sorts of problems in clinical judgment as (a) errors of omission (i.e., failure to ask about a crucial aspect of the client's life) and (b) errors of commission (i.e., focus on an issue that is not especially important, although the therapist believes that it is). With regard to people who have disabilities, one example of an error of omission is the failure to ask about clients' sexuality; therapists may mistakenly assume that people with disabilities are incapable of or not interested in sexual intimacy. In contrast, an error of commission would be a heavy focus on the disability when it is not the client's presenting problem (Kemp & Mallinckrodt, 1996, p. 378).

Finally, in assessing the normality of behaviors in children, it is important to consider the influence of developmental processes. For example, children may lack the verbal skills to express feelings of worthlessness and guilt or the intellectual ability to understand or describe death or suicidal ideation (Yamamoto, Silva, Ferrari, & Nukariya, 1997). In addition, the ages at which social and verbal skills develop may vary depending on the cultural context.

Conclusion

Effective and accurate assessment involves a systemic understanding of the whole individual in his or her historical and cultural context. Historical and cultural information is best obtained primarily outside the therapy setting and provides a template for understanding specific individual and family details. For therapists engaged in ongoing self-education, this chapter focused on specific steps they can take during the assessment, including the use of multiple sources of information obtained in multiple ways regarding multiple domains. Equally important is therapists' willingness to adapt their interviewing style to allow for different cultural norms regarding appropriate questions and response styles. The use of a client's preferred language is recommended, but when this is not possible, a number of strategies are available for facilitating work with an interpreter. Finally, culturally responsive assessment assumes a strengths-oriented approach in which therapists deliberately look for and incorporate culturally related strengths and supports at the individual, interpersonal, and environmental levels. All of this work sets the stage for the culturally responsive use of standardized questions and tests—the next chapter's topic.

Key Ideas

Strategies for Culturally Responsive Assessment

1. Recognize cultural norms that may prevent the client from answering certain types of questions or questions posed in a particular way.
2. Adapt the interviewing style and pace to fit the client's communication style.
3. Think systemically and, whenever possible, seek out multiple sources of information in multiple ways regarding multiple domains.
4. Use the cultural history as a cognitive template into which specific individual and family information can be placed to increase your understanding of the client.
5. Stay aware of changing conceptualizations and cultural differences regarding illness, health, and disability over time.
6. Ask about the client's conceptualization of his or her problem, situation, and health care (including self-care) practices.
7. When assessing for trauma, be cautious about making judgments as to what constitutes a traumatic experience until you fully understand the client's family, community, and cultural histories.
8. Facilitate use of the client's preferred language, if necessary through referral to another therapist or the involvement of a well-qualified interpreter.
9. Look for culturally related strengths and supports at the individual, interpersonal, and environmental levels.
10. In distinguishing pathological from nonpathological behaviors and beliefs, remember that the latter are usually preceded and followed by good coping, lead to increased self-esteem, and receive the support of family and community.

Putting Culture to the Test

Considerations With Standardized Testing

7

My initial exposure to cultural issues in testing occurred during my doctoral studies at the University of Hawaii in the mid-1980s. My focus there was on cultural issues in clinical psychology. Through academic lectures and reading, I became aware of the continued lack of consensus on the definition of intelligence. I learned that definitions vary across cultures because different cultures value different skills and knowledge (Berry, 2004; Sternberg & Grigorenko, 2004). For example, in some traditional African cultures, a person who is cognitively quick but lacks social responsibility is generally not considered intelligent (Serpell & Haynes, 2004). Even within cultures, the most appreciated skills and knowledge can change across historical periods and over the life span of an individual (Anastasi, 1992). Although it is possible with deep knowledge of a culture to delineate such skills and knowledge, the most commonly used tests of intelligence come from the United States or Great Britain and represent knowledge and competencies relevant to urban industrialized societies (Poortinga & Van De Vijver, 2004).

With this knowledge in hand, I was granted a 1-year practicum that primarily involved testing children in Hawaii public schools. Most of these children were of Asian, Pacific Island, or mixed cultures. After my first couple of months, I asked my supervisor, a thoughtful Japanese American woman with children of her own, about the ethics of using such Eurocentric tests with children who were not European American. The gist of her reply was that this is not an ideal world, and if these children were to get anywhere in life, they had to first succeed in the European American-dominated school system. She went on to say that the tests we were conducting helped to demonstrate these childrens' specific learning needs so that they could get the help they needed. Her response underscores the complexity of issues involved in the use of psychometric tests with people of minority cultures.

This chapter begins with an overview of four common approaches to decreasing Eurocentric bias that have been presented in the testing literature. The suggestions that follow move beyond critiques to a description of specific strategies for using standardized tests in a culturally responsive way, including tests of intellectual abilities, mental status, neuropsychological functioning, and personality assessment. I also describe a case example of an older Korean man brought in for an assessment by his adult daughter, who was concerned about his memory difficulties.

Decreasing Test Bias

Most standardized tests originate from a European American worldview that permeates procedural norms in the research and development of such instruments. Items are chosen according to the rational analysis and judgments of a panel of experts who usually hold European American perspectives (Rogler, 1999), and instruments are validated through correlation with other instruments based on European American cultural views (Pace et al., 2006). Furthermore, by design, standardized instruments impose a response set on the client, limiting the individual's choices to those provided by the instrument (Pace et al., 2006).

One of the most common approaches to the problem of test bias involves the use of restandardized instruments. *Restandardization* is a complex process that includes the collection of norms from samples that are more representative of the population at large. It can lead researchers to make changes in the original test, including deletion or modification of items that are found to be invalid across cultures and the addition of items that are more cross-culturally valid. It may also involve the development of new scales and subtests. This approach offers the advantage of a starting point for cross-cultural assessments—a starting point that has been well established with at least one group (i.e., European Americans). Furthermore, it is possible that an instrument developed for the dominant culture could be relevant to some other cultures. For example, research has found that the extensively restandardized Wechsler Adult Intelligence Scale (Wechsler, 1981, 1997) and the Minnesota Multiphasic Personality Inventory—2 (MMPI–2; Butcher et al., 1989) to be valid with some ethnic minority groups (Nagayama Hall, Bansal, & Lopez, 1999; Suzuki & Kugler, 1995). However, restandardization does not address all potential forms of bias, particularly when tests are translated from English into another language. (See Butcher, Coelho Mosch, Tsai, & Nezami, 2006, and Geisinger, 1992; also see Hambleton, Merenda, & Spielberger, 1996, for a detailed explanation of the International Test Commission guidelines on adapting English-language educational and psychological instruments for cross-cultural assessment.)

The second solution to biases in testing is to create new tests that emanate from the value systems of minority cultures (Lindsey, 1998). This approach includes the use of a test medium that is familiar to members of that culture. For example, in their development of a culture-specific measure of intelligence in Zambian children, Kathuria and Serpell (1998) took into account prior research showing that Zambian children more accurately reproduced patterns using twisted strips of wire than did their English counterparts, whereas the English children surpassed their Zambian peers when reproducing the same patterns using paper and pencil. The authors developed the Panga Munthu Test, which involves showing children a model of a person, then asking them to build (*panga*) their own model of a person (*munthu*) using clay. The test was designed to tap into a set of skills that are actively cultivated in the daily lives of Zambian children, particularly those growing up in rural areas, where the authors noted that making models of people, animals, and domestic items such as pots and bowls may serve a developmental function comparable to the activity of drawing in Western societies.

This second solution of developing culture-specific approaches has also been used to develop instruments that assess affective constructs such as depression (Geisinger, 1992). Examples include the Hispanic Stress Inventory (Cervantes, Padilla, & Salgado de Snyder, 1990), the Vietnamese Depression Scale (Kinzie et al., 1982), and some of the instruments described in the *Handbook of Tests and Measurements for Black Populations* (R. L. Jones, 1996).

The third approach involves the use of an index of correction for culture (ICC; Cuéllar, 2000), which is derived by correlating a measure of acculturation with the criterion variable; an individual's score on the test is then adjusted by this correction factor. The greater the cultural difference between the person taking the test and the standardization sample, the greater the ICC. The direction of the correction is determined "by the direction of the correlation between acculturation and the criterion variable" for that ethnic group (Cuéllar, 2000, p. 124). However, as Cuéllar noted, standardized procedures for this approach have not been established. An additional problem is the conceptualization of acculturation as a linear process rather than as a complex variety of adaptations (Roysircar, 2004b).

The fourth approach to test bias involves a more fluid, dynamic approach, in which specific strategies are added on to standardized procedures. These strategies are aimed at gathering "additional qualitative data about the examinee" that help with a fuller understanding of the client's test performance (Cuéllar, 1998, p. 76). They may include a number of procedures known as "testing the limits" (described later in this chapter) as well as information obtained through interviews, active listening, direct observation, informant reports, and culture-specific tests. It is important to note that with this approach, test selection is not arbitrary, but rather involves a clear rationale for one's choice of tests and procedures.

Rethinking the Assessment of Intellectual Abilities

Too often, educational level and experience have been confounded with culture, resulting in the interpretation of lower test scores as evidence of lower intelligence in people of minority cultures. For example, some immigrants from rural areas of Latin America have limited literacy skills and are unfamiliar with the procedures and skills taught in school, which negatively affect their performance on U.S. tests of intellectual abilities. However, many of these same individuals are able to survive and thrive in a foreign and often hostile new country, find jobs, obtain a driver's license, buy a home, and sponsor family members to come to the United States—activities that require exceptional flexibility and intelligence (Pérez-Arce & Puente, 1996).

A relatively recent development in cognitive research involves the distinction between academic intelligence (used to solve academic questions and typically measured by quantitatively oriented instruments) and practical intelligence (used to solve day-to-day problems and performance in real-life situations; Sternberg & Grigorenko, 2004; Sternberg, Wagner, Williams, & Horvath, 1995). Whereas academic intelligence is facilitated by academic knowledge, practical intelligence increases with one's *tacit knowledge*, or common sense.

Tacit knowledge is action oriented (i.e., it involves knowing how to do things), is practical (in contrast to academic knowledge, which is often irrelevant to people's daily lives), and is usually acquired without the help of others, which means that it is often unspoken and poorly articulated (unlike academic knowledge, which is practiced and reinforced by the academic environment and the dominant culture; Sternberg et al., 1995). Research has shown that it is possible to develop measures of tacit knowledge relevant to job and school performance (Sternberg, Wagner, & Okagaki, 1993).

Along the same lines, in assessing everyday-life functioning among Aboriginal Australians, Davidson (1995) suggested that what is needed is an ideographic approach in which the skills and knowledge used to assess a client's functioning are those considered important for that particular person and should be measured in relation to his or her baseline; thus, what is assessed may vary with each client.

> Those who quibble with the notion that cognitive assessment can be ideographic may consider the possibility of a psychologist asking the question "Which of these two individuals is more schizophrenic?" When it comes to clinical diagnosis we are more concerned about whether, and the extent to which, both individuals are functional in everyday-life contexts rather than whether one individual has more psychopathology than the other. Why then are we not prepared to adopt an ideographic approach to cognitive assessment? The question in cognitive assessment should be, To what extent is the individual functioning cognitively in particular contexts? and not, Which of these two individuals is more cognitively capable? (Davidson, 1995, p. 32)

Obviously, such an approach does not address all of the issues involved in the diversity of purposes for which tests are used. For example, as my former supervisor suggested, children need to be able to perform at a certain level in the mainstream educational system to gain access to future opportunities. Thus, it is still necessary to assess children's performance in relation to the dominant curricula. However, even with children, an additional emphasis on practical intelligence can be helpful in calling attention to a child's strengths, avoiding the pathologization of difficulties, and thinking beyond numerically based assessments of a child's functioning.

In the past, the misguided equation of IQ with intelligence led to the misclassification of many African, Latino, and Native American children as mentally retarded or learning disabled (Suzuki & Valencia, 1997). Some psychologists and educators now emphasize the need to move beyond a focus on *classification and rating* (exemplified by the IQ score) to an approach that emphasizes understanding and guidance, or *description and prescription* (Samuda, 1998, p. 173). This latter approach involves more than simply evaluating whether a person can perform a task or not. Rather, the focus is on understanding the reasons for individuals' performance with the goal of providing recommendations for helping them.

With regard to the assessment of intelligence, this approach may involve dropping the concept of IQ, which represents only a composite of one's scores on a variety of tasks. Instead, the results of specific subtests may be used to provide details about what the individual can do, cannot do, and might be able to do with help. This approach also involves considering cultural influences on a person's test performance and functioning. For example, the emphasis of U.S.-based tests on speed of response and completion of tasks without help corresponds to the value European Americans place on cognitive quickness, personal independence, and competitiveness (Pérez-Arce & Puente, 1996). In contrast, many cultures place a higher value on careful thought, cautious behavior, and cooperation with others—values that may negatively affect their test performance but facilitate functioning in their own environments.

Recognizing that European American instruments are commonly exported and used in many nonindustrialized countries, researchers must continue to look for ways to increase the validity of intellectual assessment across diverse cultures around the world. In many previously colonized countries (as well as in U.S. history), intellectual testing was used primarily for selection purposes, namely, to deliberately eliminate poor and Indigenous people from the formal educational system. Unfortunately, even when such exclusion is no longer the intention, it can still have the same result when standardized tests are used to determine advancement to the next grade or level. As Serpell and Haynes (2004) noted with regard to African countries, a more socially productive and less culturally invasive approach involves prioritizing the guidance function of assessment over the selection function—advice that is similar to the description and prescription emphasis.

Wong, Strickland, Fletcher-Janzen, Ardila, and Reynolds (2000) made the following four practical suggestions for cross-cultural neuropsychological assessments; they seem equally relevant to most testing situations:

1. Make sure the testing environment is culturally sensitive. Many of the suggestions described in chapter 5 regarding physical space, arrangement of chairs, titles of address, and so on are applicable. In addition, the tester should provide a thorough explanation of the testing procedures so that the client knows what to expect, keeping in mind that some clients will be uncomfortable with, unfamiliar with, and even fearful of testing.

2. Always conduct a thorough clinical interview in conjunction with testing. An interview allows the tester to obtain information regarding cultural influences on the client that may affect test scores. For example, level of education has been shown to have a significant effect on test scores. It is important to understand not only the number of years of education but also the nature and structure of and expectations regarding education in the client's culture. The quality of education is also a consideration; for instance, African Americans are more likely to receive a less adequate education than are European Americans, even though they live in the same country (Nabors, Evans, & Strickland, 2000).

3. Do not use translated versions of tests unless their validity and reliability have been clearly established. In general, standardized tests (particularly intelligence and neuropsychological instruments) should be administered by a tester who speaks the client's language (i.e., not with an interpreter), because understanding the nuances of a client's language and subtle behaviors is key to accurate interpretations.

4. When writing the report, include information on potential cultural biases in the test and tester, and in the report authors' interpretations.

Mental Status Evaluations

With clients of minority identities and experiences, it is important to recognize that the questions included in standardized mental status evaluations are not reliable indicators of every client's functioning (Paniagua, 1998). For example, in a study of Native and non-Native elders in Manitoba, 45% of the Native elders had no formal schooling at all, and dates were considered less important as time markers than events such as the beginning of hunting and fishing season (Kaufert & Shapiro, 1996). The Native elders had difficulty naming the current and former prime ministers of Canada (questions on the adapted Mental Status Questionnaire developed by Kahn, Goldfarb, Pollack, & Peck, 1960). When the elders were asked what year they gained voting rights and when the community obtained electricity, relatively few could answer the first question, but a higher proportion answered the second correctly (Kaufert & Shapiro, 1996). The authors attributed these findings to the cultural and ecological significance of electrification: the hydroelectric dam that produced electricity resulted in the flooding of hunting, trapping, and fishing territories, which in turn contributed to decreased self-sufficiency and a sense of alienation among community members.

One of the most commonly used questionnaires for assessing mental status is the Folstein Mini Mental Status Exam (MMSE; Folstein, Anthony, Parhad, Duffy, & Gruenberg, 1985). The MMSE is only a screening test and has limitations in assessing individuals who have not had formal schooling in North America. For example, this test requires individuals to draw geometric designs as a screen for visuospatial perceptual difficulties. But nonliterate people with normal visuospatial abilities may have difficulty with this task because they rarely use a pencil. Basic questions concerning orientation may be misleading with clients who do not use watches or the Christian calendar, or with those who do not follow a structured daily routine (Jewell, 1989). For Spanish-speaking people, the MMSE has been found to yield higher error rates on questions as simple as "Can you tell me the season?" and "What state are we in?" (Escobar et al., 1986). Many Spanish-speaking people come from tropical and subtropical areas, which have two seasons—rainy and dry—rather than the four seasons of temperate climates. And the term *state* can be interpreted to mean both a country and divisions within a country (Ardila, Rosselli, & Puente, 1994).

Again, knowledge of the client's cultural history and context is important in making accurate interpretations of clients' responses to standardized questions. Take the case of an older man from Mauritania (a predominantly Muslim country in western Africa) who was deeply religious, worked as a farmer, and came to the United States after his wife died to live with his son. The man subsequently had a stroke, and the psychologist needed to assess whether there had been a change in his cognitive functioning.

Knowing that the man had 5 years of schooling, the psychologist could easily have underestimated his premorbid level of functioning based on the European American view of 5 years as a low level of education. However, the psychologist did his homework and learned that this man came from an area where 5 years in a strict Koranic school (which emphasized memorization and recitation of the Koran) was highly respected, particularly for a man born in Mauritania in the 1930s. He also learned from the client's son that in addition to being a farmer, the man was an imam whose advice was sought by many. This information helped the psychologist (with the help of the son and a cultural consultant) to develop questions that more accurately assessed the man's mental status.

As this example illustrates, with immigrant clients who are not educated in the European American school system, another strategy (in addition to learning about the cultural history) is to enlist the help of a family member or someone else who has an intimate knowledge of the client's culture (i.e., a cultural consultant). In some cases, the cultural consultant may be another therapist who does not know the client, and no personal identifying information is needed or given. In other situations, the cultural consultant may be the client's case manager or interpreter, and a release of information may be necessary. If the cultural consultant is not a family member, involving the family member in addition to the cultural consultant is helpful, because family members can often provide personal details the cultural consultant doesn't know.

When standardized procedures and tests are too culturally inappropriate or irrelevant, it may be helpful to hold a preassessment meeting with the cultural consultant with the goal of figuring out a way to assess the client's mental status and general functioning as accurately as possible. Let's return to the case of the Cambodian (Khmer) woman, Mrs. Sok, who I described in chapter 2. Before the preassessment meeting, the therapist would do her own independent research to educate herself about Mrs. Sok's culture, including experiences common to nonliterate women of her generation (e.g., farm work, motherhood, forced labor in camps during the war, the experiences of being a refugee and of immigrating). Then, during the preassessment meeting, the therapist could ask the cultural consultant questions to help her better understand the specific skills and knowledge valued in Khmer society over the course of Mrs. Sok's life and what Mrs. Sok might be reasonably expected to know.

The therapist might use the standard mental status categories of orientation, attention, speech, language, short- and long-term memory, visuospatial abilities, psychomotor functioning, and executive functions to initially generate relevant questions. However, the content of these questions would need to reflect Mrs. Sok's sociocultural upbringing and environment rather than the therapist's. In addition, the therapist should include categories of questions that reflect the client's culture's values (e.g., questions that assess good social judgment). She would need to keep in mind that speed (of cognitive processing and responses) would not be as important in Mrs. Sok's culture of origin as in European American culture.

The questions would also need to be framed so that the therapist could obtain confirmation of correct answers. Asking Mrs. Sok to recall her own or her children's birth dates as a screen for long-term memory difficulties would not be particularly helpful, because Mrs. Sok probably wouldn't know this information, and certainly not by the European calendar. Alternatively, asking the names of her father's sisters might be one indication of her long-term memory ability, but only if this information could be confirmed by family members. Questions that would tap more commonly held knowledge and give some indication of Mrs. Sok's memory might address the name of the place in Cambodia where she was from, the name of the camp where she lived before immigrating, the foods she used to prepare a particular Khmer meal, and how she would prepare it. All of this information could be obtained from or confirmed by the cultural consultant and family members for accuracy.

However, a significant problem with the approach of simply asking Mrs. Sok a set of questions (albeit a more culturally relevant set) involves the confounding of Mrs. Sok's verbal abilities (e.g., naming, fluency, word generation, verbal memory) with her functional abilities. That is, she may know and be able to describe how a traditional Khmer meal is prepared but be unable to carry out the specific tasks involved in preparing it. Or she might be unable to describe how to prepare the meal, despite the fact that she prepares such a meal daily. Or her description of the steps or components involved in making the meal might not follow the temporal sequence expected by a non-Cambodian therapist and thus might sound disorganized or confused to the latter. The therapist would also need to consider whether Mrs. Sok was describing the meal preparation as she would to a non-Cambodian or to another Cambodian; for the latter, Mrs. Sok would probably assume a common knowledge base and thus leave out some details.

For all of these reasons, a home visit might be the most helpful approach. A home visit could allow the therapist to directly observe

Mrs. Sok's activities and thus assess more fully how Mrs. Sok functions in her own environment. The therapist might still include some of the culturally relevant questions but would not depend solely on Mrs. Sok's verbal answers as a screening for mental status.

With clients who do not reference European American norms regarding time, Manson and Kleinman (1998) suggested the use of life history charts in which clients' symptoms are tied to significant events rather than dates. The client chooses events, which may be important for either personal reasons (e.g., "the crying started the year my husband died") or larger sociocultural reasons (e.g., "I remember first feeling that way just before the last harvest"). Visual symbols and pictures could be used to make the chart more comprehensible to nonliterate clients. The timeline described in chapter 6 of this volume (with historical cultural events above the line and personal events listed beneath it) could be modified to incorporate these ideas.

With clients who are culturally Deaf or who have a hearing impairment, Leigh, Corbett, Gutman, and Morere (1996) offered several suggestions for assessing mental status. The use of written language (e.g., in an emergency room when no interpreters are immediately available) may seem like a reasonable approach but can lead to serious errors in clinical judgment. Because "ASL grammatical structures differ from English, written communication by Deaf signers who are weak in English may appear aphasic or psychotic to the unsophisticated practitioner" (Leigh et al., 1996, p. 367). Similarly, English-based tests of intellectual functioning may not accurately reflect the client's cognitive abilities because they are confounded with the client's English linguistic abilities. To decrease this problem, Leigh et al. recommended the use of the Wechsler Adult Intelligence Scale—Revised (WAIS–R) Performance Scales (Wechsler, 1981) and the Standard Progressive Matrices (Raven, 1960) for intellectual assessment. However, it is important to note that even these scales (including the updated Wechsler Adult Intelligence Scale—III [WAIS–III]; Wechsler, 1997) are not free of cultural biases (Samuda, 1998).

To avoid misunderstandings and inaccurate diagnoses, Olkin (1999) advised that "Deaf clients are best served by Deaf therapists within the Deaf community" (p. 4). This is a controversial issue, because at present the majority of therapists providing services to Deaf clients require a sign language interpreter to effectively serve their clients (C. R. Williams & Abeles, 2004). To decrease the therapist's tendency to overgeneralize the experiences and behaviors of Deaf clients to all Deaf people, it is important for hearing therapists to spend time around Deaf people outside the therapy setting (C. R. Williams & Abeles, 2004).

One helpful approach to the standardized assessment of general cognitive functioning with ethnic minority elders is the Fuld Object Memory Evaluation (FOME; Fuld, 1977). The FOME has been found to be an effective screening tool for Alzheimer's disease in older African Americans (Mast, Fitzgerald, Steinberg, MacNeill, & Lichtenberg, 2001), and useful for the evaluation of possible dementia in multiethnic populations (Fuld, Muramoto, Blau, & Westbrook, 1988). The FOME involves asking an elder to put his or her hand into a bag that contains 10 small objects (e.g., key, cup, ring) and then name the item he or she feels before pulling it out and looking at it (or if he or she cannot name it, pull it out, look at it, and then try to name it). The elder names every object in this way and then, following a distraction task (word generation), is asked to name as many objects as he or she can remember. The tester tells the client the objects he or she forgot, and another distraction task is performed, followed by the request for another recall of the 10 items. This procedure is repeated five times and yields a measure of the person's learning and memory abilities over time with practice, along with verbal fluency measures from the distraction tasks. I have found this to be a fun test that lends itself to humorous comments later (e.g., at one nursing home where I carried the FOME bag with me, one older resident affectionately referred to me as "the bag lady").

In summary, a flexible and dynamic approach to evaluations of mental status is more time consuming and does not offer the confidence level of a standardized approach. However, with clients for whom standardized tests are too culturally inappropriate or irrelevant, not using this approach may result in responses and information that are relatively meaningless. Exhibit 7.1 lists important questions for therapists to use in a dynamic and flexible approach to assessment of mental status and intellectual functioning.

EXHIBIT 7.1

Questions for Assessing Mental Status and Intellectual Functioning

1. Does the client provide a detailed personal history, or does he become confused about the sequence of events being recounted?
2. Might the client's style of recounting her personal history differ from what I would expect, but still be normal in her cultural context (e.g., in terms of the content or a style that is linear, circular, or some other form)?
3. Does the client know information that most people of his culture and age would know, and do I know enough about the client's particular cohort to assess this?
4. Does the client show communication problems such as word-finding difficulties or paraphasias (i.e., made-up or misused words), taking into account her fluency level in English?
5. Does the client show appropriate concern and knowledge about his health problems, consistent with his educational background?
6. How does the client interact with me (e.g., aggressive, hostile, disinterested, confused)? Might there be cross-cultural dynamics related to any of the ADDRESSING influences that account for this behavior?
7. Might there be cultural explanations related to any of the ADDRESSING influences for a client's behaviors or beliefs that appear to me to be unusual or abnormal?

Neuropsychological Assessment

When mental status screening suggests the possibility of a cognitive problem, a neuropsychological assessment may be necessary. Neuropsychological assessment involves the evaluation of specific cognitive functions, including attention; concentration; short- and long-term memory; language; reasoning; visuospatial perceptual and constructive abilities; psychomotor functioning; and "higher level" executive functions such as abstraction, awareness, insight, judgment, planning, and goal setting (Lezak, 1995).

For clinical purposes, neuropsychological assessment can serve a variety of functions. One of the more common is to provide help in formulating a diagnosis. Often, establishing a diagnosis involves clarifying whether the individual is experiencing impairments in cognition, behavior, emotion, or personality related to a psychological problem such as depression, or to some form of brain dysfunction caused by head injury, exposure to toxins, substance abuse, cerebrovascular disease, Alzheimer's dementia, or other disease. Neuropsychological assessment may also be helpful in determining clients' competence to manage their own affairs, handle their own finances, make life decisions, or parent effectively; in educating the family about what to expect of the individual who has experienced a head injury, stroke, or has been diagnosed with a disease that affects functioning; in determining eligibility for disability benefits; and in providing recommendations for treatment planning, rehabilitation strategies, and placement issues (i.e., how independently the person can live; Judd, 2005). Neuropsychological assessment is especially helpful when detailed information is required regarding a person's abilities, strengths, and weaknesses, and when determining the progression of his or her functioning over time (Walsh, 1987).

Ethnic differences on neuropsychological tests have been documented and may result in the overidentification of cognitive impairments in members of ethnic minority groups (Mungas, Reed, Haan, & González, 2005). Biases have been found on nonverbal as well as verbal tests. For example, the Color Trails Test (Maj et al., 1993) was designed as a culture-free analog of the Trail Making Test (Kelland, Lewis, & Gurevitch, 1992), but although the two tests were highly correlated for English speakers (indicating that they measure the same ability), they were not highly correlated for a group of Hong Kong Chinese people, suggesting that in the Hong Kong Chinese group the two tests were measuring different abilities (Lee, Cheung, Chan, & Chan, cited in A. S. Chan, Shum, & Cheung, 2003). Until very recently, research on neuropsychological assessment has paid little attention to cultural influences and non-English-speaking populations (Ardila et al., 1994; see also A. S. Chan et al., 2003, for a review of neuropsychological tests in Asian countries). But as Anastasi (1992) noted, tests measure only samples of behavior at a given time and cannot say why the person responded as he or she did. To find this out, one needs to look at other variables, such as the individual's culture, values, and beliefs (A. Campbell et al., 1996).

The hypothesis-testing approach to neuropsychological assessment provides a model for the use of standardized tests in general (Lamberty, 2002). The psychologist begins with an initial set of hypotheses based on the referral question, the client's history, and his or her initial observations. The psychologist then chooses the specific tests that will best assess the client's capabilities. As testing progresses, the psychologist refines these general hypotheses into more specific ones. Gradually, the "successive elimination of alternative diagnostic possibilities" leads to a relatively conclusive diagnosis (Lezak, 1995, p. 112).

Assuming that the psychologist has obtained cultural and personal histories for the client, the strategy known as *testing the limits* can be helpful in interpreting the results of neuropsychological tests and measures of mental status and intellectual functioning. Testing the limits of standardized tests involves exploring, beyond standard administrative procedures, the possible reasons for a client's poor performance. Because this exploration is done after the standardized test procedure for an item, testing the limits does not affect standardized scores (Lezak, 1995). In addition, testing the limits offers the opportunity to move beyond the constraints of the test and, because the tester may ask clients why they think they missed an item, can also facilitate discussion and rapport with clients (Morris, 2000).

Take a specific example: the Picture Completion subtest of the WAIS–III (Wechsler, 1997). This subtest asks the client to name the important part missing from a picture for a series of different scenes within time limits. If a client is unable to provide correct answers to the items on this subtest and the tester simply accepts the client's incorrect answers as an assessment of the client's ability, the tester may be missing a great deal of potentially valuable information. If, however, the tester recognizes that a score does not indicate how or why the person had difficulty with this task, the tester could gain more information in the following ways (keeping in mind that retesting within a few months may preclude the use of some of these strategies):

1. Following the standard administration, the tester may return to each item and ask the client to look at the picture again and describe in detail what he sees. The underlying hypothesis at this point is that the client is capable of seeing the missing piece but simply missed it when he was asked.

2. To assess the influence of time pressure, the tester can ask the client to try to answer each item again, but this time without time limits. Time limits may contribute to the underestimation of a person's

true abilities, particularly in the case of people who require additional time because of age, disability, language differences, cultural factors, chronic illness, sensory or motor impairment, or simply nervousness (Lezak, 1995). When these factors are present, testing without time limits is important to give a fuller picture of the client's capabilities. Granted, there are no normative data with which to compare time-free responses on certain items. However, the point is to find out whether or not the individual can perform the task at all. If the person can, it is then necessary to figure out whether time-limited performance of the skills is important. For example, in the case of an elder who can do picture completion only without time limits, does her performance represent a deficit that could be dangerous in an independent living situation? Or, given that she experiences little time pressure in her home environment (and does not drive), is the issue of time relatively unimportant in assessing her visuospatial abilities?

3. The tester may inform the client of the correct answer and ask if he can now see the missing piece. (This strategy should not be used if the person needs to be retested within the next year.) A look of surprised recognition is often apparent if the person then sees it. The psychologist may then ask the client to point to the missing piece to confirm that he does see it.

4. The tester may ask the client directly if she has an idea why she had difficulty with a particular item on the subtest. The answer may be as simple as fatigue, disinterest, preoccupation with a problem, or physical pain that distracted the client. Similarly, a misunderstanding of the directions or impaired vision or hearing can account for poor performance. For example, as an intern in a Veterans Administration nursing home, I used the Geriatric Depression Scale (Yesavage & Brink, 1983) in assessing some of the older male clients. The first question, "Are you basically satisfied with your life?" elicited the response, "Oh, yeah, she's been a pretty good old gal." After a couple of these responses, I learned to ask before testing whether a person used or needed a hearing aid.

5. With individuals who speak English as a second language, Cuéllar (1998) suggested that after administering the failed item in English, a bilingual psychologist may ask the client the same item in the client's native language. This questioning will indicate whether or not the problem is related to language comprehension. Similarly, on a broader scale, when assessing a bilingual child's ability to succeed in an English-language educational system, it can be helpful to have the child assessed in both languages. This approach provides the required data but also offers a fuller understanding of the child's real needs and strengths (Geisinger, 1992, p. 33).

The Case of Mr. Kim

The case of an older Korean man who was brought to a psychologist by his daughter illustrates the preceding suggestions. The psychologist was trained in standardized procedures; however, she recognized this assessment as one requiring a more dynamic approach. Because she was able to make adaptations in the moment, she was able to successfully assess the family's needs. The case description includes the key questions she used in assessing this client's mental status in the moment (see also Exhibit 7.1).

Mr. Kim, a 70-year-old, high-school-educated, second-generation Korean American man, was referred by his physician to a 37-year-old Latina psychologist for an assessment of "memory loss." Mr. Kim came to the mental health center accompanied by his 32-year-old daughter, who introduced herself as Insook. Upon meeting Mr. Kim, the psychologist was reminded of her own father, with whom she had a strained relationship. The psychologist felt uncomfortable asking Mr. Kim directly about his difficulties. She unintentionally directed several questions to Insook, whose eye contact with the psychologist was direct, whereas Mr. Kim mostly looked at the floor.

After obtaining answers to only a few questions about Mr. Kim's history, primarily from his daughter, the psychologist sensed that something was wrong. She asked Mr. Kim directly if he was experiencing memory problems. In a low voice with a slight accent, he said that he noticed "some," but that his daughter was "too bothered." This was the point at which the psychologist would normally ask the client questions to test his mental status. Taking into account Mr. Kim's educational level, language fluency, and second-generation status, the psychologist decided that the MMSE would be an adequate screening measure.

However, because she sensed that the mental status questions would alienate Mr. Kim further, the psychologist said that she would like to take a 10-minute break followed by a brief interview alone with Mr. Kim and then, if it was all right with him, an interview alone with his daughter. She offered Mr. Kim and Insook something to drink, excused herself for a few minutes, and returned with three cups of tea. During the break, the psychologist engaged Mr. Kim and Insook in a more socially oriented conversation. After the tension had subsided a little, the psychologist showed Insook to the waiting area and spoke with Mr. Kim alone for 30 minutes.

Despite her desire to ask the mental status questions, the psychologist refrained and instead engaged Mr. Kim in conversation about his family's medical history. With his help, she drew a genogram of his family on the board, which also gave them both something to look at (see McGoldrick & Gerson, 1985, regarding genograms, and chap. 10 of this volume for an example). Mr. Kim told her what he knew about the health and social histories of extended family members, including his maternal grandparents, who died in Korea. The psychologist also asked about his family's religion, which he described as Buddhist with Confucian teachings.

As Mr. Kim spoke, the psychologist realized that she had inadvertently assumed that he was more impaired than he was. Rather than ask him directly about his mental status, she watched for signs of cognitive dysfunction while they completed the genogram. She asked herself the following questions:

- *Does Mr. Kim provide a detailed personal history, or does he become confused about the sequence of events being recounted?* He provided good details for past events but couldn't recall some dates that the psychologist considered important—for example, the year he was married. However, the psychologist thought that this might not be unusual for an older Korean man who had been married for over 30 years and widowed for 10 years.

- *Might his style of recounting his history differ from what I would expect, but still be normal in his cultural context (e.g., in terms of the content or a style that is linear, circular, or some other form)?* His style of recounting events was relatively chronological. None of his responses expressed feelings; rather, they were more focused on places, events, and experiences. The psychologist hypothesized that this was normal for an older Korean American man.

- *Does he know information that most Korean American men his age would know, and do I know enough about his particular cohort to assess this?* The psychologist did not and recognized her need for consultation.

- *Does he show communication problems such as word-finding difficulties or paraphasias (i.e., made-up or misused words), taking into account his fluency level in English?* He spoke English fluently with a slight accent and occasional grammatical errors that appeared congruent with his educational level.

- *Is his understanding of his health problems consistent with his educational background?* It was.

- *How does he interact with me, and might there be a cross-cultural dynamic that accounts for his reaction?* The psychologist realized that his reserved manner might be related to any combination of his Buddhist, Confucian, or Korean heritage; his older age; and his gender in response to her identity as a younger Latina woman.

- *Might there be cultural explanations for behaviors or beliefs that appear to be unusual or abnormal—that is, explanations related to his age or generation, possible disability, religion or spiritual orientation, or any of the other ADDRESSING influences?* The psychologist correctly interpreted his lesser eye contact as a result of embarrassment about the situation; however, she overlooked her own part in their uncomfortable interactions. Otherwise, there were no beliefs or behaviors that she considered unusual.

Following the interview with Mr. Kim, the psychologist walked with him to the waiting area, offered him another cup of tea, and then met with Insook. Alone with the psychologist, Insook spoke more freely about the problems she had observed in her father (increased irritability, weight loss, and poor memory that was evident in several incidents of lost keys and leaving the stove on). She told the psychologist that she hadn't wanted to list all of these problems in front of her father, although he seemed to be aware of them at home. In response to the psychologist's questions, she noted that her father did not have any serious physical problems and did not drink alcohol or take any medications.

In a brief closing period with Mr. Kim and Insook, the psychologist thanked them for their patience and cooperation and said that she would like to consult with a colleague who had more experience with situations such as theirs. This time, she directed her comments primarily to Mr. Kim. She added that she would like to meet with them for another shorter session the next week to complete the assessment. She asked Mr. Kim first, and then Insook, if they would be willing to return. Both agreed and seemed less tense as they said good-bye.

The success of this assessment was in jeopardy from the beginning, when the psychologist posed her initial questions to the daughter. As a Latina, she was aware that in her own and Korean cultures, younger people and children, including adult children, are expected to be respectful toward elders (B. L. C. Kim, 1996; B. S. K. Kim, 1996). Her intuition was good about not pressing Mr. Kim about his memory difficulties, but her overidentification with the daughter led her to make the mistake of directing her questions to Insook in front of Mr. Kim. This was embarrassing to both father and daughter, as Insook's later comments and Mr. Kim's behavior suggested (see B. L. C. Kim, 1996, regarding therapists' demonstration of respect with Korean families).

In addition, the psychologist initially misinterpreted the father's emotional restraint, lesser eye contact, and apparent acceptance of his difficulties as signs of dementia. She later learned that Mr. Kim's demeanor is not uncommon among people of Korean and Buddhist cultures, for whom emotional restraint is often seen as a sign of maturity and problems are considered a fact of life (W. J. Kim, Kim, & Rue, 1997; Murgatroyd, 1996).

The psychologist was able to recover from her initial mistakes by taking a flexible, dynamic, hypothesis-testing approach to the situation. Her decision to meet separately with Mr. Kim and Insook, in that order, was a good one. When she did so, she immediately recognized her incorrect assumption that Mr. Kim was too impaired to speak for himself. She quickly let go of the internal demand to find out certain pieces of information in the way in which she had been trained, through direct test-type questions. Instead, she evaluated Mr. Kim through the collaborative task of completing the genogram and observing his responses to less direct questions.

Through these observations and her own internal questioning, she developed her next working hypothesis: that Mr. Kim's cognitive deficits were due to depression. (Major depression, particularly in elders, can cause cognitive deficits that are reversible if the depression is successfully treated; see American Psychological Association, 2004.) But because she realized her need for more culturally related information, she refrained from stating this hypothesis as the diagnosis. It would be a tentative one until she could consult with a Korean American clinician and possibly obtain more information through a neuropsychological evaluation.

Personality Assessment

When assessing personality, and particularly when using a standardized instrument, it is important to remember that personality is a construct. One of the more commonly used definitions of this construct is that of the *Diagnostic and Statistical Manual of Mental Disorders* (fourth edition, text revision; American Psychiatric Association, 2000), which defines personality traits as "enduring patterns of perceiving, relating to, and thinking about the environment and oneself that are exhibited in a wide range of social and personal contexts" (p. 630). Although this definition may sound so general as to be universal, the idea of the self as an "autonomous individual, free to choose and mind his own business," cut off from the interdependent whole, is not shared by all cultures (Shweder & Bourne, 1989, p. 132).

THE MINNESOTA MULTIPHASIC PERSONALITY INVENTORY

The most commonly used personality assessment is the Minnesota Multiphasic Personality Inventory (MMPI) and its revision, the MMPI–2 (Butcher et al., 1989). The original MMPI was based on a standardization sample of 724 friends and relatives of patients at the University of Minnesota hospitals. The entire sample was White, with the typical participant being married and about 35 years old, having 8 years of formal education, and residing in a small town or rural area (Graham, 1990).

In response to criticisms of the limitations of such a culturally homogeneous group, the MMPI was restandardized with new norms to include samples of African, Asian, Latino, and Native Americans representative of the U.S. population in the 1980 census. Additional improvements to the MMPI–2 included "updated and improved items, deletion of objectionable items, and some new scales" (Graham, 1990, p. 13). The MMPI–2 consists of a list of 567 true–false questions from which standard scores are derived on 13 validity and clinical scales.

Extensive research has been done to investigate the possibility of ethnic biases in the MMPI and MMPI–2. In a meta-analysis of 25 comparative MMPI and MMPI–2 studies of African Americans, European Americans, and Latino Americans, the researchers concluded that neither instrument unfairly portrays African or Latino Americans as pathological, although they also noted the need for further research on the MMPI–2 (Nagayama Hall, Bansal, & Lopez, 1999). However, considering dominant cultural influences on the development of the original test, on procedural norms in personality research, on the definition of the construct of personality, and on definitions of ethnic groups that lump together people of diverse smaller cultures and languages, extra caution is advised in the use of the MMPI–2 with members of ethnic minority cultures, particularly with individuals from countries other than the United States. The following paragraphs provide suggestions for using the MMPI–2 in culturally appropriate ways.

One of the first and most important strategies involves considering the client's symptoms and test scores in their "bio–psycho–social–cultural–historical–political–linguistic context" (Pace et al., 2006, p. 321). The interpretation of clients' scores from this holistic knowledge base opens up a much wider range of hypotheses, which in turn facilitates more accurate interpretations. Along these lines, Garrido and Velasquez (2006) provided a list of culture-specific hypotheses for therapists to consider regarding Latino clients' scale scores. One example involves the L (Lie) score, which is normally associated with test resistance, a lack of insight, an unrealistically positive self-presentation, or a lack of sophistication in creating a personal impression. The researchers noted that the L score tends to be higher in Latino than in non-Latino populations. When interpreting these higher L scores, it is important to consider the culturally sanctioned tendency to present oneself positively in structured inquiries with non-Latinos and to protect one's family's reputation. The psychologist should also consider the extent of acculturation, because less acculturation is associated with higher L scores (Garrido & Velasquez, 2006, p. 499).

Similarly, Pace et al. (2006) offered culturally relevant hypotheses for American Indians' elevated scores on several scales. For example, with regard to members of an Eastern Woodland Oklahoma tribe and a Southwest Plains Oklahoma tribe, the researchers noted that elevated scores on Scale 8 (Schizophrenia) could reflect "the alternative epistemological perspectives and religious beliefs, which constitute 'non-ordinary and ecstatic' world-views as reflected in the Native American Church and Stomp Dance" (p. 329). Therapists should take this information into account when interpreting an elevated Scale 8 score. These are just two examples; Garrido and Velasquez (2006) and Pace et al. provided many more culturally related hypotheses regarding scores on other MMPI–2 scales. See also Butcher, Cabiya, Lucio, and Garrido (2007) for more on using the MMPI–2 with Hispanic clients.

When using the MMPI–2 with people who speak English as a second language, it may be necessary to formally assess the individual's language proficiency before deciding whether to administer the test in English. This step may be necessary even with bilingual clients, because an individual's proficiency in spoken English can be quite different from the person's reading comprehension (Santiago-Rivera & Altarriba, 2002).

If the individual's preferred language is clearly not English, a number of translated versions of the MMPI–2 exist; however, it is important to remember that there are significant linguistic and cultural differences among people who speak the same language (Rogler, 1999). For example, whereas one Spanish version may be appropriate for a client of Mexican origin, it could yield inaccurate results for a Spanish speaker from Argentina (Nichols, Padilla, & Gomez-Maqueo, 2000). (For a list of translated versions and a discussion of methodological issues including several types of equivalence, see Butcher et al., 2006.)

Finally, it is important to keep in mind that clients' reactions to taking such a test may preclude its use. For example, I once worked on a geropsychiatry hospital unit where elders who had physical and mental health problems were routinely asked to complete the MMPI–2. Help was often given in the form of reading each item to each client, but still, more than 500 true–false questions can be overwhelming to such individuals, as it might be to someone who speaks English as a second language, does not like to read, or perceives taking a test as too impersonal.

PERFORMANCE-BASED PERSONALITY (PROJECTIVE) TESTS

The term *performance-based* is used in place of *projective* for these personality tests, because, unlike self-report paper-and-pencil approaches, these tests require the individual to "perform a defined activity with an examiner (i.e., generate a story or identify images)," and there is evidence that such tests do not depend on or require projections but rather reflect a person's "perceptions, classifications, and cognitive–emotional templates or internal representations" (Kubiszyn et al., 2000, p. 120). Hence, as Kubiszyn et al. noted, the descriptor *performance-based* is more accurate than *projective*.

Most of the widely used performance-based personality tests started from a European American cultural base and, as such, are also susceptible to cultural biases (Costantino, Flanagan, & Malgady, 1995; Cuéllar, 1998). For example, the Thematic Apperception Test (TAT; Murray, 1943) consists of pictures that clients are asked to describe; clients' responses are considered indicative of their beliefs and views. But the original TAT pictures were of characters and situations relevant primarily to European American culture. Over the years, the TAT pictures have been redrawn to depict people and situations of diverse cultures (see Costantino & Malgady, 2000, for an overview). However, the use of the TAT has declined significantly both in doctoral training programs and in general assessment practice (except with adolescents), and "optimism concerning TAT reliability and validity research has waned" (Dana, 1999, p. 178).

The Tell-Me-a-Story (TEMAS) test (Costantino, Malgady, & Rogler, 1988; Costantino, Malgady, & Vasquez, 1981) "was developed to revive the TAT technique for culturally and linguistically diverse children and adolescents" (Costantino & Malgady, 2000, p. 484). Research using the TEMAS suggests that the cultural identity of characters does make a difference in clients' responses (Suzuki & Kugler, 1995). The TEMAS has been described as the only "adequately validated multicultural thematic test employing cards to depict Hispanic or Black, Asian, and White adolescents" (Dana, 1998, p. 6) and has been described as an improvement over existing personality measures used by school psychologists (Flanagan & Di Giuseppe, 1999).

The Rorschach Comprehensive System (RCS; Exner, 1993) avoids the problem of respondents' perceptions of characters' identities by using inkblots. Although one might hypothesize that inkblots would be less culturally laden, the interpretation of clients' associations to these stimuli is especially susceptible to misunderstanding by clinicians whose cultures differ from their clients'. For example, the dark areas of the color cards have traditionally been associated with death and mourning, but in India, "white, not black, is the color associated with mourning and death" (Jewell, 1989, p. 306).

As Ephraim (2000) observed,

> Rorschach examiners tend to agree that common principles of Rorschach interpretation could be applied to protocols of people from any cultural background. However, there is still a need to establish, conceptually as well as empirically, which those common principles are. (p. 322)

An increasing number of normative studies internationally have found significant variations in local norms compared with norms in the United States (see Andronikof-Sanglade, 2000; Ephraim, 2000; Pires, 2000; Vinet, 2000). Controversy over the clinical usefulness of the RCS in general led to a special section on the RCS in the journal *Psychological Assessment* (December 2001) that included reviews of the literature by experts on both sides of the debate. In a summary article, Meyer and Archer (2001) concluded that the literature "does not lead to an expectation of ethnic bias" (p. 494) but added that cross-cultural applications are an understudied issue and that research regarding differential validity across large ethnic examples would be valuable. (See Dana, 2000b, for a more detailed critique of the cultural influences on the RCS.)

Conclusion

The central problem with standardized testing is that it assumes that there is a standard human being, when in reality there is not. Standardized tests can be enormously helpful in clarifying a person's diagnosis, strengths, and needs. However, if used without a solid understanding of the client's cultural identity and context, standardized instruments hold the potential for damage. In the not-too-distant past, people of ethnic and other minority identities were seriously hurt by the misuse of such tests. Thus, it is essential that psychologists be aware of the cultural biases embedded in many standardized tests of intelligence, mental status, neuropsychological functioning, and personality. This awareness, combined with specific steps aimed at obtaining culturally relevant information, can significantly improve the accuracy of one's diagnoses. And this brings us to the topic of the next chapter, namely, cultural concerns in diagnosis.

Key Ideas

Strategies for Making Standardized Tests More Culturally Responsive

1. Begin with a thorough history, both personal and cultural.
2. When available and appropriate, arrange a preassessment meeting with the client's interpreter, case manager, or a cultural consultant. For the purposes of mental status evaluation, use this meeting to develop a list of questions and confirmed answers that tap the skills and knowledge relevant to the client's experience and context.
3. Choose tests that match the referral question for the client.
4. Explore possible reasons for a client's test performance.
5. After following standardized procedures, push the limits of standardized tests.
   (a) Ask the client to look at each item again and describe in detail what she sees.
   (b) Ask the client to answer each item again, this time without time limits.
   (c) If retesting is unlikely, tell the client the correct answer, then ask and watch if he sees it or can point it out.
   (d) Ask the client why she thinks she had trouble with an item or subtest.
   (e) Ask the item in the client's native language (only if you are fluent).

6. Think ideographically—that is, whenever possible, compare clients' test performance and behaviors against their own past performance, rather than against others' performance.

7. Recognize that composite test scores say little about a client's functioning, and focus instead on specific measures of strengths and weaknesses.

8. Use standardized personality tests for diagnostic purposes in conjunction with a thorough understanding of the client's social, cultural, historical, political, and linguistic context.

Making Sense and Moving On
Culturally Responsive Diagnosis and the DSM–IV–TR

8

W hile working on a geropsychiatry unit, a physician asked me to evaluate a 63-year-old Mexican American man who had no physical or emotional complaints. Mr. García had been born in the United States, had obtained a ninth-grade education, and spoke English with an accent. In the late 1960s, he began working as a custodian for a large corporation. He was well liked and a hard worker, and over the years he was promoted to a supervisory position, which required that he keep track of equipment. However, during the past 5 years, he had begun losing requests and forgetting orders. He had also been "talked to" for some odd behaviors, such as taking his shirt off on the work floor (he said he was hot). As a result, his responsibilities had gradually been reduced to sweeping floors and other cleaning tasks.

Although Mr. García was not concerned about his work situation or health, his wife was deeply distressed. She reported that he did things that scared her—nothing abusive, but things like driving through red lights and draping a blanket over an electric heater. She had tried everything she could think of to help her husband, including rearranging things in the house and talking to his supervisors, family members, and friends. But no one had a reasonable explanation for why Mr. García was acting the way he was. She went to her priest, who prayed with her, and finally she went to the doctor, who conducted a thorough medical exam of her husband. Because the physician could find no physical reasons for the changes in Mr. García, he recommended a neuropsychological assessment.

Following a lengthy assessment, which included consultation with the physician, interviews with Mr. and Mrs. García, reports from a work supervisor, and neuropsychological testing, I concluded that Mr. García had moderate dementia probably as a result of Alzheimer's disease. Normally, I dread having to share this information with patients and their families. But because of the extent of Mr. García's impairments, I guessed that he would not be disturbed by this information, and in fact, he was not.

Telling Mrs. García, I believed, would be a different matter. I assumed that she would be crestfallen and probably angry at me, the bearer of bad news. To my surprise, she did not become upset, but rather expressed relief and appreciation. As she explained, she was exhausted from trying to figure out her husband's strange behaviors and personality changes. At least now she knew that she was not imagining things or overreacting. Although she was realistically sad about what lay ahead, she was also ready to hear about available resources and begin planning for the future.

As this case illustrates, much of the power of a diagnosis comes from the meaning it gives to a confusing situation. Ideally, this new understanding leads to specific actions that can eliminate the problem or reduce its harmful effects. Even when the problem can't be solved, an accurate diagnosis may suggest new ways of thinking about the problem and coping with it. For example, although nothing could be done to reverse Mr. García's Alzheimer's disease, as a result of learning that this was the primary problem, Mrs. García stopped questioning and blaming herself. Mr. García left his job, which he was no longer able to perform anyway, obtained disability benefits, and began attending a day program that provided social interaction for him and a break for Mrs. García.

Toward the goal of establishing a shared understanding of mental syndromes and disorders, the American Psychiatric Association [APA] developed the *Diagnostic and Statistical Manual of Mental Disorders* (DSM). The most recent major revision was the fourth edition, the *DSM–IV* (APA, 1994), followed by a minor text revision (the *DSM–IV–TR*; APA, 2000) intended to bridge the span between the *DSM–IV* and the *DSM–V*. No substantive changes in the criteria sets were made from the *DSM–IV* to the *DSM–IV–TR*, nor were any new disorders, new subtypes, or changes made in the status of the *DSM–IV* appendix categories (APA, 2000, p. xxix).

The *DSM–IV–TR* is currently the most widely used diagnostic system in the United States. However, its widespread use does not mean that it is the most sensitive, most accurate, or only approach to diagnosis. For example, five major psychoanalytic groups recently published the *Psychodynamic Diagnostic Manual*, intended to meet the need for a diagnostic system that considers the whole person and provides guidance for treatment planning (Packard, 2007). At least 18 alternative proposals have been made for a dimensional model of personality disorders to replace the categorical model used by the *DSM–IV–TR* (Widiger & Trull, 2007). In one study, a dimensional model of personality disorders was found to have greater clinical usefulness than the categorical classification of the *DSM* system (Samuel & Widiger, 2006). In many countries, the clinical modification of the *International Statistical Classification of Diseases and Related Health Problems* (*ICD–10*; World Health Organization, 1992) is preferred.

In 1991, in response to criticisms of ethnocentrism in earlier editions of the *DSM*, the National Institute of Mental Health appointed a Work Group on Culture and Diagnosis "to advise the *DSM–IV* Task Force on how to make culture more central to *DSM–IV*" (Lewis-Fernández, 1996, p. 133). Over the next 3 years, this group, composed of about 100 clinicians and social scientists, conducted extensive literature reviews and wrote detailed proposals for culturally related modifications to the new version (Kirmayer, 1998). Unfortunately, though, as one member explained later,

> Many of the substantive recommendations made by the task force—the wording of particular symptom criteria, variations in duration criteria, the inclusion of new or revised categories (a mixed anxiety–depression category, culturally distinctive forms of dissociative disorders, neurasthenia as seen and diagnosed in many Asian cultures), significant revisions of the definition of personality disorders—were not incorporated into the body of the manual, in spite of strong empirical data from the cross-cultural research literature. (Good, 1996, p. 128)

The additions to the *DSM–IV* (and the *DSM–IV–TR*) that do address cultural concerns occur primarily in five components. The first component consists of a section called "Specific Culture, Age, and Gender Features" that is included under some diagnoses, although not all. The second component consists of a revised and expanded Axis IV: Psychosocial and Environmental Problems, which includes problems relevant to minority populations such as discrimination, acculturation difficulties, homelessness, extreme poverty, inadequate health services, being the victim of a crime, and war. The third component consists of three V codes—Identity Problem, Religious or Spiritual Problem, and Acculturation Problem—that provide a way to diagnose problems that commonly affect people of minority group membership without pathologizing the individual.

The fourth component consists of an Outline for Cultural Formulation, which includes helpful questions to ask but no culture-specific information. Its placement in an appendix at the back of the manual (rather than integrated into the multiaxial system) tends to deemphasize its importance. The fifth component is a Glossary of Culture-Bound Syndromes that provides descriptions of 25 such syndromes. The separation of this section into an appendix tends to reinforce the idea that culture is relevant only to members of minority groups, when in fact no psychiatric disorder can be understood apart from the culture in which it occurs (Marsella & Yamada, 2000). For example, the symptoms of recurrent depression in a European American woman are no less linked to cultural influences than the symptoms of *nervios* in a Latina client. In summary, these components involve a mixture of helpful additions and not-so-helpful additions.

Recognizing that other approaches to diagnosis may be more valid in particular cultural contexts, this chapter focuses on the *DSM–IV–TR* because it is a requirement for so many therapists. I outline specific guidelines for making a culturally responsive diagnosis, including the use of a sixth cultural axis. A case example illustrating these suggestions describes a recently married Tunisian (Arab Muslim) couple who presented with marital distress and the wife's symptoms of depression following her recent immigration to the United States.

Making a Culturally Responsive Diagnosis

Building on the guidelines in chapter 6 of this volume for conducting a culturally responsive assessment, there are a number of additional steps that therapists can take to increase the probability of making a culturally responsive diagnosis using the *DSM–IV–TR*. The first of these is to add a sixth axis that highlights cultural influences on the client. The idea of a sixth cultural axis was one of the original suggestions proposed by the Work Group on Culture and Diagnosis. However, it was eventually rejected in favor of the Outline for Cultural Formulation, with the intention that this framework would be placed at the beginning of the manual, which did not happen (Lewis-Fernández, 1996).

One of the Work Group's primary concerns about a sixth axis was that it might "just add a sixth list of essentializing descriptors" (Lewis-Fernandez, 1996, p. 135). I share this concern, and certainly the sixth axis as I describe it in this chapter has the potential to be misused in this way. However, the uninformed application of any procedure or tool is always a problem. Because I have found the ADDRESSING acronym helpful in calling attention to cultural influences in any diagnosis, I use it as a sixth axis, as described later in this chapter. But I emphasize that this approach assumes that the therapist is engaged in the cultural self-assessment and ongoing learning process described in this book.

First, I list the *DSM* axes the way that they are listed in most intake reports—vertically on the left side of the page (see Table 8.1). However, the first axis that I fill in is Cultural Axis VI: ADDRESSING Influences. I do this by listing the ADDRESSING acronym vertically next to Axis VI. Then, next to each influence, I note the salient cultural influences and

TABLE 8.1

Diagnosis Example: Mouna

DSM–IV–TR axis	Details
Axis I	309.0 Adjustment Disorder With Depressed Mood
	V62.4 Acculturation Problem
	V61.10 Partner Relational Problem
Axis II	V71.09 No Diagnosis
Axis III[c]	None
Axis IV[b]	Problems With Primary Support (loss of primary support group secondary to immigration)
	Problems Related to Social Environment (inadequate support for new role as wife, new social and cultural environment, language barrier, racism in dominant U.S. culture)
	Occupational problems (loss of previous work due to immigration)
	Other problems (family pressure to become pregnant)
Axis V	Global Assessment of Functioning (GAF) = 65 (current)
	GAF = 90 (highest level in past year)
Axis VI[a]	Age and generational influences: 27 years old; born in 1980 (24 years after Tunisian independence). Mouna was in an early generation of girls to enter school after it became mandatory. She is the youngest child and only daughter in a Tunisoise (upper-middle-class, urban) family.
	Developmental disabilities: none reported or apparent
	Disabilities acquired later in life: none reported or apparent
	Religion and spiritual orientation: parents both Muslim but nonpracticing; Mouna's personal beliefs are Muslim, but she has a secular lifestyle.
	Ethnic and racial identity: mother and father both of Arab Tunisian heritage; family of Tunisoise heritage; first language Tunisian Arabic, but French also spoken in the home; Mouna does not yet speak English.
	Socioeconomic status: parents both university educated and are of upper-middle-class backgrounds.
	Sexual orientation: probably heterosexual
	Indigenous heritage: none
	National origin: Tunisian; recent immigrant living as a permanent resident in the United States.
	Gender: female; youngest child and only daughter in family of origin; newly married with no children, but has expectations of motherhood as central to her life and identity as a woman.

Note: DSM–IV–TR = *Diagnostic and Statistical Manual of Mental Disorders, Fourth Edition, Text Revision* (American Psychiatric Association, 2000).
[a]Complete this axis first.
[b]Complete this axis second.
[c]Complete this axis third.

identities for that client. At the time of the initial assessment, I list only those influences and identities of which I am aware; later, as I learn more about the client and his or her culture, I add in information that is then visible to anyone looking at the report. Because information needs to be abbreviated in this format, you may be unsure of what to include next to each ADDRESSING category. As a guide, I suggest returning to the questions outlined in Exhibits 4.1 and 4.2 (chap. 4 of this volume) on understanding clients' identities.

Second, I fill in Axis IV: Psychosocial and Environmental Problems. Because I have just listed cultural influences on Axis VI, many of which may be strengths, it does not seem so skewed to focus here on the problems related to clients' sociocultural contexts. To be sure that I have thought to include or ask about all relevant stressors, I again use the ADDRESSING acronym as a reminder of problems that may be related to clients' age or generation, visible or nonvisible disability, religious upbringing or current identity, ethnic and racial identity, socioeconomic status, and so on.

After filling in Axis VI: ADDRESSING Influences and Axis IV: Psychosocial and Environmental Problems, the third axis to be completed is Axis III: General Medical Conditions. Completing these three axes first gives a fuller picture of the client's context, facilitating a more accurate diagnosis on Axis I and II and a more accurate rating on Axis V: Global Assessment of Functioning.

In making an Axis I or II diagnosis, it is important to recognize the legitimacy of the client's conceptualization of the problem from his or her perspective. Equally important is the ability to explain the meaning of a diagnosis in language the client understands. Although the use of theoretical language may facilitate the therapist's understanding, it will not necessarily increase the client's (Holiman & Lauver, 1987). Moreover, it assumes a conceptualization of the problem that the client may not share.

With regard to Axis II, caution is advised in diagnosing personality disorders. Because a personality disorder "reflects difficulties in how an individual behaves and is perceived to behave by others in the social field" (Alarcón & Foulks, 1995, p. 6), the specific criteria constituting a personality disorder will vary depending on the interpersonal skills and attitudes valued by a culture at any given point in time (Alarcón, 1997). Consider, for example, the attitudes and behaviors constituting a paranoid personality disorder as defined by the *DSM–IV–TR:* "a pervasive distrust and suspiciousness of others such that their motives are interpreted as malevolent, beginning by early adulthood and present in a variety of contexts, as indicated by four (or more) of the following criteria" (p. 694). These criteria include (among others) preoccupation with unjustified doubts about the trustworthiness of others, a reluctance to confide in others because of unwarranted fear that information may be used against one, and a tendency to perceive attacks on one's character or reputation that are not apparent to others.

Without a consideration of cultural influences, these criteria might seem reasonable. But who decides whether or not a client's suspiciousness, doubts, and fears are justified or unwarranted? Suspiciousness, fear, and distrust have been described as a realistic reaction to the racism experienced by African Americans (Grier & Cobbs, 1968) and Middle Eastern immigrants currently living in the United States (Bushra, Khadivi, & Frewat-Nikowitz, 2007). Even the *DSM–IV–TR* notes that such attitudes and behaviors may be normal in anyone persistently exposed to oppressive conditions (e.g., members of ethnic and other minority groups, immigrants, and refugees; APA, 2000, p. 692).

To illustrate how dominant cultural values (particularly masculine-biased assumptions) regarding personality traits and styles have affected *DSM* categories, Kaplan (1983) noted that despite the existence of a dependent personality disorder, which is disproportionately diagnosed in women, there is no such thing as an independent personality disorder; apparently, one can be too dependent but never too independent. Similarly, the *DSM–IV–TR* does not have a diagnosis for individuals who are racist, misogynistic, or homophobic (McGoldrick, 1998). Although such beliefs and behaviors are considered offensive, undesirable, and even dangerous, they are generally not seen as evidence of any mental disorder by mainstream culture.

To accurately diagnose a personality disorder, the therapist needs to know the client's culture well enough to judge whether the client's behavior represents a marked deviation from it. In addition, because personality disorders by definition involve disturbed interpersonal functioning and misperceptions about the actions of others, the therapist may also need information from people who have known the client for many years in a variety of situations. Because such information is rarely available in an initial assessment, the diagnosis of a personality disorder will often be premature.

Finally, the last suggestion in making a culturally responsive diagnosis is to move beyond the *DSM* focus on individualistic diagnoses to think systemically and consider relational disorders (Kaslow, 1993). This is no easy task because, as Kirmayer (1998) explained, diagnosis is in itself an "essentializing" process; the *DSM–IV–TR* reinforces the focus on "decontextualized entities whose characteristics can be studied independently of the particulars of a person's life and social circumstances" (p. 342).

Although the *DSM–IV–TR* includes categories of Relational Problems (Parent–Child, Partner, Sibling, and Not Otherwise Specified), these diagnoses are all listed as V codes (i.e., under Other Conditions That May Be a Focus of Clinical Attention). Relational Problems may be listed on Axis I if they are the focus of clinical attention; however, because they are placed in an appendix at the end of the *DSM–IV–TR*, the implication is that these diagnoses are of secondary importance. Given this bias, the therapist needs to work hard to maintain a systemic perspective.

One additional dilemma for systems-oriented therapists concerns reimbursement. Many insurance and managed care companies do not reimburse for V codes. When this is the case, and one is assessing a family or couple, it may be necessary to diagnose one individual (assuming that the person's symptoms match a *DSM–IV–TR* diagnosis) while conceptualizing the problem as primarily an interpersonal one. (More on the practical considerations of this issue are discussed in the case example later in this chapter.)

In summary, I believe that it is possible, although not ideal, to make a culturally responsive diagnosis using the *DSM–IV–TR*. The likelihood of such a diagnosis is increased by completion of the Cultural Axis VI first (i.e., the ADDRESSING outline), followed by the Psychosocial and Environmental Problems on Axis IV second and the General Medical Conditions on Axis III third. This sequence allows for more fully informed diagnoses on Axis I, II, and V. Recognition of the legitimacy of clients' conceptualizations is also important. Using diagnostic language that is clear and comprehensible to clients, being cautious about the diagnosis of personality disorders, and thinking systemically about clients' presenting problems will help to increase the helpfulness and accuracy of one's diagnosis.

Case Example: Mouna and Majid

To give an idea of how these suggestions may work in practice, the following case description illustrates a therapist's diagnostic process with a couple. At the time of the initial assessment, the therapist, a European American woman in her early 50s, had little knowledge of the clients' cultures. However, she was committed to the learning process and was able to use the suggestions regarding diagnosis outlined in this chapter to make a helpful and culturally responsive diagnosis.

Majid, a 34-year-old Tunisian man, brought his wife, Mouna, a 27-year-old Tunisian woman, to his female physician for an appointment. In fluent English with an Arabic accent, Majid explained to the physician that during the past 5 months, Mouna had been "very unhappy, sleeping too much, and crying every day." Mouna did not speak English, but through Majid's interpretation, she appeared to confirm his description. The physician knew that Majid and Mouna had recently been married and that Mouna had moved to the United States to live with

Majid 8 months earlier. Following a medical checkup that ruled out any hormonal, neurological, or nutritional deficiencies that might have contributed to Mouna's mood change and hypersomnia, the physician referred the couple to a psychologist who specialized in women's issues and couples therapy.

FIRST ASSESSMENT SESSION

At the initial assessment session, the psychologist greeted Mouna and Majid warmly and introduced herself as Dr. Kate Smith. They chatted briefly, with Majid interpreting for Mouna, about the difference between the weather in the northeastern United States and Tunisia. Kate observed to herself that Mouna appeared very dressed up, with carefully done makeup, a stylish short haircut, and noticeable perfume. Mouna was alert and her affect seemed sad, but she smiled at appropriate times and, despite the language difference, always looked directly at Kate when Kate spoke. Majid was dressed neatly, although more casually. He showed a full range of affect but appeared tense. The couple seemed comfortable interacting with each other; for example, twice Mouna spoke sharply to Majid, and he responded with an irritated look.

Kate began the assessment by asking Majid to explain why they had come in to see her. Majid said that he did not think they needed a psychologist but that the doctor couldn't find anything wrong with Mouna and told them they ought to see her. Kate sensed some embarrassment on his part. She said that she hoped she could be helpful and that she would like to start by hearing a bit more about their concerns. As Majid repeated the information he had told the physician, Kate periodically made eye contact with Mouna.

After about 15 minutes of talking with Majid, Kate asked him if he would interpret a few questions for her directly to Mouna. He agreed, and through this process, Kate learned that before marrying Majid, Mouna had lived with her parents and two brothers in the capital city of Tunis. Through a meeting arranged by family members, she was introduced to Majid on one of his visits home; they corresponded for a year and then married. Mouna left her work in a hospital and moved to the United States with Majid. During their first few months together, she was happy with her new life, but then she began to miss her family, her friends, and her home. She also began to worry about not being able to have children, because after 8 months of marriage she had not yet become pregnant. When asked what she wanted, she said that she wished to return to Tunisia with Majid, but in the same sentence she acknowledged that she knew he couldn't leave his work.

Because of the interpretation process, this initial assessment took the full 90 minutes scheduled. Although she did not complete her evaluation, Kate considered the meeting successful because Mouna brightened a little when questioned directly about her thoughts and feelings, and Majid appeared less tense than when he had arrived. When asked, both Mouna and Majid agreed to return for a second assessment session.

CONSULTATION TIME

At this point, Kate was well aware of her own limitations in working with Mouna and Majid. She had some experience working with people who had immigrated from South America and Europe, and she was familiar with some of the values and behaviors more common in Mediterranean cultures (e.g., the emphasis on family, the value placed on motherhood, and expectations of marriage and children for both men and women; see Abudabbeh & Hays, 2006; Ali, Liu, & Humedian, 2004; Bushra et al., 2007). However, Kate had no personal or professional experience with Tunisian, Arab, or Muslim people.

After listening to Majid, Kate realized that she held some assumptions about Arab and Muslim men's attitudes toward women. For example, she was surprised by the sincerity of Majid's concern for Mouna and by their apparent comfort level with one another. In thinking about her surprise, she realized that she had assumed that given their arranged marriage, the couple would be quite formal with one another and that Majid would care about Mouna's health only insofar as it affected his needs. But this was clearly not the case. Kate realized that changing her biases would require work outside the therapy session.

Before their next session, Kate found information about Tunisia. She learned that Tunisia is a North African country of approximately 10 million people who are predominantly Arab and Sunni Muslim. The country was colonized by France (technically a protectorate) until it gained independence in 1956. Tunisia has a high literacy rate and mandatory schooling for boys and girls, and French is a commonly spoken second language. During the past 40 years, Tunisia has become a leader in the Arab world on the subject of women's rights; minimum ages have been set for marriage, the consent of both women and men is required for marriage, abortion and divorce initiated by women have been legalized, and family planning services offer free contraceptives across the country. The Tunisian government sends university students abroad for graduate study in particular fields. Although most go to France, some are sent to the United States, and many of these individuals become permanent residents (Hays & Zouari, 1995; World Almanac Education Group, 2007).

Kate also consulted with an Arab American therapist, who advised her that she should have arranged for an interpreter before their first session. Kate telephoned Majid to talk with him about this, but he reacted defensively. Kate realized that he took her suggestion to mean that he was not sufficiently fluent in English or that he could not represent

Mouna's views fairly. Kate explained that neither was the case, but rather that she wanted Majid to feel free to express his own concerns without the pressure of needing to attend to Mouna's needs simultaneously. Majid finally agreed to an interpreter on one condition—that he know the name of the person beforehand to be sure that they were not in the same social circle, the Tunisian community in their city being relatively small. He and Kate agreed on a Lebanese woman who spoke Arabic and did interpretation for a large hospital. Before their next assessment session, Kate talked with the interpreter on the telephone, asking questions about her expertise, confirming her understanding of confidentiality, and generally establishing rapport.

During her consultation with the Arab American therapist, Kate described her impressions of Mouna and Majid and mentioned their arranged marriage. The consultant sensed some judgmentalism on Kate's part and explained that arranged marriages are still common in Tunisia and that they help to ensure that families as well as individuals are well matched. She added that divorce is relatively uncommon. Her comments challenged Kate to think further about her assumptions regarding arranged marriages.

Kate also expressed concerns about the impact on Mouna and Majid of current political events. She said that she had not been sure of whether to ask about this, so she refrained, but at the same time she did not want them to think that she agreed with the U.S. government's actions in Iraq. The consultant validated Kate's wish to be respectful but said that given the pervasiveness of anti-Arab and anti-Muslim sentiment and its possible effects on a person's mental health, this topic was an important cause of stress to consider. The consultant explained that in addition to the U.S. invasion of Iraq, Kate needed to consider an ongoing series of events affecting Arab and Muslim people. She named the U.S.-led coalition against the Iraqi invasion of Kuwait during the Gulf War that resulted in the deaths of thousands of Arab people, the abuse of Arab Muslim prisoners by U.S. soldiers at Abu Ghraib, the ongoing U.S. support of Israel over the Palestinians, and the U.S. supply of weapons to Israel during the latter's bombing of Lebanon in 2006. She added that following the attacks on the World Trade Center, hate crimes in the United States against Muslims and Arab people increased dramatically (Zogby, 2003). The consultant explained how all of these actions, on top of a history of negative stereotypes and prejudice against Arabs and Muslims, could contribute to feelings of anger, frustration, distrust (i.e., of Americans), and hopelessness among Arab and Muslim people.

The consultant suggested asking Mouna and Majid, "Have you experienced discrimination or racism during your time here in the United States?" as part of the assessment of chronic and acute stressors in the couple's lives. She said that if Mouna or Majid did not want to talk about this, Kate would probably sense it from their responses, and she could refrain from further exploring the topic until trust was more firmly established. (Muslims and Arab people may be slow to disclose information related to religion or politics until trust has been established; Ali et al., 2004; Erickson & Al-Timmimi, 2001.)

The consultant also called Kate's attention to the assumption embedded in Kate's statement that she did not want Mouna and Majid to assume that she agreed with the U.S. government's actions. The consultant told Kate that although it was likely (considering the couple's more recent immigration, Majid's strong Muslim identity, and the current political climate) that the couple disagreed with U.S. policies, it was also possible that they did not. The consultant explained that although more recently immigrated Arabs and Muslims tend to be less satisfied with U.S. foreign policy, up until the 1980s the majority of Arab Americans were Republican and tended toward assimilation into the dominant culture (Erikson & Al-Timmimi, 2001). The consultant reminded Kate that there can be just as much diversity in the way Arab and Muslim people see the world and themselves as there is between ethnic and religious cultures. She encouraged Kate to continue her reading and look for community events at which she might meet a wide variety of Arab and Muslim people.

SECOND ASSESSMENT SESSION

At the second session, Kate introduced the interpreter, who was about 50 years old and preferred to be addressed as Mrs. Salem. Mrs. Salem shared that she was married to a Lebanese man with whom she had immigrated to the United States as an adult. She was familiar with the Tunisian dialect of Arabic (something Kate then realized she had not thought to ask), because she had worked in a Tunisian-owned travel agency for many years. She had also been trained as a peer counselor and worked as a volunteer at the local mental health center. Kate reiterated their commitment to confidentiality, primarily to reassure Majid; she and Mrs. Salem had already discussed this before the session. The assessment resumed with an emphasis on completing the histories of Mouna and Majid.

Mouna's History

Mouna reported that she was born and grew up in the same house in Tunis, along with her parents, two older brothers, and paternal grandmother. Her father was a university professor and her mother an elementary school principal. Her two older brothers (ages 28 and 30) left home in their early 20s to attend university in Paris. Mouna wanted to join them but said that her parents worried too much about her safety to allow her to move to France. While living at home, Mouna completed a master's degree in biology at the University of Tunis and then obtained a position as a research assistant in a hospital, where she worked for a year before marrying Majid.

Mouna described her family as very close, noting her parents' pride in her educational accomplishments. Because everyone except her grandmother spoke French fluently, the family's language was a mixture of Tunisian and French. Although they observed religious holidays and never drank alcohol in their home, Mouna's family members were not practicing Muslims (i.e., they did not perform the prayers five times a day, nor did they intentionally follow a religious diet). Mouna referred to her family and herself as "Tunisoise" (pronounced *too-neez-wahz*), the feminine form of a term used to describe the well-educated middle- and upper-middle class of the capital city.

To better understand the meaning of Mouna's identity, Kate asked Mouna to describe her life as a young woman in a Tunisoise family. Mouna responded by describing her typical day as "busy and mostly happy." After waking early to help her mother prepare a breakfast of bread, olive oil, and coffee for the family, Mouna would then get dressed and go to work. She enjoyed the walk to the hospital and being part of the hustle and bustle of the city. She liked her work, too, where she had many female friends. She would return home to have lunch with her family (the largest meal of the day, prepared by the maid), then take a nap and talk a little with her mother before returning to the hospital to complete her work there. In the evenings after dinner, she and her mother frequently entertained at home or visited female friends and relatives while Mouna's father and brothers went to the café to see their male friends.

In response to Kate's questions about Mouna's experience in the United States, Mouna said that during her first few months, she continued to awaken early to prepare Majid's breakfast and sit with him while he ate. However, getting up in the morning became increasingly difficult for her, and she eventually stopped. She tended to wake up closer to noon now and described her only activities as cleaning the house, watching television (although she understood little), and preparing dinner beginning in the late afternoon. She said that she'd gone out a few times but that when she tried to buy something at the local grocery store, the clerk was rude to her. Another time, she was frightened when a man in a car shouted something angry at her (she didn't understand the words). Now she didn't like going out alone and mostly stayed in the apartment. Although she looked forward to Majid's return all day, she felt angry when he arrived home, especially when he didn't want to take her out. She did admit that he drove her to English classes two nights each week, went out with her most Saturdays and Sundays, and had arranged several dinners with couples who were his friends.

Majid's History

Majid reported that he, too, grew up in a close family. His grandparents on both sides were poor but very religious. His father attended Koranic school and eventually bought and ran his own small grocery store, which provided a modest income for the family. Majid's mother completed elementary school and worked in the home preparing meals, maintaining the household, and caring for Majid and his older brother and younger sister. Majid's parents were both practicing Muslims, and he himself had practiced the prayers and followed the required diet until he left home.

Majid's parents held high expectations of him, and at school he was known for his intelligence and hard work. He won a government scholarship to a U.S. university, where he completed a master's degree in electrical engineering. He subsequently obtained work as an engineer in a medium-sized company, which allowed him to obtain permanent residence status in the United States. He worked for 4 years, saving money for a dowry and a nice apartment, and then began looking for a wife. He stated that his family was very proud of him but also disappointed that he did not return home after university.

Majid described his early years in the United States as "hard" but added that "everybody has to go through the same thing when they move here." In response to Kate's questions about his experiences of racism, he said that he'd had people be rude, stare at him, ignore him, and shout things like "Go home!" at him from a distance. He said that most Americans he met "just don't know any Muslim people personally, so they have some pretty strange ideas about Islam." He said that generally he found most Americans to be respectful once they got to know him, although he added, "but then there are always those crazy people on the edge that you have to be on the lookout for."

In response to Kate's questions about what had helped him to adjust, Majid said that he considered a key element to be his focus on learning English, because "once you speak English, you can do almost anything." When pressed by Kate to think of other things that had helped him adjust, he recalled learning to cook some Tunisian dishes, playing Tunisian music, and finding a café frequented by North Africans. In addition, a "turning point" occurred when his brother came to visit; Majid said that showing his brother around the city made Majid realize how much he liked living in the United States. Although Majid intended to return to Tunisia to retire, he did not want to live and work there now, because he said that even during visits, he became impatient with "the slow pace" and could no longer stand the heat in summer.

When asked about his marriage, Majid said that despite their frequent arguments, he thought he and Mouna had a good relationship and that the problem was her homesickness. He had tried everything he could to help her: He took her out as much as possible and encouraged her to take more English classes. He was starting to worry about their ability to have a baby, and he was beginning to think that she might have some sort of physical problem.

UNDERSTANDING THE CLIENTS' IDENTITIES

As Kate listened and recorded information about Mouna's and Majid's lives, she began forming hypotheses about their identities and the salient cultural influences in their lives. She used the ADDRESSING framework to help her organize this information and be sure that she was not ignoring potential influences.

Mouna's Identity

For Mouna, Kate asked herself which of the ADDRESSING factors Mouna had mentioned and which she had not. (See Axis VI in Table 8.1.) Although Mouna had mentioned influences related to age and generation, nationality, religion, and social status, she did not mention those related to disability, ethnicity, sexual orientation, gender, and Indigenous heritage. Kate was guided by her own general knowledge, sensitivity, and intuition to ask about some of these factors and to refrain from asking about others. As a part of her history-taking, Kate did ask more detailed questions about Mouna's religious upbringing. But she did not ask about Mouna's ethnicity (because she already knew that Mouna was ethnically Tunisian Arab), gender (which she hypothesized was self-evident), disability or Indigenous heritage (because these did not appear to be relevant), or sexual orientation (which she knew was a topic too sensitive to explore with an Arab heterosexual couple in an initial assessment).

To gain a better understanding of the meaning of the cultural influences salient in Mouna's life, Kate sought information about Tunisian cultural norms in three ways. First, she asked Mouna about her friends' situations. For example, with regard to Mouna's wish to study in France, Kate learned that in Mouna's social circle, her parents' insistence that she stay in Tunisia was considered well intentioned and reasonably protective, rather than sexist or punishing. Second, Kate listened for differences between Mouna's and Majid's descriptions of their situations. Hearing Majid's description of his Muslim upbringing alerted Kate to the differences in practices among Muslims and, more important, the differences between Mouna's family and Majid's. Third, between and after sessions, Kate consulted with the Arab American therapist and Mrs. Salem.

By the end of the second session, it was clear that Mouna's personal norms regarding women's roles and behaviors corresponded closely to those of the dominant Tunisian class. Kate hypothesized that Mouna's attitudes and worldview would soon be challenged by her new cultural context. However, she understood that although she was there to help this couple consider possible new behaviors and views, she would need to be careful not to impose her own beliefs regarding relationships and men's and women's roles.

Majid's Identity

Although Majid's identity was as firmly connected to his culture and family of origin as was Mouna's, the meaning of this connection was quite different. Majid was not from a Tunisoise family; the lower social class and the strict religious practice of his family set them apart from Tunisian society's more secular ideal of the 1960s and 1970s, just after independence from France. Even before he moved to the United States, Majid had felt "different."

Through his family, Majid had developed a deep sense of himself as a religious and spiritual person. Although nearly all of the Muslims he met growing up were Tunisian, his parents taught him to think about Muslims around the world as one community. After arriving in the United States, he attended a mosque for a few years and was delighted to meet Muslims who were Cambodian, Indonesian, Nigerian, and African American.

Majid identified himself primarily as a Tunisian man; however, during his 14-year residence in the United States, he had learned that most Americans know little if anything about Tunisia. Thus, when describing himself to Kate, he added information that he would not have added for a Tunisian listener (e.g., that he was Arab and Muslim). Although he did not specifically refer to himself as a member of an ethnic minority culture in the United States, his experiences had led him to identify with diverse people of color rather than with the European American majority.

With regard to his expectations and beliefs about marriage and the influence of gender, Majid's point of reference was a mélange of Tunisian, Muslim, and American influences. He described his belief in the equality of men and women and his marriage as an egalitarian relationship in which he and Mouna should "support each other to be good people and to do our best." From his years of living alone, he was used to cooking and cleaning up after himself, although Mouna always made dinner now. He wanted Mouna to make friends and return to working outside the home again, even after having children, if that would make her happy. He assumed that he would be the primary breadwinner but imagined that once Mouna was fluent in English, she would manage their money, as his mother had in his family. Since their marriage, he had tried to make important decisions in collaboration with Mouna (e.g., about decorating the apartment, where to go on outings, planning for the future), and he expected that she would start driving once her English was sufficient to pass the driver's test. Table 8.2 summarizes the salient ADDRESSING influences in Majid's life.

TABLE 8.2

Cultural Influences in Majid's Life

Cultural influences	Details
Age and generational influences	34 years old; born in 1973; middle child of three. Majid was in an early generation of boys educated after independence for whom expectations of success were extremely high. His generation expected to live a secular lifestyle, but Majid was not brought up this way.
Developmental disabilities	None reported or apparent
Disabilities acquired later in life	None reported or apparent
Religion and spiritual orientation	Parents both practicing Muslims; Majid has a deep sense of himself as a religious and spiritual person, although not currently practicing.
Ethnic and racial identity	Mother and father both Arab Tunisian; Arabic is spoken in their home; Majid is fluent in French and English, too.
Socioeconomic status	Parents had elementary school educations and were working poor; family lived in Tunis but was not Tunisoise.
Sexual orientation	Probably heterosexual
Indigenous heritage	None
National origin	Tunisian; living as a permanent resident in the United States; has considered obtaining U.S. citizenship as well.
Gender	Male; middle child but youngest son; newly married, with a strong desire to be a "good husband" (meaning in an egalitarian, mutually supportive relationship, as primary breadwinner); no children, but has expectations of fatherhood as central to his life and identity as a man.

CASE CONCEPTUALIZATION AND DIAGNOSIS

With this understanding of the salient cultural influences on Mouna and Majid, Kate was in a position to consider what would be the most accurate and useful conceptualization and diagnosis for their case. She was knowledgeable enough about the stressors involved in immigration to realize that Mouna's depressive symptoms (crying, excessive sleeping, sad mood and affect) are common responses to the enormous changes involved in such a transition. She understood how Mouna's acculturation difficulties might be exacerbated by the current political climate and racism in the dominant culture. Thinking systemically, Kate also recognized the adjustment difficulties that Majid was experiencing as a result of the marriage and his new role as a husband. And from the consultant, she learned that a huge missing piece in the adjustment of both Mouna and Majid was the social support from extended families that they would have received as a newly married couple in Tunisia.

Majid's distress did not meet criteria for a *DSM–IV–TR* diagnosis. For Mouna, the V code Acculturation Problem was clearly justified, but the question remained whether this would be a sole, primary, or secondary diagnosis. Mouna's symptoms suggested the possibility of a Major Depressive Episode or Adjustment Disorder With Depressed Mood. Kate ruled out the first diagnosis because Mouna did not report at least five of the required symptoms, but the decision to rule out an Adjustment Disorder was more complex.

Diagnosis of an Adjustment Disorder requires the development of "clinically significant emotional or behavioral symptoms" (p. 679) within 3 months of the onset of a stressor (APA, 2000). The symptoms or behaviors must be "in excess of what would be expected given the nature of the stressor" or result in "significant impairment in social or occupational (academic) functioning" (p. 679). Immigration and discrimination qualify as stressors (or more accurately, a collection of stressors), and Mouna's symptoms had begun within 3 months after her move. However, her distress was not in excess of what one would expect in the face of such a transition.

The difficult question was deciding whether or not her symptoms were significantly impairing her social, occupational, or academic functioning. Mouna was not impaired in her ability to relate to people or to form new relationships; she simply lacked opportunities and was limited by the language barrier. She continued to carry out most of her household responsibilities (although she no longer cooked breakfast), and she was progressing in her English class. However, one could argue that her depressive symptoms were interfering with her marital relationship.

With this information in mind, Kate chose to conceptualize the case as one in which extraordinary stressors were affecting both Mouna and Majid individually and in their relationship as a couple. Mouna was clearly more expressive of her distress and thus more easily seen as "the patient." Her symptoms were marginally diagnosable as an Adjustment Disorder. In an ideal world, Kate noted to herself, she would not diagnose Mouna so as to avoid pathologizing her. However, in their current situation, the managed care company would pay only for treatment of a clinical or personality disorder (i.e., not for a V code such as Acculturation or Partner Relational Problem). In addition, Kate suspected that Mouna and Majid would not return if their insurance did not cover the therapy. (See Cooper & Gottlieb, 2000, and Eisman et al., 2000, regarding reimbursement and ethical issues related to managed care.)

CONSIDERING THE CLIENTS' VIEWS

Toward the end of their second assessment session, Kate summarized the information in the preceding paragraphs. She reviewed with Mouna and Majid the social and cultural stressors in their lives and talked about common responses to those stressors. Kate stated that she saw Mouna's difficulties as primarily caused by the stressors related to immigration and their relationship difficulties as a result of the challenges of beginning a marriage without the usual social support. She added that the current political climate in the United States was also an ongoing stressor. She validated the need for Mouna to develop a level of caution about going out alone that acknowledged real dangers but at the same time was not unreasonably limiting. She explained how important social support is as a counter to such stressors and how the absence of their immediate family support probably made the stressors feel even greater.

At the same time, Kate said, she saw Mouna and Majid as having many strengths. She cited their strong family ties, despite the physical distance from Tunisia; their faith, particularly Majid's involvement with the Muslim community; their commitment to and caring for one another; their intelligence and histories of success in education and work; and their willingness to try new things—for example, counseling. She added that with all of these strengths, she was confident that they could find ways to help Mouna feel happier and to help the two of them get along better.

Majid and Mouna appeared relieved by Kate's summary. They agreed that they would be willing to attend several counseling sessions. Kate then explained that their insurance would cover only the diagnosis and treatment of one person. She described two solutions to this dilemma: (a) They could pay for couples therapy themselves or (b) because Mouna could technically be diagnosed with an Adjustment Disorder, Kate could make this diagnosis and be paid by the managed care company. In the latter case, the stated goal would be to facilitate Mouna's adjustment to a new country, life, and marriage, but couples counseling could be the method chosen to address this goal and their relationship. Mouna and Majid chose the latter option and returned for couples counseling.

Conclusion

Kate was not the ideal therapist in this case. She did not speak her clients' language, she had only a general familiarity with Arab cultures, and she held some prejudices about Arab Muslim men and about arranged marriages. In addition, she made some significant mistakes. For one, she neglected to obtain an interpreter before the first session, an oversight that might have ended the chance of therapy with some clients. She also forgot to ask about the Lebanese interpreter's familiarity with Tunisian Arabic; fortunately, the interpreter was aware enough to have thought about dialect differences. However, Kate was committed to providing culturally responsive services to Mouna and Majid. She did her homework in learning about her clients' cultures (i.e., reading, consulting with an Arab American therapist, and obtaining the help of an interpreter). She was also careful to obtain a detailed history, including information about each person's cultural context and identity. And she paid attention to differences between Mouna's and Majid's stories as cues about what was normative in their families' contexts.

With regard to the diagnosis, Kate started with the Cultural Axis VI and considered the salience of each ADDRESSING influence in Mouna's and Majid's lives. Although she recognized that Mouna's symptoms met criteria for an Adjustment Disorder, she was quick to see the larger context, including contradictory pressures (e.g., that the diagnosis of Mouna would reinforce the idea that Mouna was the problem, but that finances were also a concern for the couple). She included both Mouna and Majid in the diagnostic process using straightforward language and a systemic perspective that acknowledged the impact on both Mouna and Majid of Mouna's recent immigration, racism in the dominant U.S. culture, their newly married status, and decreased social support. And in her final assessment, she gave special attention to the couple's culturally related strengths and supports. In sum, Kate's diagnosis was not ideal, but it was ethical, culturally responsive, and likely to lead to help for this couple. As the next chapter illustrates, culturally responsive assessment and diagnosis pave the way for more effective interventions.

Key Ideas

Making a Culturally Responsive Diagnosis

1. Start with the Cultural Axis VI: ADDRESSING Influences to describe identities, contexts, and strengths.
2. Next, complete Axis IV: Psychosocial and Environmental Problems using the ADDRESSING acronym as a reminder of problems that may be related to clients' age or generation, visible or nonvisible disability, religious upbringing and current identity, ethnic and racial identity, socioeconomic status, and so on.
3. Third, complete Axis III: General Medical Conditions.
4. After completing Axes VI, IV, and III, in that order, consider possible diagnoses on Axes I, II, and V.
5. Recognize the legitimacy of the client's conceptualization of the problem.
6. Be able to explain the meaning of your conceptualization and diagnosis in language that the client understands.
7. Be cautious about diagnosing personality disorders.
8. Move beyond the *DSM–IV–TR* focus on individualistic diagnoses to think systemically and consider relational disorders.

CULTURALLY RESPONSIVE PRACTICE V

How to Help Best
Culturally Responsive Therapy

9

When I was living in North Africa, an Arab Muslim man who knew that I was a psychologist asked if he could talk with me about a problem he was having. He told me that he was experiencing anxiety related to worries about money and his work. He had always been an intense person, and these were ongoing worries, but suddenly he found that he was unable to swallow. He would put food or drink in his mouth but couldn't get it to go down. As a result, he had lost quite a bit of weight, and he was extremely uncomfortable because it was summer and the heat made him unbearably thirsty. (During the summer, he also had more free time to sit and worry.) He did not want to talk about his feelings in any depth, and I was not in a position to be of any help professionally. However, I listened, encouraged him by saying that this was a problem that could be solved, and suggested that he see his doctor (there were no psychologists in his country at the time).

Several months later, when I was back in the United States, I learned that although the problems in his life were still there, his anxiety had decreased, and he was no longer having difficulty swallowing. He had gone to see a doctor, but that was not what had helped. What made the difference was that he began practicing the religious requirements of

Islam. The essentials of these requirements are commonly called the "five pillars of Islam" and include the following:

1. the *Shahaada*, a profession of faith in the one God and Mohammed as his prophet;
2. the daily prayers;
3. giving alms to the poor (*zakat*), a form of worship also intended to correct social inequalities;
4. fasting during the holy month of Ramadan, which celebrates Mohammed's initial revelation from God and his journey from Mecca to Medina; and
5. the *hajj*, a pilgrimage to Mecca, made toward the end of one's life if at all possible. (Ali, Liu, & Humedian, 2004)

Of these requirements, the prayers involve the greatest commitment of time and effort on a daily basis. In Muslim countries, the call to prayer is made from the mosques (more recently, over loudspeakers) at regular intervals five times each day. In response to the call, devout believers stop what they are doing and perform special washing rituals, which cleanse one's body and also symbolically purify the soul. The prayer

> begins in dignified, upright posture but climaxes when the supplicant has sunk to his or her knees with forehead touching the floor. This is the prayer's holiest moment for it carries a twofold symbolism. On the one hand, the body is in a fetal position, ready to be reborn. At the same time it is crouched in the smallest possible space, signifying human nothingness in the face of the divine. (H. Smith, 1991, p. 246)

The act of praying in the direction of Mecca, along with the knowledge that Muslims around the world are also turned toward Mecca, and the act of saying the same prayers at similar intervals, "creates a sense of participating in a worldwide fellowship, even when one prays in solitude" (H. Smith, 1991, p. 246).

With regard to this man and his anxiety, one could view his healing from a strictly cognitive behavioral perspective. It could be that the prayers and social support for his religious practice provided sufficient cognitive restructuring and behavioral change to reduce his anxiety. However, one could also view his healing from a spiritual perspective and emphasize the comfort, peace, and possibly transcendence he obtained through his efforts. Whatever one's view, the practice worked for him.

In many cultures, psychotherapy is a treatment of last resort because it is unavailable, because shame prevents people from accessing services, or because there are other treatments that are more effective or preferred (Yeh, Inman, Kim, & Okubo, 2006). For these reasons, it is important that therapists be eclectic in their knowledge about coping strategies and diverse forms of therapy practiced in various cultures. At the same time, as long as the therapist stays flexible, a particular theoretical orientation can provide a direction and specific tools that may be helpful to clients of minority and dominant cultures.

Eclecticism in psychotherapy can take two general forms. The first involves an integration of diverse theories into one *transtheoretical model* (Consoli & Jester, 2005; Prochaska & Norcross, 1994). The second, known as *technical eclecticism*, describes the increasingly common practice of systematically choosing and using a wide range of interventions and procedures (Lazarus & Beutler, 1993). The practice of multicultural therapy (MCT) is probably best described as technical eclecticism. Although there are theoretical premises unique to MCT (e.g., that cultural differences between the therapist and client affect therapy), it is far from an integrated, transtheoretical model, probably because unlike the major schools (e.g., psychodynamic, behavioral, cognitive behavior, family systems, and humanistic–existential therapies), which began from a place of describing how therapy is done, MCT began from the question, "With whom is it done?" MCT certainly involves a paradigm shift in that it calls into question the usefulness of all preceding theories, but the diversity and complexity of clients' identities rule out the possibility of one therapeutic approach for all.

What MCT uniquely offers is a perspective that opens up an enormous set of questions and considerations that may otherwise be ignored. These new considerations point to the inadequacy of any sole conceptualization, approach, or strategy. This perspective means thinking about therapy in new ways that include interventions that may not fit mainstream conceptualizations but that may benefit people of minority and dominant groups.

This chapter begins with some examples of therapies and coping strategies that are indigenous to particular minority cultures and groups. Next is a section on the expressive and creative arts therapies (e.g., art, music, and body movement therapies), which can be helpful with people who speak English as a second language, have language deficits (e.g., people who have dementia), or are simply less verbally oriented. Within this section, some suggestions regarding play therapy with children of diverse identities are included. The next sections describe the use of family, couples, and group therapies with people of diverse cultures.

The last portion of this chapter focuses on the integration of cultural considerations into cognitive behavior therapy (CBT). CBT is not the only form of psychotherapy amenable to cross-cultural adaptation, but it is one of the most widely practiced. A survey conducted for the American Psychological Association (APA) found that 89% of psychologists reported using cognitive or CBT (Myers, 2006). Because it is so widely used and understood, CBT is the focus of the last section, with the intention of providing just one example of how cultural considerations can be integrated into a mainstream psychotherapy. However, it is important to note that the integration of cultural considerations into the major psychotherapies has been addressed from diverse theoretical perspectives including psychodynamic (Berzoff, Flanagan, & Hertz, 1996; Chin, 1994); self psychology (Hertzberg, 1990); existential (Vontress, Johnson, & Epp, 1999); family systems (Boyd-Franklin, 2003; McGoldrick, Giordano, & Garcia-Preto, 2005); and feminist therapies (Brown & Ballou, 1992; Comas-Díaz & Greene, 1994). Increasing interest in the need for evidence-based practices, along with increasing awareness of the health needs of minority populations, underscore the continuing need for research on cross-cultural adaptations of all the major psychotherapies (for more on this subject, see Hwang, 2006).

Indigenous and Traditional Therapies

As the case of the Arab Muslim man illustrates, religion can be a powerful therapy that meets a person's spiritual, emotional, and social needs. There are also therapies indigenous to particular cultures that share religious assumptions while not being religions per se. For example, the five therapies of Morita, Naikan, Shadan, Seiza, and Zen are indigenous to Japan and share the goals of helping the individual refocus attention away from self and everyday self-consciousness and slow the pace of thought, which in turn helps to deepen it (Reynolds, 1980, p. 103). Like Buddhism, emphasis is placed on the acceptance of suffering as an integral part of life. In contrast to mainstream psychotherapies, talking is discouraged; instead, clients are placed in quiet isolation (with some guidance provided by the therapist) to facilitate the development of the "natural inner strength" that can lead to "a more enlightened understanding" of oneself (Reynolds, 1980, p. 104).

Drawing from Buddhist practices, "mindfulness meditation," in which one's attention is directed to the present moment, has become increasingly popular among non-Buddhists for the purposes of stress reduction and pain control and as an integral part of CBT (DeSilva, 1993, Hayes & Duckworth, 2006; Kabat-Zinn, 2005). Along with behavioral and cognitive changes, the practices of "stopping," calming oneself through conscious breathing, paying attention, and simply "being" in the present moment can facilitate a shift in consciousness. As the Vietnamese Buddhist monk Thich Nhat Hanh (1992) explained,

> If we practice mindfulness, we get in touch with the refreshing and joyful aspects of life in us and around us, the things we're not able to touch when we live in forgetfulness. Mindfulness makes things like our eyes, our heart, our non-toothache, the beautiful moon, and the trees deeper and more beautiful. If we touch these wonderful things with mindfulness, they will reveal

their full splendor. When we touch our pain with mindfulness, we will begin to transform it. (p. 29)

Traditional healers are the helpers of choice for many people of minority and dominant cultures, particularly for problems that have a psychological or psychosocial aspect (Jilek, 1994). For example, for many people of Central and Latin American cultures, *curanderos* (male healers) and *curanderas* (female healers) are sought out for help with a variety of illnesses, but especially those "with psychological components, such as *susto* (fright), *mal de ojo* (evil eye), *empacho* (indigestion), or *envidia* (envy)" (Falicov, 1996, p. 173). They may also be consulted for such problems as depression, impotence, alcoholism, and menstrual cramps (Falicov, 1998). Among Mexicans and Mexican Americans, such healers are primarily women who use practices derived from Catholicism, ancient Mayan and Aztec cultures, and herbology (Novas, 1994). In California and the southwest United States, their services are included in some innovative health care programs as complementary options that broaden the range of care available to clients (Falicov, 1998; Koss, 1980; Novas, 1994). (See Marsella & Kaplan, 2002, for a list of 27 healing systems or therapies, including curanderos, acupuncture, Ayurvedic medicine, ho'oponopono, Morita, Naikan, tai chi chuan, yoga, and Zen.)

Ho'oponopono is a family therapy developed by Native Hawaiians that involves a formally organized family meeting in which relationships are "set right" through a process of "prayer, discussion, confession, repentance, mutual restitution, and forgiveness" (Pukui, Haertig, & Lee, 1972, p. 60). In response to a problem, the family gathers together in a spirit of honesty and sincerity (Rezentes, 1996). A healer or family elder leads the meeting and guides discussions, questions participants, and controls disruptive emotions. Emphasis is placed on the value of *lokahi*, in which everything is perceived to be interconnected and one, and on a sense of balance between the person, family, nature, and spiritual world (Gaughen & Gaughen, 1996). Although it would be inappropriate for a therapist to lead a ho'oponopono unless he or she has been trained to do so, the therapist may work with a family elder or healer to arrange it. This approach has been integrated into a substance abuse program in Hawaii (Gaughen & Gaughen, 1996).

One traditional helping strategy that can be incorporated into mainstream psychotherapy is the practice of storytelling. Storytelling is one of the most common forms of verbal learning in Indigenous cultures (Brendtro, Brokenleg, & Van Bockern, 1998). Used as a helping strategy, the speaker does not directly advise the listener, but rather tells a story through a metaphor that offers a social message. The listener is then free to draw a conclusion if he or she is ready to do so (Swinomish Tribal Community, 1991).

In the movie *Smoke Signals* (Rosenfelt, Estes, & Eyre, 1998), storytelling as a therapeutic strategy is illustrated in an interaction between a handsome angry young man named Victor and his mother. In the movie, Victor lives with his mother on the Coeur d'Alene reservation in Idaho. He has painful childhood memories of his father's drinking. He pretends not to care that his father left them when Victor was a boy. But one day, when Victor is in his 20s, his mother gets a phone call. The woman on the other end says that Victor's father has died and that she has his things if someone wants to come to Arizona to get them.

There is no question that Victor will go; the problem is how. They have no money and no car. Then a nerdy young man named Thomas offers his jar of savings on one condition: Victor has to take Thomas with him. Thomas is like a pesky younger brother to Victor; his constant talking, upbeat attitude, pigtails, and goofy grin all annoy Victor to no end. Neither of them has ever been off the reservation, and Victor does not want his first trip complicated by having to deal with Thomas.

As Victor's mother is cooking fry bread in the kitchen, Victor explains his disinterest in Thomas's offer. In response, Victor's mother asks Victor if he knows how she learned to make such good fry bread. He replies that he knows she makes it all by herself. She smiles and then goes on to tell him about all the people who have helped in making her fry bread delicious—her grandmother, who taught her how to make it; her grandmother's grandmother, who passed down the recipe; and all the people who had eaten it over the years and said, "Arlene, there's too much flour" or "Arlene, you should knead your dough more." And, she adds, "I watch that Julia Child. She's a good cook too, but she gets lots of help." The point is not lost on Victor, who eventually accepts (albeit begrudgingly) Thomas's offer.

Substance Abuse Treatment

Another source of psychotherapeutic help is available through the grass-roots movement of self-help groups known as Alcoholics Anonymous, or AA. Related groups include Adult Children of Alcoholics and Narcotics Anonymous. The format and structure of AA groups vary, but in general, meetings begin with a formal statement of the purposes of AA, followed by a reading of the Twelve Steps, a set of guidelines for recovery:

> Step 1: [We] admitted we were powerless over alcohol [drugs]—that our lives had become unmanageable.
> Step 2: Came to believe that a Power greater than ourselves could restore us to sanity.
> Step 3: Made a decision to turn our will and our lives over to the care of God as we understood Him.
> Step 4: Made a searching and fearless moral inventory of ourselves.
> Step 5: Admitted to God, to ourselves, and to another human being the exact nature of our wrongs.

Step 6: Were entirely ready to have God remove all these defects of character.
Step 7: Humbly asked Him to remove our shortcomings.
Step 8: Made a list of all persons we have harmed and became willing to make amends to them all.
Step 9: Made direct amends to such people wherever possible, except when to do so would injure them or others.
Step 10: Continued to take personal inventory and when we were wrong, promptly admitted it.
Step 11: Sought through prayer and meditation to improve our conscious contact with God as we understood Him, praying only for knowledge of His will for us and the power to carry that out.
Step 12: Having had a spiritual awakening as the result of these Steps, we tried to carry this message to alcoholics [drug abusers] and practice these principles in all our affairs. (J. A. Lewis, Dana, & Blevins, 1994, pp. 119–120)

Several culture-specific groups have grown out of AA, and when referring clients, it is helpful to be familiar with the norms of these groups. In American Indian AA groups, the expectation of anonymity may be rejected, participation may be open to anyone in the community, meetings are less structured in terms of procedures and arrival and departure times, and potlatches may be held to celebrate anniversaries of sobriety (Jilek, 1994). For Native people who have limited literacy or speak English as a second language, AA meetings and 12-step programs may be conducted in the local first language and use fewer written materials (Weaver, 2001).

Men in Recovery is a 12-step program whose membership consists primarily of African American men. This group objects to the ideas of admitting one's powerlessness and "surrendering," which are seen as detrimental to African American men (Hopson, 1996). Similarly, Women for Sobriety rejects the concept of dependency and instead stresses "healthy self-esteem, autonomy, and individual responsibility" for women in recovery (Hopson, 1996, p. 538). In general, with clients who do not identify completely with the AA philosophy, Herman (1997) suggested focusing on the components that work for the individual. (For more on ethnic-specific approaches to substance abuse treatment, see Straussner, 2001.)

Expressive and Creative Arts Therapies

All of the major psychological theories are heavily language dependent. This reliance on verbal skills as the dominant mode of expression places many people at a disadvantage, including people who speak English as a second language, individuals born with certain developmental disabilities, those with dementia or brain injuries that limit their language abilities, and young children. In addition, some individuals who speak English as a first language and have no impairments are simply less verbally oriented.

Solutions to the language-centered bias of psychotherapy may be found in the expressive and creative arts therapies, which incorporate art, music, body movement, dance, and play (Dulicai & Berger, 2005; Hiscox & Calish, 1998; Hoshino, 2003; Malchiodi, 2005; O'Connor, 2005; J. P. Sutton, 2002). Such modalities can facilitate interaction and elicit responses when verbal modalities fail. With clients whose cultural frame of reference renders direct eye contact uncomfortable or inappropriate, creative arts therapies may be more effective, because they give clients something to look at and something to do with their hands. Itai and McCrae (1994) described a specific instance of the benefits of such therapy in a study of horticultural therapy, in which clinicians used gardening to engage Japanese American elders.

Another advantage to expressive and creative arts therapies is that the therapist's appreciation of a client's creation may have positive effects on the client and on the therapeutic relationship. As Wadeson (1980) noted, "Many people with whom I have worked, particularly hospitalized, depressed patients, have been convinced on entering art therapy that their art work was meaningless and inadequate (which is how they saw themselves). As a result of my interest in their art expressions they soon became interested in them themselves" (p. 38).

A common misperception regarding art therapy is that therapists directly interpret the meaning of clients' drawings (e.g., that a drawing of a person without limbs means the client feels powerless). On the contrary, art therapists are generally trained to avoid interpreting clients' creations and instead are trained to allow clients to interpret their own work (J. Hoshino, personal communication, September 25, 2006). This approach eliminates the problem of misinterpretation, which is more likely when therapists differ culturally from their clients.

Regarding the use of clients' artwork, Hammond and Gantt (1998) suggested that artwork be viewed as equivalent to verbal communication and subject to the same protections. For example, clients' artwork should not be displayed without clients' permission (and even then, with confidentiality protected), and therapists need to take special care in their inclusion of clients' artwork in clinical records, where it could be misinterpreted or "susceptible to inappropriate exposure" by others (Hammond & Gantt, 1998, p. 273).

Because clients of any age may feel inhibited, overwhelmed, or frustrated by art activities, Weiss (1999) advised that therapists give clients an explanation of the types of art media available, demonstrate their use, and offer a varied selection (e.g., colored pencils, fine-tip magic markers, pastels, acrylics, oils). Different media have varying degrees of flexibility and ease of use and thus can elicit different emotions. Weiss provided specific art exercises for work with older adults, such as "Making Your Own World," "Tree of Life," and "Draw Your Future"; these exercises may also be helpful with people of other age groups (pp. 193–195). Additional resources include Herring's (1999) description of the variety of creative arts used in American Indian cultures, the description of methods for engaging people of diverse spiritual perspectives in the creative process (Fukuyama & Sevig, 1999), and the use of the ADDRESSING framework in art therapy with families of minority cultures (Hoshino, 2003). (See also Calisch, 2003, regarding multicultural training in art therapy.)

Because children under the age of 11 generally do not have a fully developed ability to think abstractly and are thus unable to verbally express complex feelings, motives, and concerns, play therapy can provide an opportunity for them to more naturally express themselves (Bratton, Ray, Rhine, & Jones, 2005). Play therapy is therapeutic, because it provides a space in which children can act out problems or conflicts and practice possible solutions. The therapist facilitates this process by establishing a safe environment, giving his or her undivided attention to the child during play, and occasionally making well-timed interpretations or suggestions that help the child's understanding and development of new skills (Swinomish Tribal Community, 1991).

Research has shown play therapy to be effective in improving children's emotional and behavioral problems, particularly the form of play therapy known as *filial therapy*, in which therapists teach parents how to play with their own children (Bratton et al., 2006). However, play therapy research is only beginning to address cultural influences and continues to be hindered by several ethnocentric assumptions: (a) that children's play behavior is the same across cultures (there are significant cultural variations; see Roopnarine, Johnson, & Hooper, 1994); (b) that the direct expression of feelings is essential for effective conflict resolution (in contrast to preferences for more indirect and subtle solutions in other cultures); and (c) that a relatively unstructured and casual relationship with the play therapist is preferable (O'Connor, 2005).

Countering these assumptions, O'Connor (2005) suggested the following strategies:

- Include a selection of culture-specific and culture-neutral toys and materials in the therapy setting. Canes, wheelchairs, and adaptive devices for pretend play figures can reflect different physical abilities; dolls of different ethnicities and genders should include enough of each gender for the possibility of two mothers, two fathers, and extended family members; and religious symbols should include decorations that celebrate a variety of religious traditions and holidays. Keep in mind that the typical dollhouse reflects a middle-class, single-family environment, and include house-type structures with relevant furnishings (e.g., a piece of felt with a Navajo design on it for a rug).

- Recognize that some parents (e.g., of Asian heritage) may expect a more active, directive, and goal-oriented approach that helps their children build specific skills; they may also expect the therapist to tell them what has happened in each session. Some Asian parents may disagree with the practice of teaching children to directly and overtly express their opinions, viewing this behavior as confrontational or disrespectful. Similarly, some African American parents may consider children calling the therapist by his or her first name to be disrespectful. Recognizing these cultural preferences, O'Connor (2005) encouraged therapists to "negotiate a balance between the needs of their child clients and the families and the community systems in which they are embedded" (p. 569). Part of this balance involves emphasizing the strengths of each child's culture, a practice that can occur naturally when the child mentions something unique about his or her culture and through the use of culture-specific stories, games, songs, and poems (O'Connor, 2005; see also Gil, 2006).

Finally, when using expressive and creative arts therapies, the setting may play a role in clients' comfort level with these approaches. Whereas these therapies may be viewed as "normal" in residential or educational facilities, adult and elder clients in behavioral health or medical clinics may view these approaches as the therapist treating them like children. To avoid this assumption, a thorough introduction and explanation of the approach is important. In addition, if you intend to use expressive and creative arts modalities in your work with clients, training in these therapies is strongly advised.

Family Therapy

For many people of ethnic minority cultures, family therapy is the therapy of choice. In working with multigenerational families, Duffy (1986) emphasized that older family members are central figures with desires and needs of their own, not simply resources for younger members. He suggested the use of telephone conference calls, letters, and audiotapes to include members who are unable to attend therapy sessions because of distance or disability. He also advised home visits and creative scheduling—for example, three 1-hour sessions on 3 consecutive days rather than one exhausting 3-hour session.

Using a combination of strategic (Haley, 1963) and structural (S. Minuchin, 1974) approaches, S. C. Kim (1985) described an approach to working with Asian American families (that may also apply to other minority cultures) in which the therapist carefully assesses the power structure of the family system, does not overtly challenge the leadership of those in authority, and uses a directive, problem-focused (rather than person-focused) approach that provides clients with a sense that practical suggestions will be aimed at changing the situation as quickly as possible. Although insights and emotional expressiveness may come as a result of these situational changes, they are not the primary focus. With South Asian (e.g., East Indian, Pakistani, Bengali) families in particular, Tewari, Inman, and Sandhu (2003) noted that it may be helpful to meet separately with each family member (in addition to family sessions) to give all members the opportunity to express their thoughts and feelings.

When working with ethnic minority families and in rural areas, it can be helpful to conceptualize one's role as similar to that of a family doctor who sees individuals and family subsystems on an as-needed basis for whatever problems may arise (Hong, 1988). It is important to recognize the variety of definitions of family; for example, children may have more than one mother or father, may consider a grandparent to be the primary parent, or may include non-blood-related individuals as family (Matthews & Lease, 2000). Particularly in rural areas, where resources are often limited, therapists need to be generalists, willing to work flexibly with families and their individual members (Harowski, Turner, LeVine, Schank, & Leichter, 2006). Advantages to being considered the family's care provider include decreased time and costs (compared with a different therapist seeing each person) and a decreased need to establish trust with every new family member.

Couples Therapy

Keeping in mind all of the ADDRESSING influences and identities that two individuals may hold, it is not surprising that couples' conflicts often emerge in relation to differences in worldviews and values. Understanding the origins of these differences as individual, familial, or cultural is often key in helping clients to accept and make changes. Recognizing that a particular behavior has come from a client's family or cultural upbringing may decrease an individual's sense of guilt and allow him or her to consciously decide whether he or she wants to continue the behavior. Similarly, recognizing cultural influences on a partner's views can facilitate the development of understanding and the acceptance of differences (Hays, 1996b).

Consider the situation of a 28-year-old Indonesian man married for 3 years to a 28-year-old European American woman. Amin left his family in Indonesia to attend university, where he met his wife, Liz, who graduated at the same time. Both biologists, they decided to forgo having children for 5 years and live in a small one-bedroom apartment to save money. Conflict arose when Amin's family decided to send his younger sister to university with the expectation that she would live with Amin and Liz. To Liz, it seemed that the decision had been made without her consent. Amin, however, could not understand Liz's resistance—it was his sister who would be living with them, not a complete stranger; furthermore, if she did not live with them, she would not be able to leave their parents' home.

In a counseling session with the couple, it became clear that Liz and Amin both placed a high value on family relationships. However, Liz's family and culture emphasized independence, self-sufficiency, and plenty of physical space as necessary ingredients for a well-functioning family. In contrast, Amin's family placed more value on physical proximity and interdependence; young adult Indonesians commonly live at home until they marry (Piercy, Soekandar, & Limansubroto, 1996).

As Falicov (1995) noted, intermarried couples may either focus on and thus overemphasize their differences or minimize these differences and fail to see the impact of culture on their interactions. For Amin and Liz, recognizing the differences in their values was the first step toward a resolution. Next, exploring the influence of culture on these values helped Liz and Amin step back from their assumptions about what "should be" or "must be." What seemed like enormous differences in their viewpoints was reconceptualized as only different degrees of emphasis. Liz also valued interdependence, just a little less than Amin. Similarly, Amin liked having his own physical space, but he didn't need as much as Liz. This reconceptualization helped the couple to come up with new ideas for solutions and eventually decide on a compromise. Because it would cost extra for his sister to live with them, Amin asked his parents for a larger monthly allowance for her living expenses, and they readily agreed. This extra money allowed them to rent a nicer two-bedroom apartment, which gave the sister her own room and satisfied Liz's need for space.

Although value differences are an obvious source of conflict for cross-cultural couples, they can be especially problematic for families with a recent history of immigration. Intergenerational conflict often occurs as older members support traditional values, language, and behaviors but younger members are pulled toward more current expressions of their own culture or the dominant culture. In such situations, it is important that therapists be clear about their own leanings and willing to share this information with families in transition. More specifically, therapists may need to let clients know when their values conflict with client goals. For example, it may be necessary for therapists to tell couples at the outset whether they lean toward placing more emphasis on the happiness of each individual or on the preservation of the relationship. This type of self-disclosure needs to be handled cautiously, however, because too much sharing can shift the focus to the therapist's unresolved value conflicts. When in doubt, the therapist should consult with someone who shares or knows the client's value system well.

Regarding issues of power in family and couples therapy, I have taken the position that therapists need to be able to accept and work with the value systems of their clients—the view promoted by the multicultural counseling field in general. For example, therapists working in families with clearly defined hierarchies may need to address elders first (i.e., parents before their children) and show respect for family members who hold more authority (S. C. Kim, 1985; Murgatroyd, 1996). Such a stance does not require that therapists completely agree with their clients; value differences can have a positive effect of opening up a wider range of options for the client's consideration. However, it does mean that therapists may have to settle for the small changes desired by clients rather than fundamental structural changes in clients' relationships.

As a feminist, this is a difficult position for me to take, because it suggests support for relationships defined by patriarchal assumptions. As L. S. Brown (1994) noted, feminist therapy aims to change patriarchal assumptions, beliefs, and structures that cause distress in people's lives: "It attends as well to prescribed 'normal' patterns of being with which people may be comfortable but which are ultimately destructive to their integrity" (p. 19).

The practical application of these ideas can be difficult, to say the least. B. L. C. Kim (1998) provided concrete examples of couples consisting of an Asian woman (Korean, Filipina, or Japanese) and an American man, both working on a U.S. military base near their home. The woman is likely to hold a low-status, low-paying job in comparison to the man, whose position, although not necessarily high status in the United States, is associated with the most powerful military presence in the world. In addition, the woman may have experienced abuse, neglect, poverty, or economic exploitation (the man may have also). In this context, "sexist expectations and cultural colonialism" create a special form of racism in which "the husband's superior and dominant position in such a couple's relationship is affirmed and reinforced" (B. L. C. Kim, 1998, p. 311):

> For a woman who comes to such a marriage with low
> socioeconomic status and low self-esteem, her dignity and identity
> are further diminished. Moreover, the arduous tasks of learning
> English and becoming acculturated to the American lifestyle are
> placed upon the wife, whereas the husband is nearly always
> exempted from learning his wife's language and culture. . . . The
> clear message to the wife is that her own heritage of language and
> culture is unworthy of her husband's attention or respect. (p. 311)

From a feminist perspective, the therapist's work with couples whose power is so imbalanced would be to help them recognize the imbalance and then consider the advantages but also the costs of maintaining such a relationship, with the ultimate goal being to help the couple become more egalitarian in their interactions (Sims, 1996). But the couple may not share the values embedded in this goal. As B. L. C. Kim (1998) noted in relation to couples in the situation described previously:

> Very often the partners are quite satisfied with small changes in the relationship, along with clarification of misunderstandings and miscommunications. Many wives are happy when their husbands move from the role of dictator to that of benevolent although still-domineering husband. Nearly three-quarters of the couples I have seen have terminated therapy at this point. Only about one-fifth are motivated to go on with treatment and seek further growth. (p. 317)

The question then becomes, "Is it possible to help people work toward 'better' relationships when their definition of *better* is different from the therapist's?" I believe that it is, but at the same time, I recognize that therapists vary in what they are willing (and not willing) to help clients do. For example, some feminist therapists may believe that it compromises their ethics to work with couples who prefer a power differential in their relationship. However, I also think that it is important to consider how therapists' own cultural heritage and context influence their sense of what is ethical.

There is one exception to my suggestion that therapists try to avoid imposing their values on the client, and that is when there is a risk of harm to the client or someone else. Such a statement might seem obvious, but there seems to be a perception among many European Americans that minority groups, particularly those with patriarchal traditions (e.g., Latino, Asian, Arab, Muslim), condone domestic violence. But one could make the same observation regarding European American culture, which also has patriarchal traditions and a high rate of violence against women (APA, 1996). Although patriarchal relationships tend to increase the likelihood of violence, just because a culture is patriarchically organized does not mean that violence is normative or that a given family will view it as such.

In therapeutic settings, domestic violence is largely a hidden problem; clients rarely come to therapy stating that they are being abused or abusing someone else. Rather, they bring other problems that are often related to, caused by, or exacerbated by abuse. For this reason, therapists need to be sensitized to the signs and symptoms of abuse. One of the best ways for female therapists to gain this sensitivity is to work or volunteer in a shelter for abused women and children. For male therapists, such experience is usually less easily obtained; however, men may gain a knowledge base through volunteer work with a women's resource center, reading, and consultation. (For information on programs across many cultures, see L. Walker, 1999, special edition of *American Psychologist* titled "International Perspectives on Domestic Violence.")

Culture should never be used as an excuse for violence, but the ways in which a therapist addresses domestic violence may vary depending on the culture (C. K. Ho, 1990). For example, the involvement of community and family elders may be helpful in cases of domestic violence in Asian and Asian American communities. By giving the woman permission from a position of authority to escape the dangerous situation, elders can help to bypass the problem of a woman's loyalty to an abusive husband (C. K. Ho, 1990, p. 146).

Although research on power in relationships has traditionally focused on heterosexual couples, power differentials related to gender role socialization may be equally influential for same-sex couples. As Farley (1992) noted with regard to gay men, therapists should consider how each partner defines masculinity, including how they view competition and aggression within relationships. Because men are more often socialized to fear a loss of control or power, holding back from a commitment to intimacy may be an issue for male couples. In contrast, because women are more often socialized to make relationships their center, bonding in lesbian couples may result in "fusion, with the struggle becoming one of individuation" (Farley, 1992, p. 235).

With clients of all cultural identities, it is important to look for the ways in which power is organized in the family. Although one might be inclined to assume a patriarchal organization, the variation between and within cultures is so great that it is safer to start with well-informed questions. These questions may be generated using the ADDRESSING framework:

- **A**ge and generational influences—for example, does the couple have a large age difference that contributes to a power differential?
- **D**evelopmental disabilities—for example, is power held or withheld on this basis?
- **D**isabilities acquired later in life—for example, is power held or withheld on this basis?
- **R**eligion and spiritual orientation—for example, do religious beliefs dictate that certain members have more authority?
- **E**thnic and racial identity—for example, who holds the dominant cultural identity in bicultural or multicultural couples and families? Are there differences in status related to skin color or other physical or ethnic characteristics?
- **S**ocioeconomic status—for example, who makes the money or holds the highest status by income, education, or occupation?
- **S**exual orientation—for example, does one family member receive less social support or status on the basis of his or her sexual orientation?

■ **I**ndigenous heritage—for example, does one family member hold greater authority or status related to a stronger Native heritage (e.g., both parents are Native vs. one Native parent and one non-Native parent, or someone with a more traditional upbringing)?

■ **N**ational origin—for example, who is a citizen or holds a work visa? Who speaks English most fluently?

■ **G**ender—for example, is power based on gender identity?

With some families, therapists may be able to ask and discuss these questions directly. However, with others, such an approach would be much too threatening, and these questions are best used to raise therapists' awareness of possibilities. Whenever a therapist suspects that violence may be occurring, the first priority is always to ensure the safety of the abused individual. Couples counseling is not an appropriate modality when violence between partners is ongoing, because "the dynamics of abusive relationships preclude the feasibility" of a safe, therapeutic setting for both individuals (Farley, 1992, p. 241).

Group Therapy

Group therapy is another systemic intervention that can be helpful in creating an environment in which clients can learn from others, practice new behaviors, and obtain support. Culturally diverse therapy groups have the added advantage of increasing members' opportunities for growth through interactions with people of different perspectives. When problem solving is a focus, diverse therapy groups offer a broader information base and a wider range of potential solutions for group members.

Of course, diversity has its down side, namely, the conflict that often occurs with differences. Because groups can easily replicate oppressive conditions in the larger society, therapists must pay special attention to the needs of individuals who are in the minority in a group. For example, in referring a gay African American man to a predominantly White gay and lesbian group, the counselor would first need to find out whether the group therapist is knowledgeable about and sensitive to African American culture. Otherwise, as Gutiérrez and Dworkin (1992) noted, "the referral could backfire if [the client] experiences insensitivity from the other group members and/or the facilitator" (p. 149).

Group therapy may be problematic in rural areas or within close-knit minority groups, because confidentiality is difficult to ensure (Schank & Skovholt, 2006). For example, Paradis, Cukor, and Friedman (2006) described the particular challenges in conducting group therapy with Orthodox Jewish patients who live in close-knit communities, including the task of ensuring confidentiality, patients' discomfort with therapy groups, and cultural restrictions regarding the appropriateness of certain topics. One way around the limitations of small communities is to offer time-limited educational or experiential classes or workshops that provide information and allow a structured format for discussion as well as indirectly involve social support (Droby, 2000; LaFromboise, Berman, & Sohi, 1994; Organista, 2006).

In addition to family and group therapies, systems-level interventions can include social programs and political action aimed at preventing mental illness rather than treating it after the fact (Cardemil, Kim, Pinedo, & Miller, 2005). The type of action a therapist chooses depends on his or her experience and concerns. For example, a therapist frustrated by the limitations of being a professional for Child Protective Services may become involved in lobbying to increase legal protections for children. A psychologist who works with crime victims may work to pass a law that ensures compensation by offenders to those who have lost property or a loved one. A school counselor who works with the children of Latino migrant workers may become involved in protests against inhumane housing and working conditions in the farming business. Such activities can have the added advantage of energizing therapists who feel discouraged by the slow pace of psychotherapeutic change.

Culturally Responsive Cognitive Behavior Therapy

People often assume that CBT simply focuses on positive thinking, but it involves much more (Greenberger & Padesky, 1995). Cognitive behavior assessment involves a careful evaluation of the client's thoughts, feelings, behaviors, physical symptoms, and environment in relation to the presenting problem (and the interaction between these components). The therapeutic process of CBT involves problem solving, including making practical changes in the client's physical and social environments, increasing coping skills, making behavioral changes, building social support, and fostering cognitive restructuring. The goal of cognitive restructuring is not simply positive thinking, but rather more realistic and helpful thinking that enables clients to manage overwhelming emotions, replace self-defeating behaviors with helpful behaviors, and minimize or eliminate distressing physical symptoms.

As stated earlier, CBT is not the only form of psychotherapy that has been adapted for cross cultural use. However, because it is so widely practiced and understood, it is described here as just one example of how cultural considerations can be integrated into a mainstream theoretical orientation.

Although CBT is my primary theoretical orientation, because the phrase *cognitive behavior therapy* leaves out the words *spiritual, family,* and *cultural,* I rarely use it in my rural practice with Native and non-Native people. When I explain what I do in an initial assessment, I say the following:

> I use an approach that divides problems into two main categories. The first category consists of those problems that are in your environment or more external to you. With these kinds of problems, there is usually some action you can take that will make the problem better. For example if your child gets into trouble at school, you may talk with your child, or go to see his teacher, or discipline your child in some way. You may also make some changes in your environment that decrease your overall stress level—for example, making changes in your work schedule, exercising, increasing self-care activities, or seeking support from others. With these kinds of problems, counseling can help people figure out what can be done, come up with a plan, and then carry it out.
>
> The second category of problems consists of those things that you can't change or for some reason decide not to. I call these problems the "givens," because we all have them and have to find a way to work around them. For example, if you have a chronic illness and you've done everything you can practically and medically to minimize your difficulties, there is still a lot of stress related to hospital visits, medication changes, the physical pain, and so on. Or you may have a supervisor who is very unfair, but you only have 9 months until you receive a retirement pension, so you decide you cannot quit. Even though we can't change these kinds of problems (or choose not to), there is something we can do to decrease their impact. One thing we know is that the way we think affects how we feel. With this category of problems, counseling involves looking for the thoughts and images that may be contributing to your anxiety, depression, or anger and changing them to ones that help you feel less distressed. So even if the problem is still there, it doesn't bother you as much. This may sound simple, but it usually takes a lot of practice to change unhelpful self-talk, because for most of us, our immediate, automatic thoughts when we are stressed tend to be negative.

CBT fits well with a multicultural perspective for several reasons (Hays, 1995, 2006b). First, both emphasize the empowerment of clients (CBT through specific skill building, and MCT through a focus on the client's cultural identity and strengths). Both acknowledge the need to adapt therapy to the particular needs and strengths of each client (vs. one treatment modality for all). Both emphasize the role of the environment in shaping emotions, behaviors, thoughts, and physical symptoms (CBT from a behavioral perspective, and MCT from a cultural one). Both encourage the incorporation of a client's naturally occurring strengths and supports into therapy. And CBT focuses on conscious processes that can be easily articulated and assessed, which is helpful when language and cultural differences exist.

At the same time, CBT's usefulness with people of minority cultures and groups may be limited by the following factors: (a) an assumption of value neutrality when, in fact, values permeate all psychotherapies, (b) an individualistic orientation that places greater value and focus on the individual when this is not the client's orientation, and (c) a focus on the present to the neglect of the past. However, each limitation can be minimized by a careful consideration and systematic integration of cultural influences. I call this adapted version culturally responsive CBT, and it was useful with a client I shall call Dee.

Dee came to see me for help in controlling her anger following an altercation with one of her children's schoolteachers. She was a large European American woman—6 feet tall, 300 pounds—who spoke loudly and bluntly and had a few teeth missing. She lived with her two children, plus a neglected neighbor child she had taken in and a dog and two cats, in a three-bedroom trailer in an impoverished rural community in which alcoholism, drugs, guns, and sex offenders were common. She supported herself and the children on a small disability income supplemented with food stamps and occasional temporary "under the table" jobs she was able to find. Every trip into town for medical appointments and groceries was an ordeal, because her car was old and frequently broke down. Dee admitted to screaming, swearing at, and even threatening teachers, store employees, and family members who she said gave her "a hard time." However, Dee was also intelligent and insightful and had a wonderful sense of humor and a soft heart for kids.

I worked with Dee for several months, helping her to recognize that what she experienced as the "normal" difficulties of daily life (i.e., normal for her, because she'd always had such problems) would be considered chaos by most people. I reassured her that anyone living in her situation would feel stressed and that she was not crazy for feeling angry, depressed, and overwhelmed. (Lott & Bullock, 2001, and Nicolas & Jean-Baptiste, 2001, described the shame, disrespect, insecurity, hopelessness, and repeated failures experienced by women living in poverty.)

The environmental, or externally oriented, portion of our work involved looking for ways to decrease Dee's overall stress level by making practical changes in her environment, including the addition of self-nurturing activities, keeping in mind the constraints that poverty placed on her options and looking for activities that cost nothing (Scarbrough, 2001; L. Smith, 2005). For example, the commonly chosen activity of taking a hot bath to relax was not an option for Dee, because her well water smelled and was discolored. However, she was eligible for free aqua therapy at the community pool, which she found relaxing and provided the added possibility of a clean shower afterwards.

The internally oriented (cognitive) part of our work involved the normalization of Dee's feelings and some education regarding the differences between assertiveness and aggression. Dee learned to recognize a pattern in which denigrating and hopeless self-talk kept her from speaking up when she was frustrated until her feelings grew to such a level of anger that she would blow up, resulting in feelings of guilt and shame that reinforced the denigrating self-talk and further decreased her willingness to speak up. Through cognitive restructuring, she began to use more helpful and empowering self-talk to manage her emotional reactions, with an emphasis on remembering long-term goals over the short-term satisfaction of venting and getting her way immediately.

After several weeks of this work, Dee came in excited to tell me about an incident she said she had handled exceptionally well. That week, her 13-year-old daughter had told her that a 21-year-old acquaintance said he would pay her $20 if she took off her shirt for him. (Her daughter did not accept.) Dee was furious, but instead of taking her usual aggressive approach, she decided to practice her assertiveness skills. She told me,

> I remembered what we talked about, so I took three deep breaths and kept my cool. Then I marched over to the uncle's trailer where that boy was staying and knocked on the door, and when he came out, I got right up in his face. I looked him straight in the eye and said in a calm, low voice, "If you ever try anything like that again, you f—-ing son of a b—-, you're mine." I was so good; I didn't punch him or poke him in the chest with my finger, or even scream at him. I just walked away. And I got my point across—he looked really scared! You would've been so proud of me!

Needless to say, I had a little difficulty trying to decide on an appropriate response. I knew what most middle-class people would say she should have done: call the state troopers (she was out of city limits for police) and let them handle it. However, when I considered this from Dee's perspective, including her previous negative interactions with and lack of trust in the troopers as well as all of the other constraints of her social and physical environment, I could see how her particular adaptation of the skills we had discussed worked for her. Her long-range goals were to protect her daughter and permanently intimidate the guy, and she focused on these instead of doing what she felt like doing (i.e., killing him). Moreover, she did not take a gun with her, she did not physically touch him, and she did not make a specific threat of physical harm. She also added a strategy of telling everyone she met about the incident, which she said "might keep the guy in check, or maybe he'll get fed up and move out."

I tried to help Dee explore the possible ramifications of her actions. I still had some concerns for her safety and believed that she should have reported the incident to the troopers, at the least to have the incident on this young man's record, but at the same time, I did not want to dampen her sense of success. It took a lot of courage and effort to do what she did, and the last thing she needed was to be told she did something wrong. As therapists, we can teach clients specific coping skills, including new behaviors and a range of assertive responses, but ultimately it is clients who must decide how to use them. In trying out new behaviors, clients must take into account the neighborhoods in which they live, community norms, and the reliability of community supports. Sometimes clients use the skills as they are taught, sometimes they adapt those skills to their particular situation, and sometimes they decide that the risk of trying these new behaviors is too great.

Wood and Mallinckrodt (1990) emphasized the risks for members of minority groups in using dominant cultural behaviors in an example of an African American man waiting in a movie line when a White man cut in front of him. Although in some parts of the United States it would be considered appropriately assertive for the African American man to say, "Excuse me, I believe that the end of the line begins behind me," these authors made the point that in some areas of the country, such a statement could place an African American man in physical danger (Wood & Mallinckrodt, 1990, p. 6). They advised therapists to help clients develop as wide a repertoire of responses as possible, but because the client is the best judge of what is right and safe, the client is the one who should decide what constitutes appropriately assertive behavior in any given situation. LaFromboise and Rowe (1983) described their work with American Indian clients similarly, using the concept of *bicultural competence,* in which clients learn the behaviors and skills of the dominant culture while retaining their own values and behavioral preferences, then use the skills from each culture as they deem appropriate.

DEFINING THE PROBLEM

The first step in culturally responsive cognitive behavior therapy (CR–CBT) involves defining which part of the client's presenting problem is primarily environmental (including social and cultural) and which part is primarily internal to the client (i.e., emotions, behaviors, thoughts, images, physical symptoms). Often there is some overlap, but clarifying this question as early as possible can prevent the therapist from moving into cognitive restructuring inappropriately or too quickly. Trying to change a client's beliefs about an oppressive situation without first (or simultaneously) trying to change the situation may be interpreted as blaming the individual, when the real problem may be an abusive relationship or a racist, sexist, heterosexist, or disability-hostile workplace.

For example, when working with transgender clients, therapists need to recognize the objective aspects of the dominant culture that create real obstacles, including housing discrimination, ostracism by family members, workplace discrimination, loss of custody of children, difficulty obtaining legal recognition of marriage, severe ridicule, and transgender identity-related violence (APA, 2006). Attention can then be given to the ways in which these experiences shape the cognitions (beliefs) that work against a person's long-range goals (e.g., "I can't get a good job because I am transgender" or "They will never be able to accept the real me"; Maguen, Shipherd, & Harris, 2005, pp. 486–487). Similarly, Mona, Romesser-Scehnet, Cameron, and Cardenas (2006) advised therapists to be careful not to minimize the impact of physical barriers and negative social attitudes on people with disabilities.

With African Americans, S. Kelly (2006) suggested always beginning with the validation of a client's report of experiences of racism. Although such an approach may seem obvious, remember that CBT emphasizes the exploration and challenging of clients' beliefs. For therapists of dominant cultural identities, the search for alternative explanations of oppression may be an automatic response (e.g., "Could it be that they meant something else by that statement?" or "Are there any other explanations for that person's behavior?"). But clients may perceive such questioning as racist or naïve. This initial validation does not mean that therapists will never explore or question clients' reports of oppressive experiences; however, this exploration and challenging should not be attempted before a very strong trust is present. Once the client feels believed and validated, the therapist may then consider assessing the relevance of an incident to the client's presenting problem (S. Kelly, 2006).

The second step of CR–CBT involves recognizing cultural influences on the cognitive, emotional, behavioral, and physiological components of the client's problem. Culture clearly shapes cognitions in the form of values, beliefs, a person's interpretation of events, definitions of rationality, and views of what is adaptive versus maladaptive behavior (Dowd, 2003). Culture also affects the expression, reporting, and experience of emotions; for instance, studies show that people of Latin American identities tend to report high levels of positive affect, whereas East Asians tend not to (Diener, Oishi, & Lucas, 2003; Okazaki & Tanaka-Matsumi, 2006). And culture certainly accounts for differences in behavior, including the conceptualization and expression of physical and mental symptoms and illness. Examples include not only the culture-bound syndromes listed in the *Diagnostic and Statistical Manual of Mental Disorders* (American Psychiatric Association, 2000) but all disorders (e.g., consider the way that European American cultural beliefs about women's bodies contribute to anorexia).

DEVELOPING A TREATMENT PLAN

The next step in CR–CBT involves developing a treatment plan. For problems that are primarily external to the client, interventions generally involve making changes in the person's physical or social environment (e.g., expanding social support, learning coping skills, increasing self-care activities). For problems that are primarily internal, cognitive restructuring is frequently the focus. Often, these two types of interventions overlap—for example, when more constructive self-talk helps clients make changes in their behavior and environment.

It is important that therapists work collaboratively with clients to set goals and decide on interventions. (Of course, there are exceptions— for example, when a client's cognitive abilities are too impaired.) Such collaboration reinforces the idea that clients know more about their particular contexts and needs than a therapist ever can, especially a therapist who differs culturally from the client. It also means that there will be times when clients choose goals that do not fit with the therapist's expectations or preferences.

Take the case of a middle-class Greek American woman who came to therapy "for help in making my daughter behave." The mother had been separated from her husband for 10 years (they were never legally divorced), and she and their sole daughter lived together. The daughter was making good grades at the community college she was attending, but she wanted to do things that the mother did not like (e.g., go to movies with friends at night, wear baggy pants). When the daughter tried to explain her desires and reason with her mother, the mother would interpret this as "talking back" and become furious and shout at her daughter.

The therapist realized that the mother's behavior was understandable in relation to some childrearing practices and views in Greek culture (e.g., the questioning of authority and disobedience being seen as disrespectful; Tsemberis & Orfanos, 1996). With further discussion, it became clear that the mother was unwilling to change her conceptualization of the problem or her own behavior, and the father (who was contacted by phone) would not become involved in what he perceived as a "mother–daughter problem."

The therapist's initial inclination was to help the daughter become more independent and eventually move out on her own. However, neither the mother nor the daughter was interested in this solution. Thus, the therapist worked with the daughter to help her find more effective ways to interact with her mother. Through therapy, the daughter came to realize that when she spent more time with her mother, her mother was more likely to let her go out or bring friends home. The two continued to have disagreements about clothes, but the conflicts over the daughter's socializing subsided, at least to a more acceptable level for the pair. In sum, by joining with the clients in pursuing their goals, the therapist was able to help them both.

At the same time, there are situations in which behaviorally oriented goals may not be appropriate. For example, some American Indian people come to counseling primarily for support and want someone who will listen and provide encouragement, reassurance, practical suggestions, and caring but realistic feedback (Swinomish Tribal Community, 1991, p. 226). Similarly, with clients experiencing grief over the death of a loved one, the most helpful approach may be supportive counseling that provides a safe place to cry and reassurance that the experience of bereavement is a normal process. (For information on what constitutes normal bereavement in diverse minority cultures, see Irish, Lundquist, & Nelsen, 1993, and E. R. Shapiro, 1995.)

COGNITIVE RESTRUCTURING

The main task of cognitive restructuring involves recognizing the cognitions and cognitive processes that may be contributing to a client's emotional distress, unwanted behaviors, or physical symptoms. The form of cognitive restructuring known as *rational emotive behavior therapy* (REBT) focuses on changing irrational thoughts to more rational ones, with the expectation that more rational thoughts help a person to feel better and engage in more constructive behaviors (Ellis, 1997; Ellis & Dryden, 1987). The advantage of REBT is that it consists of a relatively simple model that is easy to explain and learn. However, one problem with REBT is its reliance on the concept of rationality. Definitions of rationality are heavily influenced by a person's culture, and the dominant culture tends to perceive many minority group beliefs as strange and irrational. If the therapist does not know the client's culture very well, he or she may jump to the conclusion that a client's belief is irrational, when in fact it is normal in the client's culture.

The most well-researched form of CBT is known as cognitive therapy (CT; A. T. Beck, Rush, Shaw, & Emery, 1979). Cognitive therapists generally prefer to question how *functional* or *dysfunctional* a belief is (J. S. Beck, 1995). Questions cognitive therapists commonly use to assess beliefs include, "What is the evidence for this thought or belief?" and "Is there an alternative explanation?" Theoretically speaking, these questions challenge the validity rather than the utility of a client's belief. (Other questions are used to challenge the usefulness.)

Although challenging the validity of the client's belief may be helpful in some situations, it is risky when the therapist and client differ culturally. Challenging the validity of core cultural beliefs is even riskier unless the client and family are open to this challenge. A safer approach is to avoid the question of rationality and validity altogether and focus instead on a collaborative exploration of the "helpfulness" (i.e., usefulness) of a thought. The therapist may simply ask, "Is it helpful for you to say this to yourself or to hold on to this belief or image?" This question recognizes that ultimately, the client is the judge regarding the helpfulness of thoughts and behaviors (Kemp & Mallinckrodt, 1996). Functionality is obviously implied in the concept of helpfulness, but the term *helpfulness* sounds a little less academic.

When a client has difficulty with the process of developing more helpful thoughts, it can be useful to go back to the list of culturally related strengths and supports described in chapter 6. The list of personal strengths in Table 6.1 can be used as empowering self-statements. The list of interpersonal supports can be used as evidence that the client is valued by others. And for spiritually oriented clients, the list of natural environmental supports may be a reminder that a higher power cares for them.

Finally, CR–CBT also involves weekly homework assignments with an emphasis on client direction. To facilitate the development of homework, I ask clients, "What is the smallest possible step you could take that would feel like you are making progress or healing?" (I use the term *healing* with more spiritually oriented clients; adapted from Dolan, 1991.) I explain why the step needs to be as small as possible: To make change, clients need to start with small steps that they are 100% sure they can do, because part of the process involves building a feeling of success so that they are more likely to take on the next step (a key principle of behaviorism). Then they can build on these small steps and, after a few weeks, see significant results.

These are only a few of the ways in which CBT can be made more culturally responsive (see Exhibit 9.1 for a summary). For more specific

---

EXHIBIT 9.1

Key Components of Culturally Responsive Cognitive Behavior Therapy

1. Clarify what part of the problem is primarily environmental (or external) and what part of the problem is primarily cognitive (or internal).
2. Validate the oppressive aspects of the client's environment, and look for ways to change these conditions before or in tandem with cognitive restructuring.
3. Recognize cultural influences on the client's cognitions, emotions, behaviors, and physical symptoms.
4. Work collaboratively to choose goals and interventions that fit with a client's cultural context and preferences.
5. With cognitive restructuring, focus on the collaborative exploration of the helpfulness of a belief (rather than its rationality or validity).
6. When developing more helpful self-talk, use the list of culturally related personal strengths, interpersonal supports, and environmental conditions.
7. For homework, ask, "What is the smallest possible step you could take that would feel like you are making progress or healing?"

examples in relation to a variety of cultural groups, see the book *Cultur-ally Responsive Cognitive–Behavioral Therapy* (Hays & Iwamasa, 2006).

USE OF MEDICATION

When a client's treatment plan involves medication, therapists should remember several points. First, women and ethnic minorities are at higher risk for receiving inappropriate medication because of misdiagnosis (Tulkin & Stock, 2004). Older people of any culture are more likely to be taking medications prescribed by different health care providers who are not coordinating with one another. Asking about prescription medica-tions, nonprescription treatments, and self-medication is important. When I see older clients for the first time, I ask them to put all of their medications in a bag and bring the bag to the assessment session. This way I do not depend on their understanding or recall of what they are taking.

Of equal concern are cultural differences in expectations. People of Asian, Central American, and Arab heritage are likely to expect medication and may feel that they are not being taken seriously if it is not prescribed (Gleave, Chambers, & Manes, 2005; Paniagua, 1998). Among American Indian clients, a more common view is that medica-tion is not healthy, whereas many African Americans see medication as too impersonal (Paniagua, 1998). Given the range of cross-cultural and intracultural variations, I suggest talking with clients about their expec-tations of what medications can and cannot do for them.

When medications are necessary, compliance may be complicated by the belief that "Western medicine" is too strong (particularly among people of Chinese, Southeast Asian, Indian, Pakistani, and other South Asian countries; Assanand, Dias, Richardson, Chambers, & Waxler-Morrison, 2005; Lai & Yue, 1990). It is not uncommon for people who hold this belief to reduce prescribed dosages themselves or to take the medication only until the symptoms disappear (Lai & Yue, 1990).

Clients may also hold culturally related assumptions that work against the use of medications. For example, Falicov (1998) described the case of a 9-year-old Latino boy who was diagnosed with attention deficit disorder and prescribed Ritalin. His parents were reluctant to give him the medication, because they feared that it would "begin a drug addiction and a life in the streets," as they had seen daily among young-sters in their neighborhood (Falicov, 1998, p. 142).

For all of these reasons, it is important to provide a careful explana-tion of the need for clients to take medications as instructed. When pos-sible, enlisting family support for the prescribed regimen may increase the likelihood of compliance. Sometimes therapists and clients disagree about the need for medication. When this happens, it is important to remember that ultimately, the client is the one who has to live with the results of the decision to medicate. (For a detailed consideration of cross-cultural ethical issues involved with medications, see Fadiman's 1997 book *The Spirit Catches You and You Fall Down*.)

Conclusion

Whether one's interventions are at the level of individuals, couples, families, groups, or institutions, culturally responsive therapy involves a systemic perspective that recognizes the impact of diverse cultural influences on clients' lives. With this perspective, eclecticism is helpful, because the wider the repertoire of methods and skills that a therapist holds, the more able he or she will be to work effectively with each client. Indigenous therapies, traditional healers, adaptations of mainstream theories (e.g., CR–CBT), expressive and creative arts therapies, and systems-level interventions offer enough ideas to keep therapists learning for a long time.

Key Ideas

Implementing Culturally Responsive Interventions

1. Develop a knowledge of Indigenous and traditional therapies.
2. Consider religion as a potential source of strength and support.
3. Become familiar with expressive and creative arts therapies, and obtain additional training when appropriate.
4. When using family interventions, conceptualize "family" broadly to include gay and lesbian parents, single parents, elders as central, relatives, and nonkin family members.
5. Be willing to see individual members or subsystems of the family on an as-needed basis.
6. Recognize any power differentials related to each ADDRESSING domain.
7. Adapt mainstream therapies (e.g., psychodynamic, humanistic, existential, behavioral, cognitive behavior, family systems) to the cultural context of the client.
8. Consider interventions aimed at institutional and political levels when appropriate and possible.
9. Set goals, develop treatment plans, and choose interventions in collaboration with clients.
10. Be aware of different cultural expectations and beliefs regarding medications.

Practice Doesn't Make Perfect, but It Sure Does Help
A Final Case Example

10

T he case study in this chapter pulls together the main suggestions I have made for understanding clients' identities,
establishing a respectful relationship, conducting a culturally responsive assessment, making a culturally responsive
diagnosis, and implementing culturally responsive therapies.
In this case, the therapies included a systems intervention
involving the whole family, an attempt at life review therapy
with the older family member, and individual cognitive behavior therapy with the primary caregiver. The therapist in this
case was Robert, a 33-year-old, bicultural geropsychologist.
Robert's mother was European American and his father
African American, and he grew up with close connections to
both of his parents' families. Robert was working in a mental
health center located in an ethnically diverse urban community in the Los Angeles area.

Referral

Robert received a telephone call from a woman who introduced herself as Janet and said that she was calling about her
mother. Janet told Robert that her mother, Mrs. Penn, was
80 years old, widowed for 7 years, retired, and living with

her in Janet's home, along with Janet's husband, their recently divorced 32-year-old daughter, and the daughter's 9-year-old daughter. Although Mrs. Penn had lived in her own home most of her life, Janet said that about 2 years earlier, her mother had experienced a stroke and had moved in with Janet and her husband. Janet stated that Mrs. Penn had gradually recovered most of her physical and mental abilities since the stroke but still experienced some weakness in her left leg.

Janet's present concerns had developed over the past few months. Her mother had begun sleeping more than usual, and Mrs. Penn's unwillingness to follow a diet despite her diagnosis of diabetes had resulted in several trips to the hospital when she became sick from eating too many sweet foods. Janet told the therapist that she was feeling very frustrated with her mother because "she doesn't do anything anymore. She doesn't see friends or want to go to church. She doesn't help with dinner or dishes, or even make her bed, and she'll only take a bath after I nag her for a week." She added, "I have to work all day, so I can't stay home and take care of her, but I could never put Mother in a nursing home. I don't know what to do."

Robert responded to Janet's story by suggesting that she and her mother come in for an assessment within the next week. He told Janet that he would like to talk with both her and her mother and that the meeting would take about an hour and a half. He asked that they bring with them the name, address, and telephone number of Mrs. Penn's physician, a bag with all of Mrs. Penn's current medications in it, and reading glasses or hearing aid if she used either.

Initial Assessment

Janet and Mrs. Penn arrived 15 minutes early for their appointment with the requested information and items. Robert greeted them warmly, showed them to his office, and asked if they would like a cup of tea or coffee. He noticed that Mrs. Penn, an African American woman, appeared to be of average weight and had slight difficulty walking and that her clothes were wrinkled and worn. He also noticed a slight smell of body odor and recalled Janet's comment about Mrs. Penn's resistance to taking baths. Mrs. Penn declined the cup of tea or coffee, chose to keep her coat on, and clutched her purse to her stomach throughout the session. Her demeanor was subdued. She did not seem distracted, and she answered questions when asked but volunteered no information. In contrast, Janet, an African American woman in her early 60s, appeared well dressed, talkative, and stressed; she rolled and unrolled a tissue in her hands as she spoke.

After a few minutes of social conversation about their neighborhoods, Robert explained to Mrs. Penn that Janet had called him because she was concerned about her (Mrs. Penn's) health. He said that he had told Janet that if her mother were willing, it would be a good idea for them to come in together to talk about how things were going at home. He then outlined the kinds of questions he would like to ask them so that he could have an accurate picture of their situation. As he talked, Janet seemed to relax a little, but Mrs. Penn's facial expression remained somewhat flattened.

Robert began by looking at Mrs. Penn's bottles of medications, which included insulin pills and two antidepressants. Janet said that her mother had not liked taking the antidepressants and did so irregularly, finally stopping completely several months earlier. Robert tried to ask Mrs. Penn questions about her health, but in the pause before Mrs. Penn answered, Janet frequently answered for her. Robert suggested that it would be helpful for him to gain an understanding of each person's concerns by meeting separately with each of them for about 30 minutes; then they could all meet together at the end for a final discussion. Neither Mrs. Penn nor Janet seemed bothered by this plan.

Robert met first with Mrs. Penn. He asked if anything about her health was bothering her, to which she replied, "I just don't feel good." In response to more specific questions, Mrs. Penn denied any disturbing thoughts or perceptions, but she admitted being hungry often and sleeping "a lot, except for last night, because I was worried about what this meeting would be about." She said that she had noticed her memory "isn't as good as it used to be." She denied hearing difficulties but said that she needed glasses to read.

Putting aside any mental status tests until he felt some rapport develop between them, Robert told Mrs. Penn that he would like to hear more about her life both before and after moving in with her daughter. In response to specific questions, Mrs. Penn said that she was born in Tennessee in 1927, that her father had worked at odd jobs and her mother as a housekeeper, and that they were poor. Her parents had three girls; Mrs. Penn was the youngest.

When Mrs. Penn was 14, her mother died of tuberculosis, and shortly thereafter, her father took his daughters to Los Angeles to live closer to their relatives. Mrs. Penn graduated from high school a year early because she was such a good student. She married the year of her graduation, but her husband was drafted and then killed in "the War," Mrs. Penn said, "before he could see his baby Janet." Mrs. Penn then moved back into her father's home and, with the help of her sisters, managed to care for Janet and work full-time for an office cleaning business, where she met her second husband. With him, she had a daughter, Laura. When Laura began school, Mrs. Penn obtained a job as a receptionist at a branch of the Department of Social and Health Services, where she was promoted to secretary and then administrative assistant, and she worked until her retirement at age 65. She and her second husband had been married for almost 45 years when he died of a heart attack. Mrs. Penn's sisters were both living in another state, and Mrs. Penn talked to them about twice a month, but they always called her.

The chronological ordering of Mrs. Penn's story was provided by the order of Robert's questions. Robert noticed that the only date Mrs. Penn gave was her birth year. When tactfully pressed about the years of her high school graduation; the births of her children, grandchildren, and great-grandchildren; and her first and second marriages, Mrs. Penn gave general or vague answers such as "sometime in the '40s" or "oh, too long ago." Considering her exceptional high school performance and responsible work history, Robert thought that these were all pieces of information she should know.

During the interview with Mrs. Penn, Robert sketched a timeline containing significant events in the lives of Mrs. Penn and her family (see Figure 10.1). He later filled in the dates Janet provided and added sociocultural influences and events that had occurred during Mrs. Penn's lifetime. The latter included the Great Depression, segregation, World War II, school desegregation, the Civil Rights movement, the assassination of Martin Luther King Jr., and in Los Angeles the Watts riots and later the violence related to the Rodney King incident. Recent events included the Iraq war, challenges to Social Security and company pension plans, and changes in Medicare.

Despite the hardships related to the time period in which Mrs. Penn had lived, she showed no emotion when talking about her life. Robert hypothesized that Mrs. Penn's unemotional presentation was due to some stoicism or resignation in her approach to life. When he asked if she felt sad about some of the events in her life, she said, "I learned early on that life is hard, and you better not get too happy, or you'll just get slapped down." (See Hinrichsen, 2006, regarding how, as a result of discrimination, many older people of color learn early on that their choices

FIGURE 10.1

Mrs. Penn's Timeline

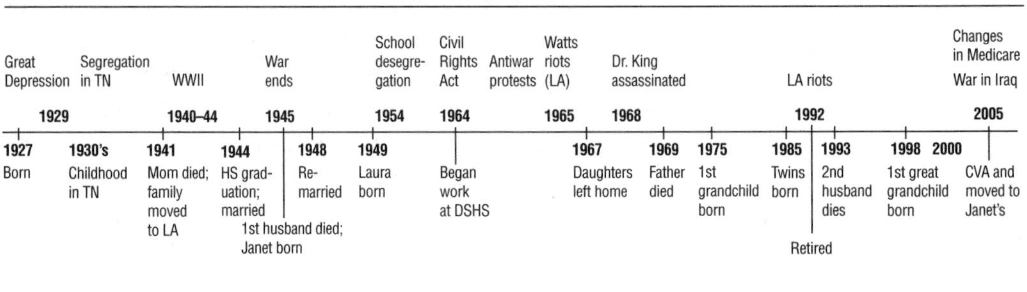

are limited, resulting in "a diminished sense of control and mastery in later life" [p. 31].) When Robert asked if she had "ever thought of ending it all," she said that she had thought about it after her mother died but not since, because it was against her religious beliefs.

Subsequently, in the interview with Mrs. Penn's daughter, Janet talked about feeling overwhelmed by her responsibilities:

> I come home from work, the phone is ringing, dinner needs fixing, my daughter is at work, and my granddaughter wants help with her homework, while my husband wants me to talk with him. Then on top of it, when Mother goes to visit my sister Laura for the weekend, Laura lets her do whatever she wants; she doesn't make Mother take a bath and lets her eat sweets, knowing that she has diabetes. And all Mother can say when she gets home is what a good time she has at Laura's and how much she wishes she could stay there longer.

At the end of the individual sessions, Robert met and talked with Janet and Mrs. Penn together about his beginning understanding of their situation. He noted that the first question that needed to be addressed concerned Mrs. Penn's memory difficulties. He explained that the difficulties Janet described, along with Mrs. Penn's inability to recall some of the things he had asked her about, suggested the need for further evaluation. He said that a thorough medical examination and a neuropsychological assessment would help to clarify whether there was a significant memory problem that needed to be addressed. He explained what a neuropsychological assessment involves and added that often what appears to be a memory problem may be something else—for example, focusing too much on one's memory, feeling depressed or worried, or just not seeing the point in remembering some things.

Robert went on to say that he was also concerned about how tired Janet seemed, at which point Janet's eyes filled with tears. From his reading of a book written for caregivers (Carter, 1994), he was aware of the pressures on caregivers and particularly of the difficulties faced by daughters caring for their parents (Hinrichsen, 1991). He said that he felt concerned that Janet was trying to do too much. Out of respect for the family's value Janet had expressed on the telephone that Mrs. Penn's place was with her family, he did not mention the idea of an alternative living arrangement for Mrs. Penn. Nor did he press the idea of a caregivers support group after Janet responded that "it would just be one more thing to do." Instead, he suggested that they might want to look as a family at some ways to lessen Janet's load. Both Mrs. Penn and Janet seemed open to this, so he suggested that they schedule a meeting in 2 weeks to discuss the results of Mrs. Penn's medical exam and neuropsychological assessment and then, afterwards, set up a family meeting. Janet agreed, and Mrs. Penn nodded that she would participate. (See Belgrave, 1998, regarding the extended family as a resource with African American clients.)

Case Formulation
and Diagnosis

Mrs. Penn's medical examination included magnetic resonance imaging of the brain, which found some slight changes related to the stroke, and a neuropsychological assessment, which found mild impairments in concentration, short-term memory, insight, judgment, and initiation. After reviewing the exam results, Robert recognized that there were several possible explanations for Mrs. Penn's presentation and Janet's complaints. Beginning with the format of the *Diagnostic and Statistical Manual of Mental Disorders* (fourth edition, text revision; [*DSM–IV–TR*]; American Psychiatric Association, 2000), he listed the salient ADDRESSING influences in Mrs. Penn's life on the Cultural Axis VI (Table 10.1). He also made an ADDRESSING outline for Mrs. Penn's family (Table 10.2). He then noted the following events under Axis IV: Psychosocial and Environmental Problems, for example, the loss of her own home and previous independence, the move to her daughter's home, the loss of daily contact with friends and church, and the absence of meaningful activity such as work. On Axis III, he noted Mrs. Penn's diabetes and the stroke. Next, on Axis I, Robert recorded Relational Problem Related to a Mental Disorder or General Medical Condition (V61.9), referring to the strained relationship between Mrs. Penn and Janet.

Diagnosing Mrs. Penn's behavioral and cognitive deficits was more complicated. Mrs. Penn's functioning was moderately impaired compared with her prestroke baseline, when she was retired but ran her own household and maintained a moderately active social life. Although Robert believed that the cumulative effects of stressors over the past few years were contributing to her current difficulties, he did not diagnose an Adjustment Disorder, because the most recent behavioral symptoms had not begun within 3 months of the stressors. He did not diagnose Dysthymia, because Mrs. Penn's attitude toward life seemed an appropriate adaptation given the hardships she had experienced, nor did this approach to life interfere with her social or occupational functioning before the stroke. Robert decided to give Mrs. Penn the diagnosis of a Major Depressive Disorder on the basis of the family's report that her poor self-care and apathetic behavior had begun or increased in the past few months and of his own knowledge that depression can cause the kind of concentration and memory problems she was having. Robert was aware that depression should not be diagnosed if the symptoms are related to a medical condition; however, the relationship in this case was not clear (and it was a greater risk to not treat her for depression—see American Psychological Association, 2004; National Institute of Health Consensus Development Panel on Depression in Late Life, 1992).

TABLE 10.1

Mrs. Penn's Diagnosis

DSM–IV–TR axis	Initial diagnosis as formulated by Robert
Axis I	296.32 Major Depressive Disorder (recurrent, moderate)
	V61.9 Relational Problem Related to a Mental Disorder or General Medical Condition (by daughter's report).
	Mild to moderate cognitive impairments with etiology unclear (possibly related to depression, cerebrovascular disease, cerebrovascular accident [CVA], diabetes).
Axis II	V71.09 No Diagnosis
Axis III	Insulin-dependent diabetes mellitus, CVA 2 years ago with residual left-leg weakness and possible cognitive impairments.
Axis IV	Problems With Primary Support (adjustment to daughter's home)
	Problems Related to Social Environment (loss of own home and previous independence; move to daughter's home; loss of daily contact with church, neighbors, and friends; no meaningful activity or work).
Axis V	Global Assessment of Functioning (GAF) = 50 (current)
	GAF = 85 (estimated baseline prior to 2 years ago)
Cultural Axis VI	Age and generational influences: grew up as an African American in the South (Tennessee) during the Depression, severe poverty, oppressive conditions; attended segregated schools.
	Developmental disabilities: none reported
	Disabilities acquired later in life: CVA 2 years ago, with recovery except for residual left leg weakness and possible cognitive impairments.
	Religion and spiritual orientation: both parents Christian; active member of a Baptist church until her stroke and subsequent move to Janet's house.
	Ethnic and racial identity: both parents African American
	Socioeconomic status: grew up in poverty; as an adult, with her second husband, had a lower-middle-class income; currently living on middle-class family income, including own pension and Social Security.
	Sexual orientation: heterosexual
	Indigenous heritage: none
	National origin: born and reared in United States; English is first language.
	Gender: woman; youngest child in a family of three daughters; mother died when Mrs. Penn was 14; married twice, two daughters; role as the family's grandmother involved "active authority" (therapist's words) before the stroke and move to Janet's, but not since.

Note. *DSM–IV–TR = Diagnostic and Statistical Manual of Mental Disorders, Fourth Edition, Text Revision* (American Psychiatric Association, 2000).

Robert agreed with the neuropsychologist's observation that Mrs. Penn's impaired judgment and insight were not well explained by a diagnosis of depression and that it was possible that her deficits were attributable to vascular dementia. However, because it was also possible that the deficits were caused primarily by the depression and thus might be reversible, he refrained from making the diagnosis of Dementia and

TABLE 10.2

ADDRESSING Outline for Mrs. Penn's Family

Cultural influences	Mrs. Penn's family
Age and generational influences	Four-generation African American family; lifetimes span 1920s to 2007.
Developmental disabilities	None reported
Disabilities acquired later in life	Only family member with disability is Mrs. Penn (left-leg weakness and cognitive impairments).
Religion and spiritual orientation	Christian family; Mrs. Penn grew up and brought up her daughters in a nondenominational African American church; as adults, she and Janet belong to a Baptist church.
Ethnic and racial identity	Everyone is African American
Socioeconomic status	Current household is middle class with four incomes: Janet's, Jim's, Clarisse's, and Mrs. Penn's pension and Social Security income; Laura and her children are low income and live in a poor neighborhood.
Sexual orientation	Adults are heterosexual.
Indigenous heritage	Native American grandfather on Jim's side of the family, but little connection to this heritage.
National origin	All born and reared in United States; English is their first language.
Gender	Household includes three adult women, one adult man, and a girl; extended family includes Mrs. Penn's daughter Laura and her two boys and Mrs. Penn's two sisters; gender roles are relatively fluid; Jim shares cleaning responsibilities with Janet and their daughter and watches his granddaughter when the women go out; Laura expects her boys to help with dinner, cleaning, and laundry; Women all work outside the home.

instead noted on Axis I the presence of mild to moderate cognitive impairments that may be related to effects of depression, cerebrovascular disease, cerebrovascular accident, or diabetes. Before diagnosing Vascular Dementia, it seemed prudent to see if counseling, family interventions, and antidepressant medication could lift the depression, in which case the cognitive impairments might improve; if they did not, at least Mrs. Penn might feel better.

During the second assessment meeting with Mrs. Penn and Janet, Robert recommended that Mrs. Penn begin antidepressant medication again and return weekly for half-hour meetings for the next 6 months. Although within himself he was pessimistic about whether Mrs. Penn would comply with the medication recommendation (given her history of noncompliance with antidepressants and her diet), he hoped that closer monitoring through counseling sessions might reinforce its importance. At the same time, he felt a positive connection with

Mrs. Penn, who seemed, even with her subdued manner, to enjoy the extra attention. Robert expected that as their rapport continued to grow, she might benefit from talking about her life, her current difficulties, and her strengths.

Individual Therapy With Mrs. Penn

Robert had recently learned about a therapeutic approach known as *life review therapy* through which older clients are helped to look back on their lives, remember, and talk about events and relationships (M. I. Lewis & Butler, 1974). One goal of this reminiscing is for clients to become more accepting of their decisions, because the choices they made in the past led to the experiences that have shaped who they are in the present. The process of integrating one's past experiences with the present can be facilitated by creating a book filled with photographs, drawings, news clippings, pressed flowers, writings, and poems, along with any other forms of documentation that the client considers meaningful (Butler, Lewis, & Sunderland, 1998).

Robert was interested in trying this collaborative intervention with Mrs. Penn. He believed that it would provide some structure to his sessions with her, and he saw it as a way to affirm her life. He also saw the benefits to her family, for whom this documentation might provide a deeper appreciation of Mrs. Penn and a reminder of their family's history to pass on to younger generations. Mrs. Penn and Janet appeared only mildly interested in the idea but said they would be willing to try it.

Over the next few weeks, Mrs. Penn did engage in the verbal review of her life. However, she never brought in pictures or any other mementos, despite Robert's reminders. After 4 weeks, Robert realized that Mrs. Penn either did not want to or simply could not do such a project, given her cognitive deficits and apathy, and expecting Janet to bring in items would just add to Janet's workload.

Recognizing that the impetus for the project was coming from his assumption that the family would value it as much as he did, Robert let go of the documentation piece of this particular intervention. However, he continued the life review process verbally with Mrs. Penn, whose mood seemed to lift slightly by the end of the second month (possibly also because of the antidepressants, which she was taking more regularly). However, no improvement occurred in her resigned attitude, her activity level, or her memory difficulties. Robert now believed that these problems were attributable to an inseparable combination of previous personality tendencies, stressful life events, and mild dementia related to the stroke.

Intergenerational Family Therapy

Recognizing that Janet's needs had not yet been addressed, Robert worked with Janet to schedule and invite all members of the family to the family meeting they had discussed. This meeting turned into three sessions attended by Mrs. Penn, Janet and her husband Jim, their daughter Clarisse, Clarisse's daughter, Mrs. Penn's daughter Laura, and Laura's twin 22-year-old sons. Mrs. Penn's sisters couldn't attend, but Janet and Laura both promised to talk with them about the sessions. (See Figure 10.2 for a genogram of the family; the circled individuals share the same household.)

The family members took turns expressing their concern about Mrs. Penn and Janet, but the support for Janet was particularly striking, as her family sympathetically noted that "she tries to take on everything." Each person subsequently volunteered for a small task that Janet had previously assumed (e.g., taking Mrs. Penn to have her eyes and glasses checked, picking up medications at the pharmacy, making sure that there were fresh vegetables cut up for snacks). Robert was impressed by the family's willingness to "come through" for Janet, and his statements to this effect clearly pleased the family.

One deeply meaningful experience occurred for Janet during the second session, when Laura explained her lesser involvement in Mrs. Penn's care:

> When Mother is with me, she always talks about Janet, how responsible Janet is, how great it is living with Janet, and how well Janet takes care of her. So I just always figured Janet didn't need my help. I know Janet gets mad at me for letting Mother eat candy and not take baths, but I want Mother to enjoy her time with me, too.

Janet was clearly surprised by this revelation, which indicated that Mrs. Penn was saying things to one about the other that made both Laura and Janet feel as though they could never do enough. Janet then shared how their mother referred to Laura as "her baby," talked about how nice Laura was to her, and said, "Laura lets me eat what I want." At this point, Mrs. Penn appeared uncomfortable, but she could not or would not engage in a discussion of her behavior.

However, the shared information clearly decreased the tension between Laura and Janet. Later, Janet reported that she and Laura had

FIGURE 10.2

Genogram: Mrs. Penn and Family

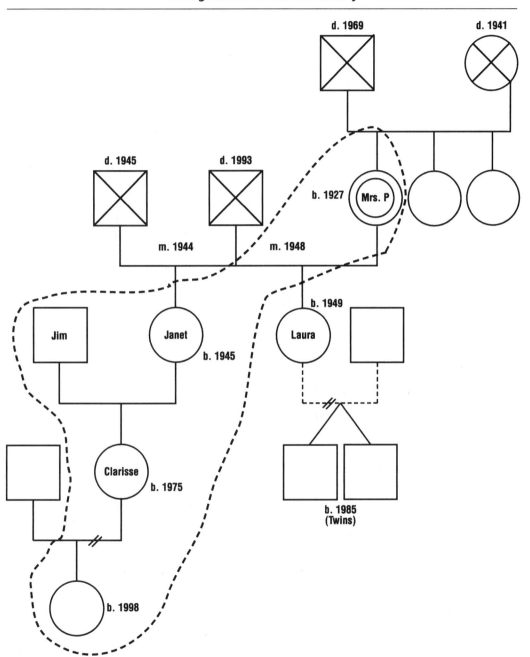

begun talking on the telephone more often. She described their conversations about Mrs. Penn as having shifted to "comparing notes instead of competing." The improvement in their relationship was a significant move forward in the family's functioning overall.

Unfortunately, the family's practical support for Janet lasted only about 2 months, after which family members, with the exception of her husband Jim, began forgetting their commitments or simply letting Janet take the tasks on again. Rather than lament the "irresponsibility" of her family members, Robert chose to reframe the situation more positively. In an individual meeting with Janet, he told her that although it seemed difficult for the family to maintain their extra efforts, it was good to know that they could be there for her in a crisis, as they had clearly demonstrated. But now it was up to Janet, who admitted to being more responsible than was always necessary, to figure out a way to take on less in her day-to-day life.

Recognizing Janet's time and financial constraints, he recommended that he and Janet meet individually for eight sessions to talk about her needs during the 45 minutes following his 30-minute sessions with Mrs. Penn. Because meeting with Janet on this subject could ethically be framed as part of helping Mrs. Penn, her time could be billed under Mrs. Penn's insurance.

Culturally Responsive Cognitive Behavior Therapy With Janet

Two main themes emerged in therapy with Janet. The first concerned her tendency to "take on too much." Janet came to understand her behavior in the context of her own upbringing; her mother and father had worked hard and expected her to share in household responsibilities, including the care of her younger sister. Janet and Robert also discussed how her tendencies were reinforced as an adult—for example, at work. As the only African American woman in her office, she knew that she was often seen, as she put it, "as the representative Black woman." She stated that she had had to work twice as hard as her White counterparts to reach and keep her managerial position.

Robert listened and affirmed her experiences. When he was sure that Janet felt heard and validated, he began asking her questions about the standards she set for herself. Janet articulated the belief that "I must *always* be responsible and hardworking to avoid disappointing others." In response to Robert's questions, Janet began to recognize how the perfectionistic nature of this belief increased her feelings of anxiety and guilt and led her to consistently put her own needs last. Robert pointed out that if she did not take care of herself by setting limits and engaging in self-care activities, she could become so physically ill that she could not take care of her mother. With some suggestions from Robert, Janet began to change her self-talk. For example, she began telling herself, "I need to take care of myself so that I can take care of my family." Also, when in doubt about what she should expect of herself, she began asking herself if she would expect the same thing of her own daughter.

A second theme involved Janet's sense of herself as a spiritual person. She told Robert that during the past few years she felt that she had "lost that part of myself." She'd become so busy that it was easier to sleep on Sundays than go to church, and she no longer prayed regularly. Using cognitive behavior strategies, Janet began using self-talk to decrease the guilt she felt. But Robert helped her go a bit further by asking her the following questions about her spirituality:

> What are your three greatest sources of strength?
> When you want to feel comforted, where do you go, or whom do you see?
> How would you describe the purpose of your life? (D. S. Smith, 1995, p. 179)

These questions led Janet to talk about what her "soul needed," which included "more quiet time in a park or by some trees, and to start praying again." She also said that she would like to find a book from which she could read an inspiring idea every morning. She had done this in the past and had liked carrying the hopeful idea or thought with her throughout the day.

Over the next few weeks, Janet talked with Robert about the importance of these needs and how she might begin to meet them. With his encouragement, she began attending church again, taking her mother with her, and the two of them would go to the park for a little while afterward. Janet also began getting up half an hour earlier to read one passage a day from a prayer book. At the end of 3 months, her schedule had not changed dramatically, but she felt more in control and hopeful about the future.

Conclusion

As the situation of Mrs. Penn and her family illustrates, culturally responsive therapy can be a complex endeavor. Robert's previous knowledge of African American culture and his professional experience with elders, including those with disabilities, enabled him to establish rapport, ask relevant questions, and obtain the necessary information. In turn, his assessment and diagnosis laid the groundwork for culturally responsive interventions. His familiarity with different theories and therapies enabled him to choose what would work best for his individual clients and their family system (i.e., life review, cognitive behavior and family systems therapies, and even a spiritual orientation). Finally, his collaborative and flexible approach facilitated therapy, particularly when something did not work (e.g., the documentation piece of the life review). In sum, Robert's assessment, diagnosis, and interventions were culturally responsive and, even more important, helpful.

Conclusion 11
Looking to the Future

The day after I began thinking about this final chapter, I was on a flight to Alaska. As the plane was taking off, I heard an angry voice and leaned forward to see what was going on. In the seats directly in front of me was a couple who appeared to be European American and in their early 60s. Earlier, I had heard them say that this was their first trip to Alaska. The wife was sitting by the window, and her husband was sitting in the middle seat. Next to him in the aisle seat was a stylishly dressed young woman, whom I guessed to be American Indian, from Los Angeles or San Francisco. This woman was angrily saying to the man, "No, that's wrong. It's just wrong." I couldn't hear the man, but I hypothesized that he had just made some well-intentioned comment about American Indian people that had offended her. They kept talking, and I heard her say something about "fishing rights . . . the American people don't know what really goes on." I hypothesized further that she was a newly appointed professor (i.e., not burned out) of American Indian studies at a university in California. At some point, the wife pretended to be taking a nap, but occasionally she would lean forward to add some benign comment like, "Well, you know, there's just good and bad in all cultures."

What subsequently amazed me about this interaction was not what they were talking about but, rather, that these two people were talking at all. Although I was uncomfortable with the angry tone in the woman's voice, as the conversation continued I thought to myself, "Why is she putting so much energy into educating this one guy?" After his initial comment, I think I would have said something polite to indicate my disagreement and then started reading a book. But she stayed in there, and so did he, and to his credit, I never heard him get defensive in response to her anger. By the end of the 3-hour flight, something had shifted, and they were laughing and sharing details about their children. When we landed, they gave each other their names, shook hands, and wished each other a good day.

While admiring these two people, I thought to myself, yes, this is what it's all about—that two people who have extremely different upbringings, identities, and views of the world can come together, interact, learn from each other, and even appreciate one another.

A Word About Conflict

The difficult thing about the field of multicultural studies (in psychology, counseling, social work, and related disciplines) is the conflict that so commonly arises. Diversity brings multiple perspectives, and multiple perspectives often lead to conflict. I suspect that this is one of the reasons why people who do not specialize in this work tend to avoid the topics of race, ethnicity, and culture. Because one can so easily offend another person even by one's choice of terms, the simplest solution often appears to be avoidance.

But as therapists, we do not have the option of ignoring cultural influences. If we are to work effectively with people of diverse identities, we must learn to deal with difference and conflict in ways that do not simply reinforce dominant power structures but rather empower and show respect for one another. In the preceding chapters, I have explained most of what I know about this work. The only additional point I make is to reiterate the role of mistakes. Just as conflict is inherent in this work, so, too, are mistakes. The challenge for therapists is to be accepting of our fallible selves and others, but at the same time be continually looking for biases that limit our thinking and work.

Education and Training

This is an exciting time to be in the field of clinical and counseling psychology, particularly in relation to cultural diversity. In the United States, the percentage of psychology 1st-year master's degree students who belong to ethnic minority cultures has risen to 21% and the percentage of 1st-year doctoral students to 27% (Norcross, Kohout, & Wicherski, 2005). (Ethnic minority cultures make up about 33% of the U.S. population.) As students and faculty become more aware of the advantages of learning in a culturally diverse environment (Iwamasa, Pai, & Sorocco, 2006), increasing attention is being given to the need for a greater diversity of practitioners, researchers, and teachers across many cultural domains (e.g., the need for more psychologists with disabilities; Gill, Kewman, & Brannon, 2003). The idea that diversity can be addressed in one multicultural counseling course has been replaced by the view that cross-cultural questions, information, and experiences must be integrated throughout the curriculum, including at the undergraduate and graduate levels and in practica and internship (Magyar-Moe et al., 2005; Roysircar, 2004). And increasing attention is being given to the need for more research on culturally responsive evidence-based practices (American Psychological Association, Presidential Task Force on Evidence-Based Practice, 2006; Nagayama Hall, 2001).

Moreover, internationally, psychology is strong. The majority of psychologists now live outside the United States (Bullock, 2006), and within the United States there appears to be increasing interest in global perspectives (Rosenweig, 1999). Many professional organizations publish information and hold regular conferences to encourage international collaboration and learning (for a list of organizations and yearly conferences, see http://www.apa.org/international/calendar.html and http://www.iupsys.org). Recognizing the disproportionate privilege and resources held by U.S. publishers and researchers, the *American Psychologist* and some other journals involve a diverse editorial board and pool of reviewers who provide extensive feedback and guidance to researchers submitting articles in English as their second language (Mays, Rubin, Sabourin, & Walker, 1996). In addition, in 2005, the American Psychological Association partnered with the Canadian Psychological Association and the publisher Hogrefe & Huber to join the World Health Organization program that provides free online journal access to students, professors, and government officials in countries in which the annual per capita income is less than $1,000 (Dingfelder, 2005). It is clear that there is still a long way to go in making psychological education, research, and practice more culturally responsive, but it appears that the field will continue to diversify and expand in response to multicultural and international influences.

Summary of the ADDRESSING Framework

If there is a central point to this book, it is this: To work effectively with people of diverse identities, we must first be willing to critically examine our own value systems, beliefs, and sociocultural contexts. To understand the impact of culture on our clients and in our work, we must also understand the impact of culture on ourselves. The ADDRESSING framework facilitates therapists' engagement in their own cultural self-assessment by providing a broad outline of influences and related identities that therapists can use to explore their own biases. As chapters 2 and 3 explained, a therapist's cultural self-assessment is facilitated by humility, compassion, and critical thinking skills. Equally key is an understanding of the relationship of privilege to culture and of the ways in which privilege separates those who hold it from those who do not. The self-knowledge that comes with such learning is essential in understanding the dynamics of therapeutic relationships and in developing the ability to comfortably discuss such dynamics with clients. Although parts of the self-assessment process may occur during sessions with clients, the bulk of this work takes place outside the therapy setting. It involves individually oriented work (e.g., introspection, self-questioning, reading, some forms of research) and learning from people of diverse identities through community activities, reading and listening to diverse media, and developing relationships.

Once therapists are engaged in this ongoing self-assessment process, the next step involves learning about and understanding the diverse identities that clients hold. The ADDRESSING outline can be a helpful reminder of influences and identities to be considered, including bicultural and multicultural identities. Although information about the person-specific meanings of identity usually comes from the client, it is the therapist's responsibility to obtain knowledge outside the therapy setting of the culture-specific meanings of a client's identity.

Knowledge of clients' salient identities gives the therapist clues about how clients see the world, what they value, how they may behave in certain situations, and how others treat them. Such knowledge can guide the therapist in developing respectful therapeutic relationships. Critical thinking about your own assumptions is important in this regard, because even if you do not know the specific meanings of clients' physical gestures, eye contact, nonverbal cues, and other culturally influenced forms of communication, simply staying aware of the diversity of meanings can help you to avoid inaccurate assumptions. Minimizing and explaining professional terminology and questioning the meaning of the terms you and the client use can also help to decrease misunderstandings.

During the assessment itself, therapists can take several practical steps to increase understanding and accuracy, including seeking out and using multiple sources of information, considering sociocultural historical events that may have affected clients during particular developmental periods in their lives, and actively looking for culturally related strengths at the individual, interpersonal, and environmental levels. Asking about clients' conceptualizations of their situations and about health care (including self-care) practices is also helpful.

The use of standardized tests for assessment purposes requires careful consideration of biases in the tests themselves, in testing procedures, in the testing environment, and in the tester. Whenever possible, it is helpful to think about clients' performance ideographically, keeping in mind the difference between academic knowledge and tacit knowledge (i.e., knowledge required in clients' everyday life functioning) and comparing clients' test performance against their own past performance rather than against the performance of others. With clients who speak English as a second language, a cultural consultant can be a valuable source of information in the development of questions that tap skills and knowledge relevant to clients' experiences and contexts. When standardized tests must be used, the relevance of responses will be greatly enhanced by an exploration of the reasons for clients' poor test performance.

In making a culturally responsive diagnosis, it can be helpful to add a sixth axis to diagnoses based on the *Diagnostic and Statistical Manual of Mental Disorders* (fourth edition, text revision [*DSM–IV–TR*]; American Psychiatric Association, 2000). This Cultural Axis VI consists of a list of the cultural influences and identities related to each of the ADDRESSING categories. Completing Cultural Axis VI first, followed by Axis IV: Psychosocial and Environmental Problems second and then Axis III: General Medical Conditions third, can facilitate a more systemic understanding of clients' problems and thus increase the accuracy of one's diagnoses on Axes I, II, and V.

Choosing the most culturally responsive interventions requires familiarity with a broad range of culturally related helping strategies, adaptations of mainstream psychotherapies, expressive and creative arts therapies, and systems-level interventions. The choice of intervention may be facilitated by a broader conceptualization of family, a willingness to see individual members and subsystems of the family on an as-needed basis, and the collaborative development of goals and treatment plans. When medications are a part of the intervention, it is important to stay aware of different cultural expectations regarding the prescription and use of medicines. Throughout one's work with individuals, couples, families, groups, and institutions, it is important to watch for power differentials between clients and between the client and the therapist. The ADDRESSING framework can be used as a reminder of the various domains in which these power differences may occur.

Conclusion

I would like to end with a story. My mother grew up during the Depression and World War II. Her father was a Presbyterian minister who believed in the equality of human beings and the importance of social responsibility. The family was of Scotch Irish descent; however, my mother believed that this was only part of her heritage. She is tall and has an olive complexion, black hair, high cheekbones, and deep-set eyes. One time when she was a child, after going to see a western at the movie theater, she and her father began talking about Indian people, and he said to her, "You know, you have some Indian blood in you." Another time, when they were living in the southern United States and talking about "Negro" people, her father told her, "You probably have some Negro blood in you, too." And still another memory she has is of her father coming home from the war, talking about the horrible things being done to Jewish people, and telling her, "You know, your ancestors were also Jewish." My mother took all of these comments literally (reinforced by an awareness of her appearance), and until her late teens, she truly believed that she was related to all of these groups. When she would see, read, or hear about some injustice that had occurred to someone of these cultures, she felt a strong sense of connection and empathy that has shaped her work and life.

Of course, in the broadest sense, my mother *is* related to each of these groups, as we are all related to one another.

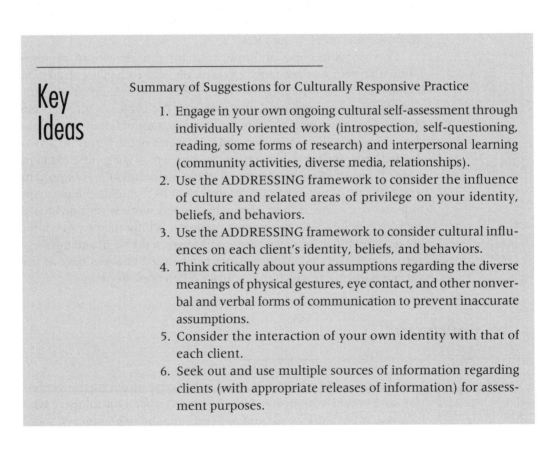

Key Ideas

Summary of Suggestions for Culturally Responsive Practice

1. Engage in your own ongoing cultural self-assessment through individually oriented work (introspection, self-questioning, reading, some forms of research) and interpersonal learning (community activities, diverse media, relationships).
2. Use the ADDRESSING framework to consider the influence of culture and related areas of privilege on your identity, beliefs, and behaviors.
3. Use the ADDRESSING framework to consider cultural influences on each client's identity, beliefs, and behaviors.
4. Think critically about your assumptions regarding the diverse meanings of physical gestures, eye contact, and other nonverbal and verbal forms of communication to prevent inaccurate assumptions.
5. Consider the interaction of your own identity with that of each client.
6. Seek out and use multiple sources of information regarding clients (with appropriate releases of information) for assessment purposes.

7. Consider sociocultural historical events that may have affected clients during particular developmental periods in their lives.

8. Deliberately look for culturally related strengths and supports at the individual, interpersonal, and environmental levels.

9. Work with cultural consultants and interpreters to develop questions that assess skills and knowledge relevant to clients' experiences and contexts.

10. Use standardized tests cautiously with consideration of possible biases in tests, testing procedures, the testing environment, and the tester.

11. Use the method of testing the limits to explore the reasons for clients' poor test performance.

12. In making a diagnosis, take into account the client's conceptualization of the problem and self-care practices.

13. Move beyond the *DSM–IV–TR*'s focus on individualistic diagnoses to think systemically and consider relational disorders.

14. When using the *DSM–IV–TR*, complete the Cultural Axis VI (ADDRESSING influences) first, Axis IV: Psychosocial and Environmental Problems second, and Axis III: General Medical Conditions third, before making diagnoses on Axes I, II, and V.

15. Take an eclectic approach to therapy, recognizing the possible usefulness of culturally related strategies and therapies, mainstream therapies adapted to minority groups, expressive and creative arts therapies, and systems-level interventions.

16. Set goals, develop treatment plans, and choose interventions collaboratively with clients.

17. Use the ADDRESSING framework as a reminder of the various domains in which power differences may exist in couple and family therapy.

18. Keep in mind culturally related expectations regarding medications.

References

aaanativearts. (2006). *Canadian Indians: First nations by culture, language, region, status, and providence.* Retrieved December 13, 2006, from http://www.aaanative arts.com/canadian_tribes_AtoZ.htm

Abudabbeh, N. (2005). Arab families. In M. McGoldrick, J. Giordano, & N. Garcia-Preto (Eds.), *Ethnicity and family therapy* (3rd ed., pp. 423–436). New York: Guilford Press.

Abudabbeh, N., & Hays, P. A. (2006). Cognitive–behavioral therapy with people of Arab heritage. In P. A. Hays & G. Y. Iwamasa (Eds.), *Culturally responsive cognitive–behavioral therapy: Assessment, practice, and supervision* (pp. 141–160). Washington, DC: American Psychological Association.

Acklin, F., Newman, J., Arbon, V., Trindal, A., Brock, K., Bermingham, M., et al. (1999). Story-telling: Australian Indigenous women's means of health promotion. In R. Barnhardt (Ed.), *Indigenous education around the world: Workshop papers from the 1996 World Indigenous Peoples Conference: Education* (pp. 1–10). Fairbanks: University of Alaska–Fairbanks, Center for Cross-Cultural Studies.

Acosta, F. X., Yamamoto, J., Evans, L. A., & Wilcox, S. A. (1982). Effective psychotherapy for low-income and minority patients. In F. X. Acosta, J. Yamamoto, L. A. Evans, & S. A. Wilcox (Eds.), *Effective psychotherapy for low-income and minority patients* (pp. 1–29). New York: Plenum Press.

Adelson, N. (2000). Re-imagining Aboriginality: An Indigenous peoples' response to social suffering. *Transcultural Psychiatry, 37,* 11–34.

Akamatsu, N. N. (1998). The talking oppression blues. In M. McGoldrick (Ed.), *Re-visioning family therapy: Race, culture, and gender in clinical practice* (pp. 129–143). New York: Guilford Press.

Alarcón, R. D. (1997). Personality disorders and culture: Conflict at the boundaries. *Transcultural Psychiatry, 34,* 453–461.

Alarcón, R. D., & Foulks, E. F. (1995). Personality disorders and culture: Contemporary clinical views (Part A). *Cultural Diversity and Mental Health, 1,* 3–18.

Ali, S. R., Liu, W. M., & Humedian, M. (2004). Islam 101: Understanding the religion and therapy implications. *Professional Psychology: Research and Practice, 35,* 635–642.

Allen, J. (1998). Personality assessment with American Indians and Alaskan Natives: Instrument considerations and service delivery style. *Journal of Personality Assessment, 70,* 17–42.

Almeida, R. (2005). Hindu, Christian, and Muslim families. In M. McGoldrick, J. Giordano, & N. Garcia-Preto (Eds.), *Ethnicity and family therapy* (3rd ed., pp. 377–394). New York: Guilford Press.

Altman, N. (2007). Toward the acceptance of human similarity and difference. In J. C. Muran (Ed.), *Dialogues on difference: Studies of diversity in the therapeutic relationship* (pp. 15–25). Washington, DC: American Psychological Association.

American Psychiatric Association. (1994). *Diagnostic and statistical manual of mental disorders* (4th ed.). Washington, DC: Author.

American Psychiatric Association. (2000). *Diagnostic and statistical manual of mental disorders* (4th ed., text rev.). Washington, DC: Author.

American Psychological Association. (1996). *Violence and the family: Report of the APA Presidential Task Force on Violence and the Family.* Washington, DC: Author.

American Psychological Association. (2000a). Guidelines for psychotherapy with lesbian, gay, and bisexual clients. *American Psychologist, 55,* 1440–1451.

American Psychological Association. (2000b). *Resolution on poverty and socioeconomic status.* Retrieved November 11, 2001, from http://www.apa.org/pi/urban/povres.html

American Psychological Association. (2002a). Ethical principles of psychologists and code of conduct. *American Psychologist, 57,* 1060–1073.

American Psychological Association. (2002b). Guidelines on multicultural education, training, research, practice, and organizational change for psychologists. *American Psychologist, 58,* 377–402.

American Psychological Association. (2004). Guidelines for psychological practice with older adults. *American Psychologist, 59,* 236–260.

American Psychological Association. (2006). *Answers to your questions about transgender individuals and gender identity.* Retrieved December 15, 2006, from http://www.apa.org/topics/transgender.html

American Psychological Association Presidential Task Force on Evidence-Based Practice. (2006). Evidence-based practice in psychology. *American Psychologist, 61,* 271–285.

American Religious Identity Survey (ARIS). (2001). *Largest religious groups in the United States of America.* Retrieved May 12, 2007, from http://www.adherents.com/rel_USA.html#religions

Anastasi, A. (1992). What counselors should know about the use and interpretation of psychological tests. *Journal of Counseling and Development, 70,* 610–615.

Andronikof-Sanglade, A. (2000). Use of the Rorschach Comprehensive System in Europe: State of the art. In R. H. Dana (Ed.), *Handbook of cross-cultural and multicultural personality assessment* (pp. 329–344). Mahwah, NJ: Erlbaum.

Anzaldua, G. (1987). *Borderlands/La Frontera: The new mestiza.* San Francisco: Aunt Lute Books.

Aponte, H. J. (1994). *Bread and spirit: Therapy with the new poor.* New York: Norton.

Aponte, J. F., & Wohl, J. (Eds.). (2000). *Psychological intervention and cultural diversity.* Needham Heights, MA: Allyn & Bacon.

Ardila, A., Rosselli, M., & Puente, A. E. (1994). *Neuropsychological evaluation of the Spanish speaker.* New York: Plenum Press.

Arredondo, P., & Pérez, P. (2006). Historical perspectives on the multicultural guidelines and contemporary applications. *Professional Psychology: Research and Practice, 37,* 1–5.

Arroyo, W. (1997). Children and families of Mexican descent. In G. Johnson-Powell & J. Yamamoto (Eds.), *Transcultural child development: Psychological assessment and treatment* (pp. 290–304). New York: Wiley.

Assanand, S., Dias, M., Richardson, E., Chambers, N. A., & Waxler-Morrison, N. (2005). People of South Asian descent. In N. Waxler-Morrison, J. M. Anderson, E. Richardson, & N. A. Chambers (Eds.), *Cross-cultural caring: A handbook for health professionals* (2nd ed., pp. 197–246). Vancouver, British Columbia, Canada: University of British Columbia Press.

Atkinson, D., Morten, G., & Sue, D. (Eds.). (1993). *Counseling American minorities: A cross-cultural perspective.* Dubuque, IA: William C. Brown Communications.

Atkinson, D. R., Wampold, B. E., Lowe, S. M., Matthews, L., & Ahn, H. (1998). Asian American preferences for counselor characteristics: Application of the Bradley–Terry–Luce model to paired comparison data. *Counseling Psychologist, 26,* 101–123.

Balsam, K. F., Huang, B., Fieland, K. C., Simoni, J. M., & Walters, K. L. (2004). Culture, trauma, and wellness: A comparison of heterosexual and lesbian, gay, bisexual, and Two-Spirit Native Americans. *Cultural Diversity and Ethnic Minority Psychology, 10,* 287–301.

Balsam, K. F., Martell, C. R., & Safren, S. A. (2006). Affirmative cognitive–behavioral therapy with lesbian, gay, and bisexual people. In P. A. Hays & G. Y. Iwamasa (Eds.), *Culturally responsive cognitive-behavioral therapy: Assessment, practice, and supervision* (pp. 223–243). Washington, DC: American Psychological Association.

Barakat, H. (1993). *The Arab world: Society, culture, and state.* Berkeley: University of California Press.

Barón, A., & Cramer, D. W. (2000). Potential counseling concerns of aging lesbian, gay, and bisexual clients. In R. M. Perez, K. A. DeBord, & K. J. Bieschke (Eds.), *Handbook of counseling and psychotherapy with lesbian, gay, and bisexual clients* (pp. 207–224). Washington, DC: American Psychological Association.

Beck, A. T., Rush, A. J., Shaw, B. F., & Emery, G. (1979). *Cognitive therapy of depression.* New York: Guilford Press.

Beck, J. S. (1995). *Cognitive therapy: Basics and beyond.* New York: Guilford Press.

Belgrave, F. Z. (1998). *Psychosocial aspects of chronic illness and disability among African Americans.* Westport, CT: Auburn House.

Bergin, A. E., Payne, I. R., & Richards, P. S. (1996). Values and psychology. In E. P. Shafranske (Ed.), *Religion and the clinical practice of psychotherapy* (pp. 297–326). Washington, DC: American Psychological Association.

Bernal, G., & Shapiro, E. (1996). Cuban families. In M. McGoldrick, J. Giordano, & J. K. Pearce (Eds.), *Ethnicity and family therapy* (2nd ed., pp. 155–168). New York: Guilford Press.

Berry, J. W. (2004). An ecocultural perspective on the development of competence. In R. J. Sternberg & E. L. Grigorenko (Eds.), *Culture and competence: Contexts of life success* (pp. 3–22). Washington, DC: American Psychological Association.

Berry, J. W., Poortinga, Y. H., Segall, M. H., & Dasen, P. R. (1992). *Cross-cultural psychology: Research and applications.* New York: Cambridge University Press.

Berzoff, J., Flanagan, L. M., & Hertz, P. (1996). *Inside out and outside in: Psychodynamic clinical theory and practice in contemporary multicultural contexts.* Northvale, NJ: Aronson.

Betancourt, H., & López, S. R. (1993). The study of culture, ethnicity, and race in American psychology. *American Psychologist, 48,* 629–637.

Beutler, L. E., & Malik, M. L. (2002). *Rethinking the DSM: A psychological perspective.* Washington, DC: American Psychological Association.

Bibb, A., & Casimir, G. J. (1996). Haitian families. In M. McGoldrick, J. Giordano, & J. K. Pearce (Eds.), *Ethnicity and family therapy* (2nd ed., pp. 86–111). New York: Guilford Press.

Blood, P., Tuttle, A., & Lakey, G. (1995). Understanding and fighting sexism: A call to men. In M. L. Anderson (Ed.), *Race, class and gender: An anthology* (pp. 154–161). New York: Wadsworth.

Boyd-Franklin, N. (1989). *Black families in therapy.* New York: Guilford Press.

Boyd-Franklin, N. (2003). *Black families in therapy* (3rd ed.). New York: Guilford Press.

Bradford, D. T., & Munoz, A. (1993). Translation in bilingual psychotherapy. *Professional Psychology: Research and Practice, 24,* 52–61.

Bratton, S. C., Ray, D., Rhine, T., & Jones, L. (2005). The efficacy of play therapy with children: A meta-analytic review of treatment outcomes. *Professional Psychology: Research and Practice, 36,* 376–390.

Brendtro, L. K., Brokenleg, M., & Van Bockern, S. (1998). *Reclaiming youth at risk: Our hope for the future.* Bloomington, IN: National Educational Service.

Brookfield, S. (1987). *Developing critical thinkers.* San Francisco: Jossey-Bass.

Brown, D. (1997). Implications of cultural values for cross-cultural consultations with families. *Journal of Counseling and Development, 76,* 29–35.

Brown, L. S. (1990). Taking account of gender in the clinical assessment interview. *Professional Psychology: Research and Practice, 21,* 12–17.

Brown, L. S. (1994). *Subversive dialogues.* New York: Basic Books.

Brown, L. S. (2004). Feminist paradigms of treatment. *Psychotherapy: Theory, Research, Practice, Training, 41,* 464–471.

Brown, L. S., & Ballou, M. (Eds.). (1992). *Personality and psychopathology: Feminist reappraisals.* New York: Guilford Press.

Bullock, M. (2006, May). Toward a global psychology. *Monitor on Psychology, 37,* 9.

Burlingame, V. S. (1999). *Ethnogerocounseling: Counseling ethnic elders and their families.* New York: Springer Publishing Company.

Bushra, A., Khadivi, A., & Frewat-Nikowitz, S. (2007). History, custom, and the twin towers: Challenges in adapting psychotherapy to Middle Eastern culture in the United States. In J. C. Muran (Ed.), *Dialogues on difference: Studies of diversity in the therapeutic relationship* (pp. 221–235). Washington, DC: American Psychological Association.

Butcher, J. N, Cabiya, J., Lucio, E., & Garrido, M. (2007). *Assessing Hispanic clients using the MMPI–2 and MMPI–A.* Washington, DC: American Psychological Association.

Butcher, J. N., Coelho Mosch, S., Tsai, J., & Nezami, E. (2006). Cross-cultural applications of the MMPI–2. In J. Butcher (Ed.), *MMPI–2: A practitioner's guide* (pp. 505–538). Washington, DC: American Psychological Association.

Butcher, J. N., Graham, J. R., Ben Porath, Y. S., Tellegen, A., Dahlstrom, W. G., & Kaemmer, B. (1989). *Minnesota Multiphasic Personality*

Inventory—2 (MMPI–2): Manual for administration, scoring, and interpretation (Rev. ed.). Minneapolis: University of Minnesota Press.

Butcher, J. N., Graham, J. R., Ben-Porath, Y. S., Tellegen, A., Dahlstrom, W. G., & Kaemmer, B. (2001). *Minnesota Multiphasic Personality Inventory—2 (MMPI–2): Manual for administration, scoring, and interpretation* (Rev. ed.). Minneapolis: University of Minnesota Press.

Butler, R. N., Lewis, M., & Sunderland, T. (1998). *Aging and mental health.* New York: Allyn & Bacon.

Calisch, A. (2003). Multicultural training in art therapy: Past, present, and future. *Art Therapy, 20,* 11–15.

Campbell, A., Rorie, K., Dennis, G., Wood, D., Combs, S., Hearn, L., et al. (1996). Neuropsychological assessment of African Americans: Conceptual and methodological considerations. In R. L. Jones (Ed.), *Handbook of tests and measurements for Black populations* (pp. 75–84). Hampton, VA: Cobb & Henry.

Campbell, C., Richie, S. D., & Hargrove, D. S. (2003). Poverty and rural mental health. In B. H. Stamm (Ed.), *Rural behavioral health care: An interdisciplinary guide* (pp. 41–51). Washington, DC: American Psychological Association.

Cardemil, E. V., Kim, S., Pinedo, T. M., & Miller I. W. (2005). Developing a culturally appropriate depression prevention program: The family coping skills program. *Cultural Diversity and Ethnic Minority Psychology, 11,* 99–112.

Carter, R. (1994). *Helping yourself help others: A book for caregivers.* New York: Times Books.

Cashwell, C. S., & Young, J. S. (2005). *Integrating spirituality and religion into counseling: A guide to competent practice.* Alexandria, VA: American Counseling Association.

Cass, V. C. (1979). Homosexual identity formation: A theoretical model. *Journal of Homosexuality, 4,* 219–235.

Cervantes, R. C., Padilla, A. M., & Salgado de Snyder, N. (1990). Reliability and validity of the Hispanic Stress Inventory. *Hispanic Journal of Behavioral Sciences, 12,* 76–82.

Chan, A. S., Shum, D., & Cheung, R. W. Y. (2003). Recent development of cognitive and neuropsychological assessment in Asian countries. *Psychological Assessment, 15,* 257–267.

Chan, C. S. (1992). Cultural considerations in counseling Asian American lesbians and gay men. In S. H. Dworkin & F. J. Gutiérrez (Eds.), *Counseling gay men and lesbians: Journey to the end of the rainbow* (pp. 115–124). Alexandria, VA: American Counseling Association.

Chin, J. L. (1994). Psychodynamic approaches. In L. Comas-Díaz & B. Greene (Eds.), *Women of color: Integrating ethnic and gender identities in psychotherapy* (pp. 194–222). New York: Guilford Press.

Chödrön, P. (2000). *When things fall apart: Heart advice for difficult times.* Boston: Shambala.

Comas-Díaz, L. (2001). Hispanics, Latinos, or Americanos: The evolution of identity. *Cultural Diversity and Ethnic Minority Psychology, 7,* 115–120.

Comas-Díaz, L. (2007). Commentary: Freud, Jung, or Fanon? The racial other on the couch. In C. Muran (Ed.), *Dialogues on difference: Studies of diversity in the therapeutic relationship* (pp. 35–39). Washington, DC: American Psychological Association.

Comas-Díaz, L., & Greene, B. (1994a). Overview: Gender and ethnicity in the healing process. In L. Comas-Díaz & B. Greene (Eds.), *Women of color: Integrating ethnic and gender identities in psychotherapy* (pp. 185–193). New York: Guilford Press.

Comas-Díaz, L., & Greene, B. (Eds.). (1994b). *Women of color: Integrating ethnic and gender identities in psychotherapy.* New York: Guilford Press.

Consoli, A. J., & Jester, C. M. (2005). A model for teaching psychotherapy theory through an integrated structure. *Journal of Psychotherapy Integration, 15,* 358–373.

Cooper, C. C., & Gottlieb, M. C. (2000). Ethical issues with managed care: Challenges facing counseling psychology. *Counseling Psychologist, 28,* 179–236.

Costantino, G., Flanagan, R., & Malgady, R. (1995). The history of the Rorschach: Overcoming bias in multicultural projective assessment. *Rorschachiana: Yearbook of the International Rorschach Society, 20,* 148–171.

Costantino, G., & Malgady, R. G. (2000). Multicultural and cross-cultural utility of the TEMAS (Tell-Me-A-Story) Test. In R. H. Dana (Ed.), *Handbook of cross-cultural and multicultural personality assessment* (pp. 481–513). Mahwah, NJ: Erlbaum.

Costantino, G., Malgady, R. G., & Rogler, L. H. (1988). *TEMAS (Tell-Me-a-Story) manual.* Los Angeles: Western Psychological Services.

Costantino, G., Malgady, R., & Vasquez, C. (1981). A comparison of the Murray–TAT and a new Thematic Apperception Test for urban Hispanic children. *Hispanic Journal of Behavioral Science, 3,* 291–300.

Courtois, C. A. (2004). Complex trauma, complex reactions: Assessment and treatment. *Psychotherapy: Theory, Research, Practice, Training, 41,* 412–425.

Criddle, J. (1992). *Bamboo and butterflies: From refugee to citizen.* Dixon, CA: East/West Bridge.

Cross, T. L. (2003). Culture as a resource for mental health. *Cultural Diversity and Ethnic Minority Psychology, 9,* 354–359.

Cross, W. E. (1991). *Shades of Black: Diversity in African American identity.* Philadelphia: Temple University Press.

Croteau, J. M. (1999). One struggle through individualism: Toward an antiracist White racial identity. *Journal of Counseling and Development, 77,* 30–32.

Cruikshank, J. (1990). *Life lived like a story: Life stories of three Yukon Native elders*. Lincoln: University of Nebraska Press.

Cuéllar, I. (1998). Cross-cultural clinical psychological assessment of Hispanic Americans. *Journal of Personality Assessment, 70,* 71–86.

Cuéllar, I. (2000). Acculturation as a moderator of personality and psychological assessment. In R. H. Dana (Ed.), *Handbook of cross-cultural and multicultural personality assessment* (pp. 113–129). Mahwah, NJ: Erlbaum.

Dana, R. H. (1998). Cultural identity assessment of culturally diverse groups: 1997. *Journal of Personality Assessment, 70,* 1–16.

Dana, R. H. (1999). Cross-cultural–multicultural use of the Thematic Apperception Test. In L. Geiser & M. I. Stein (Eds.), *Evocative images: The Thematic Apperception Test and the art of projection* (pp. 177–190). Washington, DC: American Psychological Association.

Dana, R. H. (2000). Culture and methodology in personality assessment. In I. Cuéllar & F. A. Paniagua (Eds.), *Handbook of multicultural mental health: Assessment and treatment of diverse populations* (pp. 79–120). San Diego, CA: Academic Press.

Dator, J. (1979). The futures of culture or cultures of the future. In A. J. Marsella, R. G. Tharp, & T. J. Ciborowski (Eds.), *Perspectives on cross-cultural psychology* (pp. 369–388). New York: Academic Press.

Davidson, G. (1995). Cognitive assessment of Indigenous Australians: Towards a multiaxial model. *Australian Psychologist, 30,* 30–34.

Davis, H. (1993). *Counselling parents of children with chronic illness or disability.* Leicester, England: British Psychological Society.

deShazer, S. (1985). *Keys to solution in brief therapy.* New York: Norton.

DeSilva, P. (1993). Buddhist psychology: A therapeutic perspective. In U. Kim & J. W. Berry (Eds.), *Indigenous psychologies* (pp. 221–239). Newbury Park, CA: Sage.

Dew, B. J., Myers, J. E., & Wightman, L. F. (2006). Wellness in adult gay males: Examining the impact of internalized homophobia, self-disclosure and self-disclosure to parents. *Journal of LGBT Issues in Counseling, 1,* 23–40.

Diener, E., Oishi, S., & Lucas, R. E. (2003). Personality, culture, and subjective well-being: Emotional and cognitive evaluations of life. *Annual Review of Psychology, 54,* 403–425.

Dingfelder, S. (2005, December). APA offers free journal access to world's poorest countries. *Monitor on Psychology, 36,* 14.

Dolan, Y. M. (1991). *Resolving sexual abuse.* New York: Norton.

Dowd, E. T. (2003). Cultural differences in cognitive therapy. *Behavior Therapist, 26,* 247–249.

Downing, N. E., & Roush, K. L. (1985). From passive acceptance to active commitment: A model of feminist identity development of women. *Counseling Psychologist, 13,* 59–72.

Droby, R. M. (2000). *With the wind and the waves: A guide for non-Native mental health professionals working with Alaska Native communities.* Nome, AK: Norton Sound Health Corporation, Behavioral Health Services.

Duffy, M. (1986). The techniques and contexts of multigenerational therapy. In T. Brink (Ed.), *Clinical gerontology: A guide to assessment and interventions* (pp. 347–362). New York: Haworth Press.

Duffy, M. (Ed.). (1999). *Handbook of counseling and psychotherapy with older adults.* New York: Wiley.

Dulicai, D., & Berger, M. R. (2005). Global dance/movement therapy growth and development. *Arts in Psychotherapy, 32,* 205–216.

Duran, E. (2006). *Healing the soul wound.* Williston, VT: Teachers College Press.

Dwairy, M. (2006). *Counseling and psychotherapy with Arabs and Muslims.* Williston, VT: Teachers College Press.

Dworkin, S. H., & Gutiérrez, F. J. (Eds.). (1992). *Counseling gay men and les-bians: Journey to the end of the rainbow.* Alexandria, VA: American Counseling Association.

Eisman, E. J., Dies, R. R., Finn, S. E., Eyde, L. D., Kay, G. G., Kubiszyn, T. W., et al. (2000). Problems and limitations in using psychological assessment in the contemporary health care delivery system. *Professional Psychology: Research and Practice, 31,* 131–140.

Elliott, J. E., & Fleras, A. (1992). *Unequal relations: An introduction to race and ethnic dynamics in Canada.* Scarborough, Ontario: Prentice-Hall Canada.

Ellis, A. (1997). Using rational emotive behavior therapy techniques to cope with disability. *Professional Psychology: Research and Practice, 28,* 17–22.

Ellis, A., & Dryden, W. (1987). *The practice of rational–emotive therapy.* New York: Springer Publishing Company.

Ephraim, D. (2000). Culturally relevant research and practice with the Rorschach Comprehensive System. In R. H. Dana (Ed.), *Handbook of cross-cultural and multicultural personality assessment* (pp. 303–328). Mahwah, NJ: Erlbaum.

Erikson, C. D., & Al-Timmimi, N. R. (2001). Providing mental health services to Arab Americans: Recommendations and considerations. *Cultural Diversity and Ethnic Minority Psychology, 7,* 308–327.

Escobar, J. I., Burman, A., Karno, M., Forsythe, A., Landsverk, J., & Golding, J. M. (1986). Use of the Mini-Mental State Examination (MMSE) in a community population of mixed ethnicity. *Journal of Nervous and Mental Disease, 174,* 607–614.

Exner, J. E., Jr. (1993). *The Rorschach: A comprehensive system: Vol. 1. Basic foundations* (3rd ed.). New York: Wiley.

Fadiman, A. (1997). *The spirit catches you and you fall down*. New York: Farrar, Straus & Giroux.

Falicov, C. J. (1995). Cross-cultural marriages. In N. S. Jacobson & A. S. Gurman (Eds.), *Clinical handbook of couple therapy* (pp. 231–246). New York: Guilford Press.

Falicov, C. J. (2005). Mexican families. In M. McGoldrick, J. Giordano, & J. K. Pearce (Eds.), *Ethnicity and family therapy* (2nd ed., pp. 169–182). New York: Guilford Press.

Falicov, C. J. (1998). *Latino families in therapy*. New York: Guilford Press.

Farley, N. (1992). Same-sex domestic violence. In S. H. Dworkin & F. J. Gutiérrez (Eds.), *Counseling gay men and lesbians: Journey to the end of the rainbow* (pp. 231–244). Alexandria, VA: American Counseling Association.

Fiore, J., Coppel, D. B., Becker, J., & Cox, G. B. (1986). Social support as a multi-faceted concept: Examination of important dimensions for adjustment. *American Journal of Community Psychology, 14*, 93–111.

Fiske, S. (1993). Controlling other people: The impact of power on stereotyping. *American Psychologist, 48*, 621–628.

Flanagan, R., & Di Giuseppe, R. (1999). Critical review of the TEMAS: A step within the development of thematic apperception instruments. *Psychology in the Schools, 36*, 21–30.

Foa, E. B., Keane, T. M., & Friedman, M. J. (Eds.). (2000). *Effective treatments for PTSD*. New York: Guilford Press.

Folstein, M., Anthony, J. E., Parhad, I., Duffy, B., & Gruenberg, E. M. (1985). The meaning of cognitive impairment in the elderly. *Journal of the American Geriatrics Society, 33*, 228–235.

Fong, R. (Ed.). (2004). *Culturally competent practice with immigrant and refugee children and families*. New York: Guilford Press.

Fowers, B. J., Tredinnick, M., & Applegate, B. (1997). Individualism and counseling: An empirical examination of the prevalence of individualistic values in psychologists' responses to case vignettes. *Counseling and Values, 41*, 204–218.

Frager, R., & Fadiman, J. (1998). *Personality and personal growth*. New York: Longman.

Fukuyama, M. A., & Sevig, T. D. (1999). *Integrating spirituality into multicultural counseling*. Thousand Oaks, CA: Sage.

Fuld, P. A. (1977). *Fuld Object–Memory Evaluation*. Wood Dale, IL: Stoelting Co.

Fuld, P. A., Muramoto, O., Blau, A., & Westbrook, L. (1988). Cross-cultural and multi-ethnic dementia evaluation by mental status and memory testing. *Cortex, 24*, 511–519.

Gaines, E. J. (1997). *A lesson before dying*. New York: Vintage Books.

Gaines, S. O., & Reed, E. S. (1995). Prejudice: From Allport to DuBois. *American Psychologist, 50*, 96–103.

Garrido, M., & Velasquez, R. (2006). Interpretation of Latino/Latina MMPI–2 profiles: Review and application of empirical findings and cultural–linguistic considerations. In J. Butcher (Ed.), *MMPI–2: A practitioner's guide* (pp. 477–504). Washington, DC: American Psychological Association.

Gatz, M. (1994). Application of assessment to therapy and intervention with older adults. In M. Storandt & G. R. VandenBos (Eds.), *Neuropsychological assessment of dementia and depression in older adults: A clinician's guide* (pp. 155–176). Washington, DC: American Psychological Association.

Gaughen, K. J. S., & Gaughen, D. K. (1996). The Native Hawaiian (Kanaka Maoli) client. In P. B. Pedersen & D. C. Locke (Eds.), *Cultural and diversity issues in counseling* (pp. 33–36). Greensboro: School of Education, University of North Carolina at Greensboro. (ERIC Document Reproduction Service No. ED400486)

Geisinger, K. F. (1992). *Psychological testing of Hispanics.* Washington, DC: American Psychological Association.

Gibbons, K. (1998). *Ellen Foster.* New York: McMillan.

Gil, E. (Ed.). (2006). *Cultural issues in play therapy.* New York: Guilford Press.

Gill, C. J., Kewman, D. G., & Brannon, R. W. (2003). Transforming psychological practice and society: Policies that reflect the new paradigm. *American Psychologist, 58,* 305–312.

Glasgow, J. H., & Adaskin, E. J. (1990). The West Indians. In N. Waxler-Morrison, J. M. Anderson, & E. Richardson (Eds.), *Cross-cultural caring: A handbook for health professionals in Western Canada* (pp. 214–244). Vancouver, British Columbia, Canada: University of British Columbia Press.

Gleave, D., Chambers, N. A., & Manes, A. S. (2005). People of Central American descent. In N. Waxler-Morrison, J. M. Anderson, E. Richardson, & N. A. Chambers (Eds.), *Cross-cultural caring: A handbook for health professionals* (2nd ed., pp. 11–58). Vancouver, British Columbia, Canada: University of British Columbia Press.

Gonzalez, A., & Zimbardo, P. G. (1985, March). Time in perspective: The time sense we learn early affects how we do our jobs and enjoy our pleasures. *Psychology Today,* pp. 21–26.

Good, B. J. (1996). Culture and *DSM–IV:* Diagnosis, knowledge and power. *Culture, Medicine and Psychiatry, 20,* 127–132.

Gopaul-McNicol, S. A. (1993). *Working with West Indian families.* New York: Guilford Press.

Graham, J. (1990). *MMPI–2: Assessing personality and psychopathology.* New York: Oxford University Press.

Greenberg, S., & Motenko, A. K. (1994). Women growing older: Partnerships for change. In M. P. Mirken (Ed.), *Women in context* (pp. 96–117). New York: Guilford Press.

Greenberger, D., & Padesky, C. A. (1995). *Mind over mood: Change How you feel by changing the way you think*. New York: Guilford Press.

Greene, B. (1994.) Lesbian women of color: Triple jeopardy. In L. Comas-Díaz & B. Greene (Eds.), *Women of color: Integrating ethnic and gender identities in psychotherapy* (pp. 389–427). New York: Guilford Press.

Grier, W., & Cobbs, P. (1968). *Black rage*. New York: Basic Books.

Griffin-Pierce, T. (1997). "When I am lonely the mountains call me": The impact of sacred geography on Navajo psychological well-being. *American Indian and Alaskan Native Mental Health Research, 7*, 1–10.

Guthman, D., & Sandberg, K. A. (2002). Dual relationships in the Deaf community: When dual relationships are unavoidable and essential. In A. A. Lazarus & O. Zur (Eds.), *Dual relationships and psychotherapy* (pp. 287–297). New York: Springer Publishing Company.

Gutiérrez, F. J., & Dworkin, S. H. (1992). Gay, lesbian, and African American: Managing the integration of identities. In S. H. Dworkin & F. J. Gutiérrez (Eds.), *Counseling gay men and lesbians: Journey to the end of the rainbow* (pp. 141–156). Alexandria, VA: American Counseling Association.

Haley, J. (1963). *Strategies of psychotherapy*. New York: Grune & Stratton.

Hall, C. C. I. (2003). Not just Black and White: Interracial relationships and multicultural individuals. In J. S. Mio & G. Y. Iwamasa (Eds.), *Culturally diverse mental health* (pp. 231–248). New York: Brunner-Routledge.

Hall, E. T. (1966). *The hidden dimension*. New York: Doubleday.

Hambleton, R. K., Merenda, P. F., & Spielberger, C. D. (Eds.). (1996). *Adapting educational and psychological tests for cross-cultural assessment*. Mahwah, NJ: Erlbaum.

Hamilton, D. L., & Trolier, T. K. (1986). Stereotypes and stereotyping: An overview of the cognitive approach. In J. F. Dovidio & S. L. Gaertner (Eds.), *Prejudice, discrimination, and racism* (pp. 127–163). New York: Academic Press.

Hammond, L. C., & Gantt, L. (1998). Using art in counseling: Ethical considerations. *Journal of Counseling and Development, 76*, 271–276.

Hanh, T. N. (1992). *Touching peace: Practicing the art of mindful living*. Berkeley, CA: Parallax Press.

Harowski, K., Turner, A., LeVine, E., Schank, J. A., & Leichter, J. (2006). From our community to yours: Rural best perspectives on psychology practice, training, and advocacy. *Professional Psychology: Research and Practice, 37*, 158–164.

Harper, F. D., & McFadden, J. (2003). *Culture and counseling: New approaches*. Boston: Allyn & Bacon.

Harper, G. W., Jernewall, N., & Zea, M. C. (2004). Giving voice to emerging science and theory for lesbian, gay, and bisexual people of color. *Cultural Diversity and Ethnic Minority Psychology, 10*, 187–199.

Hayes, S. C., & Duckworth, M. P. (2006). Acceptance and commitment therapy and traditional cognitive behavior therapy approaches to pain. *Cognitive and Behavioral Practice, 13,* 185–187.

Hays, P. A. (1987). *Modernization, stress, and psychopathology in Tunisian women.* Unpublished doctoral dissertation, University of Hawaii, Honolulu. (UMI No. 8722387)

Hays, P. A. (1995). Multicultural applications of cognitive behavior therapy. *Professional Psychology: Research and Practice, 26,* 309–315.

Hays, P. A. (1996a). Addressing the complexities of culture and gender in counseling. *Journal of Counseling and Development, 74,* 332–338.

Hays, P. A. (1996b). Cultural considerations in couples therapy. *Women and Therapy, 19,* 13–23.

Hays, P. A. (1996c). Culturally responsive assessment with diverse older clients. *Professional Psychology: Research and Practice, 27,* 188–193.

Hays, P. A. (2006a). Cognitive–behavioral therapy with Alaska Native people. In P. A. Hays & G. Y. Iwamasa (Eds.), *Culturally responsive cognitive–behavioral therapy: Assessment, practice, and supervision* (pp. 47–72). Washington, DC: American Psychological Association.

Hays, P. A. (2006b). Introduction: Developing culturally responsive cognitive–behavioral therapies. In P. A. Hays &G. Y. Iwamasa (Eds.), *Culturally responsive cognitive–behavioral therapy: Assessment, practice, and supervision* (pp. 3–20). Washington, DC: American Psychological Association.

Hays, P. A. (2007). Commentary: A strengths-based approach to psychotherapy with Middle Eastern people. In J. C. Muran (Ed.), *Dialogues on difference: Studies of diversity in the therapeutic relationship* (pp. 243–250). Washington, DC: American Psychological Association.

Hays, P. A., & Iwamasa, G. Y. (Eds.). (2006). *Culturally responsive cognitive–behavioral therapy: Assessment, practice, and supervision.* Washington, DC: American Psychological Association.

Hays, P. A., & Zouari, J. (1995). Stress, coping, and mental health among rural, village, and urban women in Tunisia. *International Journal of Psychology, 30,* 69–90.

Helms, J. E. (1995). An update of Helms's White and people of color racial identity models. In J. Ponterotto, J. M. Casas, L. A. Suzuki, & C. M. Alexander (Eds.), *Handbook of multicultural counseling* (pp. 181–198). Thousand Oaks, CA: Sage.

Herman, J. (1992). Complex PTSD: A syndrome in survivors of prolonged and repeated trauma. *Journal of Traumatic Stress, 5,* 377–391.

Herman, J. (1997). *Trauma and recovery.* New York: Basic Books.

Hernandez, M. (2005). Central American families. In M. McGoldrick, J. Giordano, & J. K. Pearce (Eds.), *Ethnicity and family therapy* (3rd ed., pp. 178–191). New York: Guilford Press.

Herring, R. (1999). *Counseling with Native American Indians and Alaskan Natives*. Thousand Oaks, CA: Sage.

Herrnstein, R. J., & Murray, C. (1994). *The bell curve*. New York: Free Press.

Hertzberg, J. F. (1990). Feminist psychotherapy and diversity: Treatment considerations from a self psychology perspective. In L. S. Brown & M. P. P. Root (Eds.), *Diversity and complexity in feminist therapy* (pp. 275–298). Binghamton, NY: Haworth Press.

Hill, C. E., & Lent, R.W. (2006). A narrative and meta-analytic review of helping skills training: Time to review a dormant area of inquiry. *Psychotherapy: Theory, Research, Practice, Training, 43*, 154–172.

Hinrichsen, G. A. (1991). Adjustment of caregivers to depressed older adults. *Psychology and Aging, 6*, 631–639.

Hinrichsen, G. A. (2006). Why multicultural issues matter for practitioners working with older adults. *Professional Psychology: Research and Practice, 37*, 29–35.

His Holiness the Dalai Lama. (2003). *A simple path: Basic Buddhist teachings by His Holiness the Dalai Lama*. New York: Thorsons/HarperCollins.

His Holiness the Dalai Lama, & Cutler, H. C. (1999). *The art of happiness: A handbook for living*. New York: Riverhead Books.

Hiscox, A. R., & Calish, A. C. (Eds.). (1998). *Tapestry of cultural issues in art therapy*. Philadelphia: Jessica Kingsley.

Ho, C. K. (1990). An analysis of domestic violence in Asian American communities: A multicultural approach to counseling. In L. S. Brown & M. P. P. Root (Eds.), *Diversity and complexity in feminist therapy* (pp. 129–150). Binghamton, NY: Haworth Press.

Ho, M. K. (1987). *Family therapy with ethnic minorities*. Newbury Park, CA: Sage.

Hogan, L. (1995). *Solar storms*. New York: Scribner.

Holiman, M., & Lauver, P. J. (1987). The counselor culture and client-centered practice. *Counselor Education and Supervision, 26*, 184–191.

Hong, G. K. (1988). A general family practitioner approach for Asian American mental health services. *Professional Psychology: Research and Practice, 19*, 600–605.

hooks, b. (1998). Feminism: A transformational politic. In P. S. Rothenberg (Ed.), *Race, class, and gender in the United States* (pp. 579–586). New York: St. Martin's Press.

Hopson, R. E. (1996). The 12-step program. In E. P. Shafranske (Ed.), *Religion and the clinical practice of psychology* (pp. 533–558). Washington, DC: American Psychological Association.

Hoshino, J. (2003). Multicultural art therapy with families. In C. Malchiodi (Ed.), *Clinical handbook of art therapy* (pp. 375–386). New York: Guilford Press.

Hoshmand, L. T. (Ed.). (2006). *Culture, psychotherapy, and counseling: Critical and integrative perspectives.* Thousand Oaks, CA: Sage.

Hulnick, M. R., & Hulnick, H. R. (1989). Life's challenges: Curse or opportunity? Counseling families of persons with disabilities. *Journal of Counseling and Development, 68,* 166–170.

Hwang, W. (2006). The psychotherapy adaptation and modification framework: Application to Asian Americans. *American Psychologist, 61,* 702–715.

International Policy Coordination, Citizenship and Immigration. (2004, March). *Remittances: A preliminary research.* Retrieved December 15, 2006, from http://www.rcmvs.org/investigacion/remittances_paper_april_5.doc

Irish, D. P., Lundquist, K. F., & Nelsen, V. J. (1993). *Ethnic variations in dying, death, and grief: Diversity in universality.* Washington, DC: Taylor & Francis.

Itai, G., & McRae, C. (1994). Counseling older Japanese American clients: An overview and observations. *Journal of Counseling and Development, 72,* 373–377.

Ivey, A. E., D'Andrea, M., Ivey, M. B., & Simek-Morgan, L. (2001). *Theories of counseling and psychotherapy: A multicultural perspective.* Needham Heights, MA: Allyn & Bacon.

Ivey, A. E., Ivey, M. B., & Simek-Morgan, L. (1993). *Counseling and psychotherapy: A multicultural perspective.* Needham Heights, MA: Simon & Shuster.

Iwamasa, G. Y., Hsia, C., & Hinton, D. (2006). Cognitive–behavioral therapy with Asian Americans. In P. A. Hays & G. Y. Iwamasa (Eds.), *Culturally responsive cognitive–behavioral therapy: Assessment, practice, and supervision* (pp. 117–140). Washington, DC: American Psychological Association.

Iwamasa, G. Y., Pai, S. M., & Sorocco, K. H. (2006). Multicultural cognitive–behavioral therapy supervision. In P. A. Hays & G. Y. Iwamasa (Eds.), *Culturally responsive cognitive–behavioral therapy: Assessment, practice, and supervision* (pp. 267–281). Washington, DC: American Psychological Association.

Jensen, J. P., & Bergin, A. E. (1988). Mental health values of professional therapists: A national interdisciplinary survey. *Professional Psychology: Research and Practice, 19,* 290–297.

Jewell, D. A. (1989). Cultural and ethnic issues. In S. Wetzler & M. M. Katz (Eds.), *Contemporary approaches to psychological assessment* (pp. 299–309). New York: Brunner/Mazel.

Jilek, W. G. (1994). Traditional healing in the prevention and treatment of alcohol and drug abuse. *Transcultural Psychiatric Research Review, 31,* 219–258.

Johnson-Powell, G. (1997). The culturologic interview: Cultural, social, and linguistic issues in the assessment and treatment of children. In G. Johnson-Powell & J. Yamamoto (Eds.), *Transcultural child development: Psychological assessment and treatment* (pp. 349–364). New York: Wiley.

Jones, E. (1974). Social class and psychotherapy: A critical review of research. *Psychiatry, 37,* 307–320.

Jones, E. E. (1987). Psychotherapy and counseling with Black clients. In P. Pedersen (Ed.), *Handbook of cross-cultural counseling and psychotherapy* (pp. 173–179). New York: Praeger.

Jones, R. L. (Ed.). (1996). *Handbook of tests and measurements for Black populations.* Hampton, VA: Cobb & Henry.

Judd, T. (2005). Cross-cultural forensic neuropsychological assessment. In K. Barrett & W. George (Eds.), *Race, culture, psychology, and law* (pp. 141–162). Thousand Oaks, CA: Sage.

Kabat-Zinn, J. (2005). *Wherever you go, there you are: Mindfulness meditation in everyday life.* New York: Hyperion.

Kahn, R. L., Goldfarb, A., Pollack, M., & Peck, A. (1960). Brief objective measures for the determination of mental status in the aged. *American Journal of Psychiatry, 117,* 326–328.

Kail, R. V., & Cavanaugh, J. C. (2000). *Human development: A lifespan view.* Belmont, CA: Wadsworth.

Kantrowitz, R. E., & Ballou, M. (1992). A feminist critique of cognitive–behavioral therapy. In L. S. Brown & M. Ballou (Eds.), *Personality and psychopathology: Feminist appraisals* (pp. 70–87). New York: Guilford Press.

Kaplan, M. (1983). A woman's view of the *DSM–III. American Psychologist, 38,* 786–792.

Karlsson, R. (2005). Ethnic matching between therapist and patient in psychotherapy: An overview of findings, together with methodological and conceptual issues. *Cultural Diver-sity and Ethnic Minority Psychology, 11,* 113–129.

Kaslow, F. (1993). Relational diagnosis: An idea whose time has come? *Family Process, 32,* 255–259.

Kathuria, R., & Serpell, R. (1998). Standardization of the Panga Munthu test—A nonverbal cognitive test developed in Zambia. *Journal of Negro Education, 67,* 228–241.

Kaufert, J. M., & Shapiro, E. (1996). Cultural, linguistic and contextual factors in validating the Mental Status Questionnaire: The experience of Aboriginal elders in Manitoba. *Transcultural Psychiatric Research Review, 33,* 277–296.

Kearney, L. K., Draper, M., & Barón, A. (2005). Counseling utilization by ethnic minority college students. *Cultural Diversity and Ethnic Minority Psychology, 11,* 272–285.

Kelland, D. Z, Lewis, R., & Gurevitch, D. (1992). Evaluation of the Repeatable Cognitive–Perceptual–Motor Battery: Reliability, validity and sensitivity to diazepam [Abstract]. *Journal of Clinical and Experimental Neuropsychology, 14,* 65.

Kelly, E. W., Jr. (1995). *Spirituality and religion in counseling and psychotherapy.* Alexandria, VA: American Counseling Association.

Kelly, S. (2006). Cognitive–behavioral therapy with African Americans. In P. A. Hays & G. Y. Iwamasa (Eds.), *Culturally responsive cognitive–behavioral therapy: Assessment, practice, and supervision* (pp. 97–116). Washington, DC: American Psychological Association.

Kemp, N. T., & Mallinckrodt, B. (1996). Impact of professional training on case conceptualization of clients with a disability. *Professional Psychology: Research and Practice, 27,* 378–385.

Kertesz, R. (2002). Dual relationships in psychotherapy in Latin America. In A. A. Lazarus & O. Zur (Eds.), *Dual relationships and psychotherapy* (pp. 329–334). New York: Springer Publishing Company.

Kessler, L. E., & Waehler, C. A. (2005). Addressing multiple relationships between clients and therapists in lesbian, gay, bisexual, and transgender communities. *Professional Psychology: Research and Practice, 36,* 66–72.

Kim, B. L. C. (1996). Korean families. In M. McGoldrick, J. Giordano, & J. K. Pearce (Eds.), *Ethnicity and family therapy* (2nd ed., pp. 281–294). New York: Guilford Press.

Kim, B. L. C. (1998). Marriages of Asian women and American military men. In M. McGoldrick (Ed.), *Re-visioning family therapy* (pp. 309–319). New York: Guilford Press.

Kim, B. S. K. (1996). The Korean Americans. In P. B. Pedersen & D. C. Locke (Eds.), *Cultural and diversity issues in counseling* (pp. 47–50). Greensboro: School of Education, University of North Carolina at Greensboro. (ERIC Document Reproduction Service No. ED400486)

Kim, B. S. K., Ng, G. F., & Ahn, A. J. (2005). Effects of client expectation for counseling success, client–counselor worldview match, and client adherence to Asian and European-American cultural values on counseling process with Asian Americans. *Journal of Counseling and Psychology, 52,* 67–76.

Kim, S. C. (1985). Family therapy for Asian Americans: A strategic structural framework. *Psychotherapy, 22,* 342–348.

Kim, W. J., Kim, L. I., & Rue, D. S. (1997). Korean American children. In G. Johnson-Powell & J. Yamamoto (Eds.), *Transcultural child development: Psychological assessment and treatment* (pp. 182–207). New York: Wiley.

Kim-Ju, G. M., & Liem, R. (2003). Ethnic self-awareness as a function of ethnic group status, group composition, and ethnic identity orientation. *Cultural Diversity and Ethnic Minority Psychology, 9,* 289–302.

Kimmel, M. S., & Messner, M. (Eds.). (1992). *Men's lives.* New York: Macmillan.

Kinzie, J. D., Manson, S. M., Vinh, D. T., Tolan, N. T., Anh, B., & Pho, T. N. (1982). Development and validation of a Vietnamese-language depression rating scale. *American Journal of Psychiatry, 139,* 1276–1281.

Kirmayer, L. J. (1998). Editorial: The fate of culture and *DSM–IV. Transcultural Psychiatry, 35,* 339–342.

Kiselica, M. S. (1998). Preparing Anglos for the challenges and joys of multiculturalism. *Counseling Psychologist, 26,* 5–21.

Kivel, P. (2002). *Uprooting racism.* Gabriola Island, British Columbia, Canada: New Society Publishers.

Kleinman, A. M. (1980). *Patients and healers in the context of culture.* Berkeley: University of California Press.

Kluckhohn, F., & Strodtbeck, F. (1961). *Variations in value orientations.* Evanston, IL: Row, Peterson.

Knight, B. G. (2004). *Psychotherapy with older adults.* Thousand Oaks, CA: Sage.

Koss, J. (1980). The therapist–spiritist training project in Puerto Rico: An experiment to relate the traditional healing system to the public health system. *Social Science and Medicine, 14B,* 255–266.

Kubiszyn, T. W., Meyer, G., J., Finn, S. E., Eyde, L. D., Kay, G. G., Moreland, K. L., et al. (2000). Empirical support for psychological assessment in clinical health care settings. *Professional Psychology: Research and Practice, 31,* 119–130.

LaFromboise, T. D., Berman, J. S., & Sohi, B. K. (1994). American Indian women. In L. Comas-Díaz & B. Greene (Eds.), *Women of color: Integrating ethnic and gender identities in psychotherapy* (pp. 30–71). New York: Guilford Press.

LaFromboise, T. D., & Rowe, W. (1983). Skills training for bicultural competence: Rationale and application. *Journal of Counseling Psychology, 30,* 589–595.

Lai, M. C., & Yue, K. M. K. (1990). The Chinese. In N. Waxler-Morrison, J. M. Anderson, & E. Richardson (Eds.), *Cross-cultural caring: A handbook for health professionals in Western Canada* (pp. 68–90). Vancouver, British Columbia, Canada: University of British Columbia Press.

Lamberty, G. J. (2002). Traditions and trends in neuropsychological assessment. In F. R. Ferraro (Ed.), *Minority and cross-cultural aspects of neuropsychological assessment* (pp. 3–16). Exton, PA: Swets & Zeitlinger.

Lazarus, A. A., & Beutler, L. E. (1993). On technical eclecticism. *Journal of Counseling and Development, 71,* 381–385.

Lazarus, A. A., & Zur, O. (Eds.). (2002). *Dual relationships and psychotherapy.* New York: Springer Publishing Company.

Lee, E. (Ed.). (1997). *Working with Asian Americans: A guide for clinicians.* New York: Guilford Press.

Leigh, I. W. (2003). Deaf: Moving from hearing loss to diversity. In J. S. Mio & G. Y. Iwamasa (Eds.), *Culturally diverse mental health* (pp. 323–339). New York: Brunner-Routledge.

Leigh, I. W., Corbett, C. A., Gutman, V., & Morere, D. A. (1996). Providing psychological services to deaf individuals: A response to new perceptions of diversity. *Professional Psychology: Research and Practice, 27,* 364–371.

Lemma, A. (2000). *Humour on the couch.* Philadelphia: Whurr.

Lewis, J. A., Dana, R. Q., & Blevins, G. A. (1994). *Substance abuse counseling: An individualized approach.* Pacific Grove, CA: Brooks/Cole.

Lewis, M. I., & Butler, R. N. (1974). Life review therapy: Putting memories to work in individual and group psychotherapy. *Geriatrics, 29,* 165–169.

Lewis-Fernández, R. (1996). Cultural formulation of psychiatric diagnosis. *Culture, Medicine and Psychiatry, 20,* 133–144.

Lezak, M. (1995). *Neuropsychological assessment.* New York: Oxford University Press.

Lindsey, M. L. (1998). Culturally competent assessment of African American clients. *Journal of Personality Assessment, 70,* 43–53.

Locke, D. C., & Kiselica, M. S. (1999). Pedagogy of possibilities: Teaching about racism in multicultural counseling courses. *Journal of Counseling and Development, 77,* 80–86.

López, S. R., Grover, K. P., Holland, D., Johnson, M. J., Kain, C. D., Kanel, K., et al. (1989). Development of culturally sensitive psychotherapists. *Professional Psychology: Research and Practice, 20,* 369–376.

Lopez, S. J., & Snyder, C. R. (2003). *Positive psychological assessment: A handbook of models and measures.* Washington, DC: American Psychological Association.

Lott, B. (2002). Cognitive and behavioral distancing from the poor. *American Psychologist, 57,* 100–110.

Lott, B., & Bullock, H. E. (2001). Where are the poor? *Journal of Social Issues, 57,* 189–206.

Lovinger, R. (1996). Considering the religious dimension in assessment and treatment. In E. P. Shafranske (Ed.), *Religion and the clinical practice of psychology* (pp. 327–364). Washington, DC: American Psychological Association.

Maguen, S., Shipherd, J. C., & Harris, H. N. (2005). Providing culturally sensitive care for transgender patients. *Cognitive and Behavioral Practice, 12,* 479–490.

Magyar-Moe, J. L., Pedrotti, J. T., Edwards, L. M., Ford, A. I., Peterson, S. E., Rasmussen, H. N., et al. (2005). Perceptions of multicultural training in predoctoral internship programs: A survey of interns and training directors. *Professional Psychology: Research and Practice, 36,* 446–450.

Mahrer, A. R., & Gervaise, P. A. (1994). What strong laughter in psychotherapy is and how it works. In H. Strean (Ed.), *The use of humor in psychotherapy* (pp. 209–222). Northvale, NJ: Aronson.

Maj, M., D'Elia, L. D., Satz, P., Janssen, R., Zaudig, M., & Uchiyama, C. (1993). Evaluation of two new neuropsychological tests designed to minimize cultural bias in the assessment of HIV-1 seropositive persons: A WHO study. *Archives of Clinical Neuropsychology, 8,* 123–135.

Maki, D. R., & Riggar, T. F. (Eds.). (1997a). *Rehabilitation counseling.* New York: Springer Publishing Company.

Maki, D. R., & Riggar, T. F. (1997b). Rehabilitation counseling: Concepts and paradigms. In D. R. Maki & T. F. Riggar (Eds.), *Rehabilitation counseling* (pp. 3–31). New York: Springer Publishing Company.

Malchiodi, C. A. (Ed.). (2005). *Expressive therapies.* New York: Guilford Press.

Manson, S., & Kleinman, A. (1998). *DSM–IV,* culture and mood disorders: A critical reflection on recent practice. *Transcultural Psychiatry, 35,* 377–386.

Mapes, L. V. (1998, August 2). Fruit pickers' summer of squalor: Migrant workers in Washington. *Seattle Times,* pp. Al, A14, A15.

Maracle, B. (1994). *Crazywater: Native voices on addiction and recovery.* Toronto, Ontario, Canada: Penguin.

Maramba, G. G., & Nagayama Hall, G., (2002). Meta-analyses of ethnic match as a predictor of dropout, utilization, and level of functioning. *Cultural Diversity and Ethnic Minority Psychology, 8,* 292–297.

Marsella, A. J., & Kaplan, A. (2002). Cultural considerations for understanding, assessing, and treating depressive experience and disorder. In M. Reinecke & M. Davison (Eds.), *Comparative treatments of depression* (pp. 47–78). New York: Springer Publishing Company.

Marsella, A. J., & Yamada, A. M. (2000). Culture and mental health: An introduction and overview of foundations, concepts, and issues. In I. Cuéllar & F. Paniagua (Eds.), *The handbook of multicultural mental health: Assessment and treatment of diverse populations* (pp. 3–24). New York: Academic Press.

Martell, C. R., Safren, S. A., & Prince, S. E. (2004). *Cognitive–behavioral therapies with lesbian, gay, and bisexual clients.* New York: Guilford Press.

Martin, A. (1982). Some issues in the treatment of gay and lesbian patients. *Psychotherapy Theory, Research, and Practice, 19,* 341–348.

Martínez, E. A. (1999). Mexican American/Chicano families. In H. P. McAdoo (Ed.), *Family ethnicity* (pp. 121–134). Thousand Oaks, CA: Sage.

Mast, B. T., Fitzgerald, J., Steinberg, J., MacNeill, S. E., & Lichtenberg, P. A. (2001). Effective screening for Alzheimer's disease among older African-Americans. *Clinical Neuropsychologist, 15,* 196–202.

Matheson, L. (1986). If you are not an Indian, how do you treat an Indian? In H. P. Lefley & P. Pedersen (Eds.), *Cross-cultural training for mental health professionals* (pp. 115–130). Springfield, IL: Charles C Thomas.

Matsui, W. T. (1996). Japanese families. In M. McGoldrick, J. Giordano, & J. K. Pearce (Eds.), *Ethnicity and family therapy* (2nd ed., pp. 268–280). New York: Guilford Press.

Matthews, C. R., & Lease, S. H. (2000). Focus on lesbian, gay, and bisexual families. In R. M. Perez, K. A. DeBord, & K. J. Bieschke (Eds.), *Handbook of counseling and psychotherapy with lesbian, gay, and bisexual clients* (pp. 249–274). Washington, DC: American Psychological Association.

Mays, V., Rubin, J., Sabourin, M., & Walker, L. (1996). Moving toward a global psychology: Changing theories and practice to meet the needs of a changing world. *American Psychologist, 51,* 485–487.

McAdoo, H. P. (1978). Factors related to stability in upwardly mobile Black families. *Journal of Marriage and the Family, 40,* 761–776.

McCarn, S. R., & Fassinger, R. E. (1996). Revising sexual minority identity formation: A new model of lesbian identity and its implications for counseling and research. *Counseling Psychologist, 24,* 508–534.

McClanahan, A. J. (1986). *Our stories, our lives.* Anchorage, AK: Cook Inlet Region.

McGoldrick, M. (1998). Introduction. In M. McGoldrick (Ed.), *Re-visioning family therapy: Race, culture, and gender in clinical practice* (pp. 3–19). New York: Guilford Press.

McGoldrick, M., & Gerson, R. (1985). *Genograms in family assessment.* New York: Norton.

McGoldrick, M., Giordano, J., & Garcia-Preto, N. (Eds.). (2005). *Ethnicity and family therapy* (3rd ed.). New York: Guilford Press.

McIntosh, P. (1998). White privilege and male privilege: A personal account of coming to see correspondence through work in women's studies. In M. L. Anderson & P. H. Collins (Eds.), *Race, class and gender: An anthology* (pp. 94–105). New York: Wadsworth.

Menos, J. (2005). Haitian families. In M. McGoldrick, J. Giordano, & N. Garcia-Preto (Eds.), *Ethnicity and family therapy* (3rd ed., pp. 127–137). New York: Guilford Press.

Merriam-Webster. (1983). *Webster's ninth new collegiate dictionary.* Springfield, MA: Author.

Meyer, G. J., & Archer, R. P. (2001). The hard science of Rorschach research: What do we know and where do we go? *Psychological Assessment, 13,* 486–502.

Meyers, L. (2006, June). Psychologists and psychotropic medication. *Monitor on Psychology, 37,* 46–47.

Miller, W. R. (Ed.). (1999). *Integrating spirituality into treatment: Resources for practitioners.* Washington, DC: American Psychological Association.

Minton, B. A., & Soule, S. (1990). Two Eskimo villages assess mental health strengths and needs. *American Indian and Alaska Native Mental Health Research, 4,* 7–24.

Minuchin, P., Colapinto, J., & Minuchin, S. (2007). *Working with families of the poor.* New York: Guilford Press.

Minuchin, S. (1974). *Family and family therapy.* Cambridge, MA: Harvard University Press.

Mio, J. (1989). Experiential involvement as an adjunct to teaching cultural sensitivity. *Journal of Multicultural Counseling and Development, 17,* 38–47.

Mistry, R. (2001). *A fine balance.* New York: Vintage Books.

Moghaddam, F. M. (1990). Modulative and generative orientations in psychology: Implications for psychology in the three worlds. *Journal of Social Issues, 46,* 21–41.

Mona, L. R., Romesser-Scehnet, J. M., Cameron, R. P., & Cardenas, V. (2006). Cognitive–behavioral therapy and people with disabilities. In P. A. Hays & G. Y. Iwamasa (Eds.), *Culturally responsive cognitive–behavioral therapy: Assessment, practice, and supervision* (pp. 199–222). Washington, DC: American Psychological Association.

Moore Hines, P., & Boyd-Franklin, N. (1996). African American families. In M. McGoldrick, J. Giordano, & J. K. Pearce (Eds.), *Ethnicity and family therapy* (2nd ed., pp. 66–84). New York: Guilford Press.

Morales, P. (1999). The impact of cultural differences in psychotherapy with older clients: Sensitive issues and strategies. In M. Duffy (Ed.), *Handbook of counseling and psychotherapy with older adults* (pp. 132–153). New York: Wiley.

Morris, E. (2000). Assessment practices with African Americans: Combining standard assessment measures within an Africentric orientation. In R. H. Dana (Ed.), *Handbook of cross-cultural and multicultural personality assessment* (pp. 573–604). Mahwah, NJ: Erlbaum.

Morrow, S. (2000). First do no harm: Therapists issues in psychotherapy with lesbian, gay, and bisexual clients. In R. M. Perez, K. A. DeBord, & K. J. Bieschke (Eds.), *Handbook of counseling and psychotherapy with lesbian, gay, and bisexual clients* (pp. 137–156). Washington, DC: American Psychological Association

Muecke, M. (1983a). Caring for Southeast Asian refugee patients in the USA. *American Journal of Public Health, 73,* 431–437.

Muecke, M. (1983b). In search of healers—Southeast Asian refugees in the American health care system. *Western Journal of Medicine: Cross-Cultural Medicine, 139,* 835–840.

Mungas, D., Reed, B. R., Haan, M. N., & González, H. (2005). Spanish and English neuropsychological assessment scales: Relationship to demographics, language, cognition, and independent function. *Neuropsychology, 19,* 466–475.

Muran, C. (2007). *Dialogues on difference: Studies of diversity in the therapeutic relationship.* Washington, DC: American Psychological Association.

Murgatroyd, W. (1996). Counseling Buddhist clients. In P. B. Pedersen & C. Locke (Eds.), *Cultural and diversity issues in counseling* (pp. 69–72). Greensboro: School of Education, University of North Carolina at Greensboro. (ERIC Document Reproduction Service No. ED400486)

Murray, H. A. (1943). *The Thematic Apperception Test.* Cambridge, MA: Harvard University Press.

Nabors, N. A., Evans, J. D., & Strickland, T. L. (2000). Neuropsychological assessment and intervention with African Americans. In E. Fletcher-Janzen, T. L. Strickland, & C. R. Reynolds (Eds.), *Handbook of cross-cultural neuropsychology* (pp. 31–42). New York: Kluwer Academic/Plenum Publishers.

Nagayama Hall, G. C. (2001). Psychotherapy research with ethnic minorities: Empirical, ethical, and conceptual issues. *Journal of Consulting and Clinical Psychology, 69,* 502–510.

Nagayama Hall, G. C., Bansal, A., & Lopez, I. R. (1999). Ethnicity and psychopathology: A meta-analytic review of 31 years of comparative MMPI/MMPI–2 research. *Psychological Assessment, 11,* 186–197.

National Association of Social Workers. (2001). *Standards for cultural competence in social work practice.* Retrieved March 18, 2005, from http://www.social workers.org/pressroom/2001/090601.asp

National Institute of Health Consensus Development Panel on Depression in Late Life. (1992). Diagnosis and treatment of depression in late life. *Journal of the American Medical Association, 268,* 1018–1024.

Newman, B. M., & Newman, P. R. (1999). *Development through life: A psychosocial approach.* Belmont, CA: Wadsworth.

Newton, N. A., & Jacobowitz, J. (1999). Transferential and counter-transferential processes in therapy with older adults. In M. Duffy (Ed.), *Handbook of counseling and psychotherapy with older adults* (pp. 21–40). New York: Wiley.

Nichols, D. S., Padilla, J., & Gomez-Maqueo, E. L. (2000). Issues in the cross-cultural adaptation and use of the MMPI–2. In R. H. Dana (Ed.), *Handbook of cross-cultural and multicultural personality assessment* (pp. 247–266). Mahwah, NJ: Erlbaum.

Nicolas, G., DeSilva, A. M., Grey, K. S., & Gonzales-Eastep, D. (2006). Using a multicultural lens to understand illness among Haitians living in America. *Professional Psychology: Research and Practice, 37,* 702–707.

Nicolas, G., & JeanBaptiste, V. (2001). Experiences of women on public assistance. *Journal of Social Issues, 57,* 299–309.

Norcross, J. C., Hedges, M., & Prochaska, J. O. (2002). The face of 2010: A Delphi poll on the future of psychotherapy. *Professional Psychology: Research and Practice, 33,* 316–322.

Norcross, J. C., Kohout, J. L., & Wicherski, M. (2005). Graduate study in psychology: 1971 to 2004. *American Psychologist, 60,* 959–975.

Nordhus, I. H., VandenBos, G. R., Berg, S., & Fromholt, P. (1998). *Clinical geropsychology.* Washington, DC: American Psychological Association.

Norris, F. H., & Alegría, M. (2006). Promoting disaster recovery in ethnic-minority individuals and communities. In E. C. Ritchie, P. J. Watson, & M. J. Friedman (Eds.), *Interventions following mass violence and disasters* (pp. 319–342). New York: Guilford Press.

Novas, H. (1994). *Everything you need to know about Latino history.* New York: Plume/Penguin.

O'Connor, K. (2005). Addressing diversity issues in play therapy. *Professional Psychology: Research and Practice, 36,* 566–573.

Okazaki, S., & Tanaka-Matsumi, J. (2006). Cultural considerations in cognitive–behavioral assessment. In P. A. Hays & G. Y. Iwamasa (Eds.), *Culturally responsive cognitive–behavioral therapy: Assessment, practice, and supervision* (pp. 247–266). Washington, DC: American Psychological Association.

Olkin, R. (1999). *What psychotherapists should know about disability.* New York: Guilford Press.

Olkin, R. (2002). Could you hold the door for me? Including disability in diversity. *Cultural Diversity and Ethnic Minority Psychology, 8,* 130–137.

Organista, K. C. (2006). Cognitive–behavioral therapy with Latinos and Latinas. In P. A. Hays & G. Y. Iwamasa (Eds.), *Culturally responsive cognitive–behavioral therapy: Assessment, practice, and supervision* (pp. 73–96). Washington, DC: American Psychological Association.

Organista, K. C. (2007). Commentary: The need to explicate culturally competent approaches with Latino clients. In C. Muran (Ed.), *Dialogues on difference: Studies of diversity in the therapeutic relationship* (pp. 168–175). Washington, DC: American Psychological Association.

Pace, T. M., Robbins, R. R., Choney, S. K., Hill, J. S., Lacey, K., & Blair, G. (2006). A cultural-contextual perspective on the validity of the MMPI–2 with American Indians. *Cultural Diversity and Ethnic Minority Psychology, 12,* 320–333.

Packard, E. (2007, January). A new tool for psychotherapists. *Monitor on Psychology, 38,* 30–31.

Paniagua, F. A. (1998). *Assessing and treating culturally diverse clients* (2nd ed.). Thousand Oaks, CA: Sage.

Paniagua, F. A. (2005). *Assessing and treating culturally diverse clients* (3rd ed.). Thousand Oaks, CA: Sage.

Paradis, C. M., Cukor, D., & Friedman, S. (2006). Cognitive–behavioral therapy with Orthodox Jews. In P. A. Hays & G. Y. Iwamasa (Eds.), *Culturally responsive cognitive–behavioral therapy: Assessment, practice, and supervision* (pp. 161–176). Washington, DC: American Psychological Association.

Pauwels, A. (1995). *Cross-cultural communication in the health sciences: Communicating with migrant patients.* Melbourne, Australia: Macmillan Education Australia.

Payne, R. K. (2003). *A framework for understanding poverty* (3rd ed.). Highlands, TX: aha! Process, Inc.

Pedersen, P. (1987). Ten frequent assumptions of cultural bias in counseling. *Journal of Multicultural Counseling and Development, 15,* 16–24.

Pedersen, P. B., Draguns, J. G., Lonner, W. J., & Trimble, J. E. (Eds.). (2002). *Counseling across cultures.* Thousand Oaks, CA: Sage.

Pedersen, P. B., Fukuyama, M., & Heath, A. (1989). Client, counselor, and contextual variables in multicultural counseling. In P. B. Pedersen, J. G. Draguns, W. J. Lonner, & J. E. Trimble (Eds.), *Counseling across cultures* (pp. 23–52). Honolulu: University of Hawaii Press.

Perez, R. M., DeBord, K. A., & Bieschke, K. J. (2000). *Handbook of counseling and psychotherapy with lesbian, gay, and bisexual clients.* Washington, DC: American Psychological Association.

Pérez-Arce, P., & Puente, A. E. (1996). Neuropsychological assessment of ethnic minorities: The case of Hispanics living in North America. In R. J. Sbordone & C. J. Long (Eds.), *The ecological validity of neuropsychological testing* (pp. 283–300). Delray Beach, FL: GR Press/St. Lucie Press.

Pérez Foster, R. (1996). What is the multicultural perspective for psychoanalysis? In R. Pérez Foster, M. Moskowitz, & R. A. Javier (Eds.), *Reaching across boundaries of culture and class: Widening the scope of psychotherapy* (pp. 3–20). Northvale, NJ: Aronson.

Phinney, J. S. (1996). When we talk about American ethnic groups, what do we mean? *American Psychologist, 51,* 918–927.

Piercy, F., Soekandar, A., & Limansubroto, C. D. M. (1996). Indonesian families. In M. McGoldrick, J. Giordano, & J. K. Pearce (Eds.), *Ethnicity and family therapy* (2nd ed., pp. 333–346). New York: Guilford Press.

Pires, A. A. (2000). National norms for the Rorschach normative study in Portugal. In R. H. Dana (Ed.), *Handbook of cross-cultural and multicultural personality assessment* (pp. 366–392). Mahwah, NJ: Erlbaum.

Pollard, R. Q., Jr. (1996). Professional psychology and deaf people. *American Psychologist, 51,* 389–396.

Poortinga, Y. H., & Van de Vijver, F. J. R. (2004). Cultures and cognition: Performance differences and invariant structures. In R. J. Sternberg & E. L. Grigorenko (Eds.), *Culture and competence: Contexts of life success* (pp. 139–162). Washington, DC: American Psychological Association.

Pope, M. (1995). The "salad bowl" is big enough for us all: An argument for the inclusion of lesbians and gay men in any definition of multiculturalism. *Journal of Counseling and Development, 73*, 301–304.

Prochaska, J. O., & Norcross, J. C. (1994). *Systems of psychotherapy: A transtheoretical analysis*. Pacific Grove, CA: Brooks/Cole.

Pukui, M. K., Haertig, E. W., & Lee, C. A. (1972). *Nana I Ke Kumu* [*Look to the source*] (Vol. 1). Honolulu, HI: Queen Lili'uokalani Children's Center.

Puryear Keita, G. (2006, September). The many faces and foci of PI. *Monitor on Psychology, 37*, 27.

Quiñones, M. E. (2007). Reply: Are we bridging the gap yet? A work in progress. In J. C. Muran (Ed.), *Dialogues on difference: Studies of diversity in the therapeutic relationship* (pp. 181–184). Washington, DC: American Psychological Association.

Rao, K. R. (1988). Psychology of transcendence: A study in early Buddhistic psychology. In A. C. Paranjpe, D. Y. F. Ho, & R. W. Rieber (Eds.), *Asian contributions to psychology* (pp. 123–148). New York: Praeger.

Rastogi, M., & Wampler, K. S. (1998). Couples and family therapy with Indian families: Some structural and intergenerational considerations. In U. P. Gielen & A. L. Comunian (Eds.), *The family and family therapy in international perspective* (pp. 257–274). Milan, Italy: Edizioni Lint Trieste.

Raven, J. C. (1960). *Guide to the Standard Progressive Matrices*. London: H. K. Lewis.

Reid, P. T. (2002). Multicultural psychology: Bringing together gender and ethnicity. *Cultural Diversity and Ethnic Minority Psychology, 8*, 103–114.

Rennick, P. (1996). *Native cultures in Alaska*. Anchorage, AK: Alaska Geographic Society.

Reynolds, D. K. (1980). *The quiet therapies: Japanese pathways to personal growth*. Honolulu: University of Hawaii Press.

Rezentes, W. C., III. (1996). *Ka Lama Kukui Hawaiian psychology: An introduction*. Honolulu, HI: 'A'ali'i Books.

Richards, P. S., & Bergin, A. E. (2005). *A spiritual strategy for counseling and psychotherapy* (2nd ed.). Washington, DC: American Psychological Association.

Richmond, J. (1999). Psychotherapy with the suicidal elderly: A family-oriented approach. In M. Duffy (Ed.), *Handbook of counseling and psychotherapy with older adults* (pp. 650–661). New York: Wiley.

Ridley, C. R., Liddle, M. C., Hill, C. L., & Li, L. C. (2001). Ethical decision-making in multicultural counseling. In J. G. Ponterotto, J. M.

Casas, L. A. Suzuki, & C. M. Alexander (Eds.), *Handbook of multicultural counseling* (2nd ed., pp. 165–188). Thousand Oaks, CA: Sage.

Robinson, T. L. (1999). The intersections of dominant discourses across race, gender, and other identities. *Journal of Counseling and Development, 77,* 73–79.

Robinson, T. L., & Howard-Hamilton, M. F. (2000). *The convergence of race, ethnicity, and gender: Multiple identities in counseling.* Columbus, OH: Merrill/Prentice-Hall.

Rogler, L. H. (1999). Methodological sources of cultural insensitivity in mental health research. *American Psychologist, 54,* 424–433.

Rogler, L. H. (2002). Historical generations and psychology: The case of the Great Depression and World War II. *American Psychologist, 57,* 1013–1023.

Roopnarine, J., Johnson, J., & Hooper, F. (Eds.). (1994). *Children's play in diverse cultures.* Albany, NY: SUNY Press.

Root, M. P. P. (1992). Reconstructing the impact of trauma on personality. In L. S. Brown & M. Ballou (Eds.), *Personality and psychopathology: Feminist reappraisals* (pp. 229–265). New York: Guilford Press.

Root, M. P. P. (1996). The multiracial experience: Racial borders as a significant frontier in race relations. In M. P. P. Root (Ed.), *The multiracial experience: Racial borders as the new frontier* (pp. xiii–xxviii). Thousand Oaks, CA: Sage.

Rosenfelt, S., Estes, L. (Producers), & Eyre, C. (Director). (1998). *Smoke signals* [Motion picture]. United States: Miramax.

Rosenweig, M. R. (1999). Continuity and change in the development of psychology around the world. *American Psychologist, 54,* 252–259.

Royce-Davis, J. (2000). The influence of spirituality on community participation and belonging: Christina's story. *Counseling and Values, 44,* 135–142.

Roysircar, G. (2004a). Cultural self-awareness assessment: Practice examples from psychology training. *Professional Psychology: Research and Practice, 35,* 658–666.

Roysircar, G. (2004b). Counseling and psychotherapy for acculturation and ethnic identity concerns with immigrant and international student clients. In T. Smith (Ed.), *Practicing multiculturalism: Affirming diversity in counseling and psychology* (pp. 255–275). Boston: Pearson Education.

Roysircar, G., Arredondo, P., Fuertes, J. N., Ponterotto, J. D., & Toporek, R. L. (2003). *Multicultural counseling competencies.* Alexandria, VA: Association of Multicultural Counseling and Development/American Counseling Association.

Roysircar, G., Sandhu, D. S., & Bibbins, V. (2003). *Multicultural competencies: A guidebook of practices.* Alexandria, VA: American Counseling Association.

Rumbaut, R. G. (1985). Mental health and the refugee experience: A comparative study of Southeast Asian refugees. In T. C. Owan (Ed.), *Southeast Asian mental health: Treatment, prevention, services, training, and research* (pp. 433–486). Rockville, MD: National Institute of Mental Health.

Samuda, R. J. (1998). *Psychological testing of American minorities: Issues and consequences.* Thousand Oaks, CA: Sage.

Samuel, D. B., & Widiger, T. A. (2006). Clinicians' judgments of clinical utility: A comparison of the *DSM–IV* and five-factor models. *Journal of Abnormal Psychology, 115,* 298–308.

Sanders, K., Brockway, J. A., Ellis, B., Cotton, E. M., & Bredin, J. (1999). Enhancing mental health climates in hospitals and nursing homes: Collaboration strategies for medical and mental health staff. In M. Duffy (Ed.), *Handbook of counseling and psychotherapy with older adults* (pp. 335–349). New York: Wiley.

Sang, B. E. (1992). Counseling and psychotherapy with midlife and older lesbians. In S. H. Dworkin & F. J. Gutiérrez (Eds.), *Counseling gay men and lesbians: Journey to the end of the rainbow* (pp. 35–48). Alexandria, VA: American Counseling Association.

Santiago-Rivera, A., & Altarriba, J. (2002). The role of language in therapy with the Spanish–English bilingual client. *Professional Psychology: Research and Practice, 33,* 30–38.

Santiago-Rivera, A., Arredondo, P., & Gallardo-Cooper, M. (2002). *Counseling Latinos and* la familia*: A guide for practitioners.* Thousand Oaks, CA: Sage.

Scarbrough, J. W. (2001). Welfare mothers' reflections on personal responsibility. *Journal of Social Issues, 57,* 261–276.

Schank, J. A., & Skovholt, T. M. (1997). Dual-relationship dilemmas of rural and small-community psychologists. *Professional Psychology: Research and Practice, 28,* 44–49.

Schank, J. A., & Skovholt, T. M. (2006). *Ethical practice in small communities: Challenges and rewards for psychologists.* Washington, DC: American Psychological Association.

Schoonmaker, C. (1993). Aging lesbians: Bearing the burden of triple shame. *Women and Therapy, 14,* 21–31.

Serpell, R., & Haynes, B. P. (2004). The cultural practice of intelligence testing: Problems of international export. In R. J. Sternberg & E. L. Grigorenko (Eds.), *Culture and competence: Contexts of life success* (pp. 163–186). Washington, DC: American Psychological Association.

Shapiro, E. R. (1995). Grief in family and cultural context: Learning from Latino families. *Cultural Diversity and Mental Health, 1,* 159–176.

Sherman, W. J., Stroessner, S. J., Conrey, F. R., & Azam, O. A. (2005). Prejudice and stereotype maintenance processes: Attention, attribution, and individuation. *Journal of Personality and Social Psychology, 89,* 607–622.

Shweder, R. A., & Bourne, E. J. (1989). Does the concept of the person vary cross-culturally? In A. J. Marsella & G. M. White (Eds.), *Cultural conceptions of mental health and therapy* (pp. 97–140). Dordrecht, Holland: D. Reidel.

Sims, J. M. (1996). The use of voice for assessment and intervention in couples therapy. *Women and Therapy, 19,* 61–77.

Smedley, A., & Smedley, B. D. (2005). Race as biology is fiction, racism as a social problem is real. *American Psychologist, 60,* 16–26.

Smith, A. (1997). Cultural diversity and the coming-out process. In B. Greene (Ed.), *Ethnic and cultural diversity among lesbian and gay men* (pp. 279–300). Thousand Oaks, CA: Sage.

Smith, D. S. (1995). Exploring the religious–spiritual needs of the dying. In M. T. Burke & J. G. Miranti (Eds.), *Counseling: The spiritual dimension* (pp. 177–182). Alexandria, VA: American Counseling Association.

Smith, H. (1991). *The world's religions.* New York: HarperCollins.

Smith, L. (2005). Psychotherapy, classism, and the poor: Conspicuous by their absence. *American Psychologist, 60,* 687–696.

Smith, P. B., & Bond, M. H. (1999). *Social psychology across cultures.* Needham Heights, MA: Allyn & Bacon.

Snowden, L. R., Masland, M., & Guerrero, R. (2007). Federal civil rights policy and mental health treatment access for persons with limited English proficiency. *American Psychologist, 62,* 109–117.

Sotnik, P., & Jezewski, M. A. (2005). In J. H. Stone (Ed.), *Culture and disability: Providing culturally competent services* (pp. 15–36). Thousand Oaks, CA: Sage.

Sperry, L., & Shafranske, E. P. (Eds.). (2005). *Spiritually oriented psychotherapy.* Washington, DC: American Psychological Association.

Spickard, P. R. (1992). The illogic of American racial categories. In M. P. P. Root (Ed.), *Racially mixed people in America* (pp. 12–23). Newbury Park, CA: Sage.

Stamm, B. H. (Ed.). (2003). *Rural behavioral health care: An interdisciplinary guide.* Washington, DC: American Psychological Association.

Stepakoff, S., Hubbard, J., Katoh, M., Falk, E., Mikula, J. B., Nkhoma, P., et al. (2006). Trauma healing in refugee camps in Guinea. *American Psychologist, 61,* 919–932.

Stephan, W. G. (1989). A cognitive approach to stereotyping. In D. Bar-tal & C. Graumann (Eds.), *Stereotyping and prejudice* (pp. 37–57). New York: Springer-Verlag.

Sternberg, R. J., & Grigorenko, E. L. (2004). Why cultural psychology is necessary and not just nice: The example of the study of intelligence. In R. J. Sternberg & E. L. Grigorenko (Eds.), *Culture and competence: Contexts of life success* (pp. 207–223). Washington, DC: American Psychological Association.

Sternberg, R. J., Grigorenko, E. L., & Kidd, K. K. (2005). Intelligence, race, and genetics. *American Psychologist, 60,* 46–59.

Sternberg, R. J., Wagner, R. K., & Okagaki, L. (1993). Practical intelligence: The nature and role of tacit knowledge in work and at school. In H. Reese & J. Puckett (Eds.), *Advances in life span development* (pp. 205–227). Hillsdale, NJ: Erlbaum.

Sternberg, R. J., Wagner, R. K., Williams, W. M., & Horvath, J. A. (1995). Testing common sense. *American Psychologist, 50,* 912–927.

Straussner, S. L. A. (Ed.). (2001). *Ethnocultural factors in substance abuse treatment.* New York: Guilford Press.

Struwe, G. (1994). Training health and medical professionals to care for refugees: Issues and methods. In A. J. Marsella, T. Bornemann, S. Ekblad, & J. Orley (Eds.), *Amidst peril and pain: The mental health and well-being of the world's refugees* (pp. 311–326). Washington, DC: American Psychological Association.

Sue, D. W., & Sue, D. (1999). *Counseling the culturally different* (3rd ed.). New York: Wiley.

Sue, D. W., & Sue, D. (2003). *Counseling the culturally different* (4th ed.). New York: Wiley.

Sue, S. (1998). In search of cultural competence in psychotherapy and counseling. *American Psychologist, 53,* 440–448.

Sundberg, N. D., & Sue, D. (1989). Research and research hypotheses about effectiveness in intercultural counseling. In P. B. Pedersen, J. G. Draguns, W. J. Lonner, & J. E. Trimble (Eds.), *Counseling across cultures* (pp. 355–370). Honolulu: University of Hawaii Press.

Sussman, N. M., & Rosenfeld, H. M. (1982). Influence of culture, language, and sex on conversational distance. *Journal of Personality and Social Psychology, 42,* 66–74.

Sutton, C. T., & Broken Nose, M. A. (1996). American Indian families: An overview. In M. McGoldrick, J. Giordano, & J. K. Pearce (Eds.), *Ethnicity and family therapy* (2nd ed., pp. 31–44). New York: Guilford Press.

Sutton, J. P. (2002). *Music, music therapy and trauma: International perspectives.* London: Jessica Kingsley.

Suzuki, L. A., & Kugler, J. F. (1995). Intelligence and personality assessment. In J. G. Ponterotto, J. M. Casas, L. A. Suzuki, & C. M. Alexander (Eds.), *Handbook of multicultural counseling* (pp. 493–515). Thousand Oaks, CA: Sage.

Suzuki, L. A., & Valencia, R. R. (1997). Race–ethnicity and measured intelligence: Educational implications. *American Psychologist, 52,* 1103–1114.

Swan Reimer, C. (1999). *Counseling the Inupiat Eskimo.* Westport, CT: Greenwood Press.

Swinomish Tribal Community. (1991). *A gathering of wisdoms: Tribal mental health: A cultural perspective.* LaConnor, WA: Author.

Takaki, R. (1993). *A different mirror: A history of multicultural America* (reissue ed.). Boston: Little, Brown/Bay Back Books.

Taylor, S. E., Kemeny, M. E., Reed, G. M., Bower, J. E., & Gruenewald, T. L. (2000). Psychological resources, positive allusions, and health. *American Psychologist, 55,* 99–109.

Tewari, N., Inman, A. G., & Sandhu, D. S. (2003). South Asian Americans: Culture, concerns, and therapeutic strategies. In J. S. Mio & G. Y. Iwamasa (Eds.), *Culturally diverse mental health* (pp. 191–209). New York: Brunner-Routledge.

Thomas, A., & Sillen, S. (1972). *Racism and psychiatry.* Toronto, Ontario, Canada: Citadel Press.

Triandis, H. C. (1996). The psychological measurement of cultural syndromes. *American Psychologist, 51,* 407–415.

Trimble, J. E., & Fleming, C. M. (1989). Providing counseling services for Native American Indians: Client, counselor, and community characteristics. In P. B. Pedersen, J. G. Draguns, W. J. Lonner, & J. E. Trimble (Eds.), *Counseling across cultures* (pp. 177–204). Honolulu: University of Hawaii Press.

Troiden, R. R. (1979). Becoming homosexual: A model of gay identity acquisition. *Psychiatry, 42,* 362–373.

Tsemberis, S. J., & Orfanos, S. D. (1996). Greek families. In M. McGoldrick, J. Giordano, & J. K. Pearce (Eds.), *Ethnicity and family therapy* (2nd ed., pp. 517–529). New York: Guilford Press.

Tseng, W. (1999). Culture and psychotherapy: Review and practical guidelines. *Transcultural Psychiatry, 36,* 131–179.

Tulkin, S. R., & Stock, W. (2004). A model for predoctoral psychopharmacology training: Shaping a new frontier in clinical psychology. *Professional Psychology: Research and Practice, 35,* 151–157.

Uba, L. (1994). *Asian Americans: Personality patterns, identity, and mental health.* New York: Guilford Press.

U.S. Census Bureau. (2000a). *Adopted children and stepchildren: Special reports.* Retrieved November 27, 2005, from http://www.census.gov/prod/2003pubs/censr-6.pdf and http://lehd.dsd.census.gov/led/library/workshops/2003/Workshop2003-Immigration_Research 2.pdf

U.S. Census Bureau. (2000b). *Married-couple and unmarried-partner households: Special reports* (Table 5, p. 12). Retrieved April 4, 2006, from http://www.uscensus.gov/prod/2003pubs/censr-5.pdf

U.S. Census Bureau. (2000c). *United States population by race.* Retrieved October, 2004, from http://www.censusscope.org/us/chart_race.html

U.S. Department of the Interior. (2002). Bureau of Indian Affairs. In *Bureau highlights* (pp. 77–85). Washington, DC: Author. Retrieved October 25, 2004, from http://www.doi.gov/budget/2003/03hilites/bh77.pdf

U.S. Department of Labor, Employment and Training Administration. (2002). *The national agricultural workers survey.* Retrieved December 15, 2006, from http://www.doleta.gov/agworker/report9/chapter1.cfm

Vernon, M. (2006). The APA and Deafness. *American Psychologist, 61,* 815–824.

Vinet, E. V. (2000). The Rorschach Comprehensive System in Iberoamerica. In R. H. Dana (Ed.), *Handbook of cross-cultural and multicultural personality assessment* (pp. 345–366). Mahwah, NJ: Erlbaum.

Vontress, C. E., Johnson, J. A., & Epp, L. R. (1999). *Cross-cultural counseling: A casebook.* Alexandria, VA: American Counseling Association.

Wade, J. C. (1998). Male reference group identity dependence: A theory of male of identity. *Counseling Psychologist, 26,* 349–383.

Wadeson, H. (1980). *Art psychotherapy.* New York: Wiley.

Walker, K. L., & Chestnut, D. (2003). The role of ethnocultural variables in response to terrorism. *Cultural Diversity and Ethnic Minority Psychology, 9,* 251–262.

Walker, L. (Ed.). (1999). International perspectives on domestic violence. *American Psychologist, 54,* 21–65.

Walsh, K. (1987). *Neuropsychology: A clinical approach.* New York: Churchill Livingstone.

Wang, V. O., & Sue, S. (2005). In the eye of the storm: Race and genomics in research and practice. *American Psychologist, 60,* 37–45.

Watt, S. K. (1999). The story between the lines: A thematic discussion of the experience of racism. *Journal of Counseling and Development, 77,* 54–61.

Waxler-Morrison, N., & Anderson, J. M. (2005). Introduction. In N. Waxler-Morrison, J. M. Anderson, E. Richardson, & N. A. Chambers (Eds.), *Cross-cultural caring: A handbook for health professionals* (2nd ed., pp. 1–10). Vancouver, British Columbia, Canada: University of British Columbia Press.

Waxler-Morrison, N., Anderson, J. M., Richardson, E., & Chambers, N. A. (2005). (Eds.). (2005). *Cross-cultural caring: A handbook for health professionals* (2nd ed.). Vancouver, British Columbia, Canada: University of British Columbia Press.

Weaver, H. N. (2001). Native Americans and substance abuse. In S. L. A. Straussner (Ed.), *Ethnocultural factors in substance abuse treatment* (pp. 77–96). New York: Guilford Press.

Wechsler, D. (1981). *Wechsler Adult Intelligence Scale—Revised.* New York: Psychological Corporation.

Wechsler, D. (1997). *Wechsler Adult Intelligence Scale—Third edition.* New York: Psychological Corporation.

Weeber, J. E. (1999). What can I know of racism? *Journal of Counseling and Development, 77,* 20–23.

Weisman, A., Feldman, G., Gruman, C., Rosenberg, R., Chamorro, R., & Belozersky, I. (2005). Improving mental health services for Latino and Asian immigrant elders. *Professional Psychology: Research and Practice, 36,* 642–648.

Weiss, J. C. (1999). The role of art therapy in aiding older clients with life transitions. In M. Duffy (Ed.), *Handbook of counseling and psychotherapy with older adults* (pp. 182–196). New York: Wiley.

West, C. (1993). *Race matters.* Boston: Beacon Press.

Westbrooks, K. (1995). *Functional low-income families.* New York: Vantage Press.

Westermeyer, J. (1987). Cultural factors in clinical assessment. *Journal of Consulting and Clinical Psychology, 55,* 471–478.

Westermeyer, J., & Janca, A. (1997). Language, culture and psychopathology: Conceptual and methodological issues. *Transcultural Psychiatry, 34,* 291–311.

Widiger, T. A., & Trull, T. J. (2007). Plate tectonics in the classification of personality disorder: Shifting to a dimensional model. *American Psychologist, 62,* 71–83.

Wilgosh, L., & Gibson, J. T. (1994). Cross-national perspectives on the role of assessment in counseling: A preliminary report. *International Journal for the Advancement of Counseling, 17,* 59–70.

Williams, C. B. (1999). Claiming a biracial identity: Resisting social constructions of race and culture. *Journal of Counseling and Development, 77,* 32–35.

Williams, C. R., & Abeles, N. (2004). Issues and implications of Deaf culture in therapy. *Professional Psychology: Research and Practice, 35,* 643–648.

Witko, T. M. (Eds.). (2006). *Mental health care for urban Indians: Clinical insights from Native practitioners.* Washington, DC: American Psychological Association.

Wong, T. M., Strickland, T. L., Fletcher-Janzen, E., Ardila, A., & Reynolds, C. R. (2000). Theoretical and practical issues in the neuropsychological assessment and treatment of culturally dissimilar patients. In E. Fletcher-Janzen, T. L. Strickland, & C. R. Reynolds (Eds.), *Handbook of cross-cultural neuropsychology* (pp. 3–18). New York: Kluwer Academic/Plenum Publishers.

Wood, P. S., & Mallinckrodt, B. (1990). Culturally sensitive assertiveness training for ethnic minority clients. *Professional Psychology: Research and Practice, 21,* 5–11.

World Almanac Education Group. (2007). *The World Almanac 2007.* New York: Author.

World Health Organization. (1992). *International statistical classification of diseases and related health problems* (10th ed., Vol. 1). Geneva, Switzerland: Author.

Wrenn, G. C. (1962). The culturally encapsulated counselor. *Harvard Educational Review, 32,* 441–149.

Yamamoto, J., Silva, J. A., Ferrari, M., & Nukariya, K. (1997). Culture and psychopathology. In G. Johnson-Powell & J. Yamamoto (Eds.), *Trans-cultural child development: Psychological assessment and treatment* (pp. 34–57). New York: Wiley.

Yeh, C. J., Inman, A. G., Kim, A. B., & Okubo, Y. (2006). Asian American families' collectivistic coping strategies in response to 9/11. *Cultural Diversity and Ethnic Minority Psychology, 12,* 134–148.

Yesavage, J. A., & Brink, T. L. (1983). Development and validation of a geriatric depression screening scale: A preliminary report. *Journal of Psychiatric Research, 17,* 37.

Young, E. (1995). *Third World in the first: Development and indigenous peoples.* New York: Routledge.

Younggren, J. N., & Gottlieb, M. C. (2004). Managing risk while contemplating multiple relationships. *Professional Psychology: Research and Practice, 35,* 255–260.

Zinn, H. (2005). *The people's history of the United States: 1492–present.* New York: HarperPerennial.

Zogby, J. (2003). *Hearing on America after 9/11: Freedom preserved or freedom lost? (The statement before the United States Senate Committee on the Judiciary, November 18).* Retrieved August 12, 2004, from http://www.aaiusa.org/PDF/JZtestimony111803.pdf

Author Index

Subject Index

Aboriginal peoples, 12–13. *See also* Indigenous heritage
Acculturation, assessment considerations, 131–132
ADDRESSING framework, 4, 18
  applications, 10, 222, 223
  categories of work, 4–5
  client identity assessment, 7, 74–76, 81, 83, 220
  couple and family assessment, 189–190
  cultural heritage self-assessment, 42–45, 49–50
  in diagnostic practice, 156–160
  interpersonal work in, 4, 6–8
  personal work in, 4, 6
  privilege self-assessment, 45–46
  purpose, 4, 219–220
Adoption, 10
Advocacy, 191
African American
  case example, 203–216
African Americans, 12
Age-related issues
  in ADDRESSING framework, 4, 7
  cultural heritage self-assessment, 44
  demographic patterns, 11
  family assessment, 108–109
  See also Older persons

Alaska Native, 13
Alcoholics Anonymous, 180–181
American Association of People with Disabilities, 57
American Counseling Association, 4
American Psychological Association, 4, 57
American Sign Language, 11
Arab
  case example, 160–172
Art therapies, 181–183
Asian ethnicity, 13
Assessment
  avoiding premature judgments, 31
  case examples, 143–146, 161–167, 204–208
  client identity, 7, 69–73, 74–76, 81, 83, 167–168, 220
  client's historical and sociocultural milieu, 109–112
  cognitive behavior therapy, 191, 195–196
  cultural influences on client problem, 196, 220
  cultural sensitivity in, 26, 106, 127–128
  errors of omission and commission, 126
  families, 108–109

About the Author

P amela A. Hays holds a PhD in clinical psychology from the University of Hawaii in Honolulu, an MS in counseling from the University of Alaska in Anchorage, a BA in psychology from New Mexico State University in Las Cruces, and a certificate in French from La Sorbonne in Paris. From 1987 through 1988, she served as a National Institute of Mental Health postdoctoral fellow in geropsychology at the University of Rochester School of Medicine in Rochester, New York. From 1989 through 2000, she worked as a core faculty member of the graduate psychology program at Antioch University in Seattle, Washington. Her research has included work with Arab women in North Africa and Vietnamese, Lao, and Cambodian refugees living in the United States. She is coeditor with Gayle Y. Iwamasa of *Culturally Responsive Cognitive–Behavioral Therapy: Assessment, Practice, and Supervision* (American Psychological Association, 2006), and her articles on couples therapy, older adults, and multicultural and feminist issues have appeared in *Professional Psychology: Research and Practice,* the *Journal of Counseling and Development,* the *International Journal of Psychology,* and *Women and Therapy.* She is a licensed clinical psychologist who currently lives in rural Alaska and works with Central Peninsula Counseling Services and the Kenaitze Tribe's Nakenu Family Center in Kenai, Alaska. She serves as adjunct faculty for Antioch University Seattle and conducts workshops internationally.